LOAN FORGIVENESS AND LOAN REPAYMENT PROGRAMS

BANKS AND BANKING DEVELOPMENTS

Additional books and e-books in this series can be found
on Nova's website under the Series tab.

BANKS AND BANKING DEVELOPMENTS

LOAN FORGIVENESS AND LOAN REPAYMENT PROGRAMS

VIRGIL DAVIDSON
EDITOR

NOTICE TO THE READER

Library of Congress Cataloging-in-Publication Data

ISBN: 978-1-53615-181-7

Published by Nova Science Publishers, Inc. † *New York*

CONTENTS

PREFACE

Student loan forgiveness and loan repayment programs provide borrowers a means of having all or part of their student loan debt forgiven or repaid in exchange for work or service in specific fields or professions or following a prolonged period during which their student loan debt burden is high relative to their income. In both loan forgiveness and loan repayment programs, borrowers typically qualify for benefits by working or serving in certain capacities for a specified period or by satisfying other program requirements over an extended term. Upon qualifying for benefits, some or all of a borrower's student loan debt is forgiven or paid on his or her behalf. Some of these programs are intended to support goals such as providing a financial incentive to encourage individuals to enter into and/or remain in a particular profession or public service. One such federal program that has received considerable attention in recent years is the Public Service Loan Forgiveness (PSLF) program. The PSLF program forgives borrowers' federal student loans after they make at least 10 years of qualifying payments while working for certain public service employers.

Chapter 1 - Student loan forgiveness and loan repayment programs provide borrowers a means of having all or part of their student loan debt forgiven or repaid in exchange for work or service in specific fields or professions or following a prolonged period during which their student loan debt burden is high relative to their income. In both loan forgiveness and loan repayment programs, borrowers typically qualify for benefits by working or serving in certain capacities for a specified period or by satisfying other program requirements over an extended term. Upon qualifying for benefits, some or all of a borrower's student loan debt is forgiven or paid on his or her behalf. A key distinction among these types of programs is whether the availability of benefits is incorporated into the loan terms and conditions and thus considered an entitlement to qualified borrowers, or whether benefits are made available to qualified borrowers at the discretion of the entity administering the program and subject to the availability of funds. For the purposes of this chapter, the former types of programs are referred to as *loan forgiveness* while the latter are referred to as *loan repayment*. Loan forgiveness and loan repayment programs typically are intended to support one or more of the following goals:

- Provide a financial incentive to encourage individuals to enter public service or a particular profession, occupation, or occupational specialty.
- Provide a financial incentive to encourage individuals to remain employed in a high-need profession or occupation—often in certain locations.
- Provide debt relief to borrowers who, after repaying their student loans as a proportion of their income for an extended period of time, have not completely repaid their entire student loan debt.

The number and availability of loan forgiveness and loan repayment programs have expanded considerably since the establishment of the first major federal loan forgiveness program by the National Defense Education Act of 1958. Currently, over 50 such programs are authorized at the federal level, approximately 30 of which were operational as of October 1, 2017. While existing loan forgiveness and loan repayment programs may support similar broader goals, there is great variety across programs in their design and scope. Some programs are widely available to all borrowers who meet program eligibility criteria. However, many programs are narrowly focused on supporting specific public service or workforce needs and are available only to individuals serving in certain occupations or working in certain geographic regions, or individuals employed by certain federal agencies. In some programs, the availability of benefits is incorporated into the terms and conditions of borrowers' loans and is more certain, but in other programs, the availability of benefits is subject to discretionary funding and award criteria. Programs are also distinguished by types of loans that qualify for forgiveness or repayment, qualifying periods of service, the amount of debt that may be discharged, and the tax treatment of discharged indebtedness. Congress may explore whether loan forgiveness and loan repayment programs are effectively achieving policy objectives. Several issues might be examined. For instance, should multiple loan forgiveness and loan repayment programs continue to exist to provide debt relief to borrowers who engage in similar types of activities? Does the structure of some programs lead to a financial windfall for borrowers who engage in the same type of activity they might otherwise have in the absence of program benefits? Are programs appropriately targeted? Is sufficient information available to assess whether existing programs are effectively achieving their intended purposes?

Chapter 2 - The Public Service Loan Forgiveness (PSLF) program provides Direct Loan borrowers who, on or after October 1, 2007, are employed full-time in certain public service jobs for 10 years while making 120 separate qualifying monthly payments on their Direct Loans with the opportunity to have any remaining balance of principal and interest on their loans forgiven. The program was enacted under the College Cost Reduction and Access Act of 2007 (P.L. 110-84) to encourage individuals to enter into and remain employed in public service and to alleviate the potential financial burdens associated with federal student loans of borrowers in public service occupations who were presumed generally to earn less than their counterparts in other occupations.

With the opportunity to apply for program benefits first being made available on October 1, 2017, based on service completed and payments made prior to that date, many issues that span several aspects of the program have been raised and have garnered congressional interest. This chapter addresses numerous issues, which are highlighted below. Program

Virgil Davidson

implementation issues that have surfaced relate to how the PSLF program's statutory requirements have been operationalized, difficulties experienced by borrowers in participating in the program, and difficulties in administering the program. Some of these issues include:

- Operationally defining what constitutes a "public service job." This includes whether the definition in use is sufficiently targeted to meet congressional intent for the program and whether it has created inequities among types of borrowers. There have also been administrative difficulties associated with identifying and certifying qualifying employment.
- Determining what constitutes a "qualifying payment." Multiple criteria related to on-time payments, time periods over which payments must be made, and specific payment amounts must be met for a payment to be considered qualifying, which may cause confusion among borrowers and create administrative difficulties.
- Difficulties borrowers may face when determining which repayment plan to enroll in to maximize PSLF benefits. Payments made according to an income-driven repayment (IDR) plan may decrease the monthly dollar amount of payments made, which may ultimately lead to greater amounts of PSLF forgiveness benefits. Payments made under other plans may also qualify for PSLF but may not be as valuable to borrowers in terms of eventual PSLF forgiveness benefits.
- The effects of loan consolidation on a borrower's progress toward receiving PSLF benefits. Of particular importance, PSLF qualifying payments made prior to consolidation do not count toward forgiveness of the resulting Direct Consolidation Loan.
- The complexities and challenges that administering the program may present for the Department of Education, loan servicers, and borrowers. These include issues of communication among the parties regarding program requirements and processes, lack of coordination among loan servicers, loans servicers making errors or not completing

tasks associated with the program in a timely manner, and the lack of automation of some administrative functions.

Issues pertaining to PSLF program interactions with other programs and benefits relate to whether borrowers understand the interactions well enough to make rational choices and maximize available benefits and, from the federal government's perspective, questions have arisen regarding whether the desired targeting of benefits is being achieved and about the potential costs associated with such interactions. Some of these issues include:

- There is no limit to the amount of loan forgiveness benefits an individual may realize under the PSLF program. While it is possible that many borrowers may receive limited benefits, some Direct Loan borrowers may realize large forgiveness benefits under the program. This outcome may be more likely to occur for borrowers of Direct PLUS Loans for graduate and professional students, which have no aggregate borrowing limits, and which were newly authorized to be made just prior to the enactment of PSLF. Also, the variety of IDR plans has expanded greatly since the PSLF program's inception, with several of the new IDR plans providing for lower monthly payments than under the Income-Based Repayment plan the primary IDR plan available when the PSLF program was enacted. This expansion may allow borrowers to lower monthly payments and potentially realize larger forgiveness benefits under the program. The current borrowing limits and variety of IDR plans, coupled with PSLF program benefits, have raised questions about whether certain types of students are not incentivized to limit borrowing and whether they may be less sensitive to the price of postsecondary education.
- Borrowers may receive benefits under a number of federal student loan repayment programs. Borrowers may also be able to avail themselves of certain income tax provisions to maximize PSLF program benefits. For borrowers, understanding whether the same service that qualifies for

PSLF may also qualify for other loan repayment benefits is important, as is their understanding of how other benefits and tax provisions may interact with PSLF. From the perspective of the federal government, a key consideration may relate to what constitutes a "double benefit" for service performed by borrowers and the extent to which overlapping benefits might be provided.

Broad program-related issues relate to (1) how the program fits into the overall suite of federal student aid benefits and (2) the difficulty of estimating the potential participation in and costs of the program.

1) The enactment of the PSLF program is reflective of a broadening of the federal approach to student aid, providing more widely available assistance to individuals after a postsecondary education's costs have been incurred. This approach may place greater emphasis on providing aid on the basis of economic circumstances after enrollment, rather than at the time of enrollment. It also makes some aid available on a targeted basis providing relief to individuals who pursue certain types of service or occupations, rather than providing aid more broadly to individuals who enroll in postsecondary education.

2) The granting of loan forgiveness benefits results in costs to the federal government, and there has been some speculation that the cost of PSLF could be much higher than anticipated. Limited information is available on the actual and future costs to the government of the PSLF program. It has just recently become possible to claim program benefits; thus, little is known about what the costs associated with the program will be based on the experiences of actual cohorts of borrowers. In addition, estimating potential costs may prove difficult as borrowers are not required to submit information on their intent to participate in the program until they seek forgiveness benefits after 10 years of service and qualifying payments.

In: Loan Forgiveness …
Editor: Virgil Davidson

ISBN: 978-1-53615-181-7
© 2019 Nova Science Publishers, Inc.

Chapter 1

FEDERAL STUDENT LOAN FORGIVENESS AND LOAN REPAYMENT PROGRAMS (UPDATED)*

Alexandra Hegji, Elayne J. Heisler and David P. Smole

ABSTRACT

Student loan forgiveness and loan repayment programs provide borrowers a means of having all or part of their student loan debt forgiven or repaid in exchange for work or service in specific fields or professions or following a prolonged period during which their student loan debt burden is high relative to their income. In both loan forgiveness and loan repayment programs, borrowers typically qualify for benefits by working or serving in certain capacities for a specified period or by satisfying other program requirements over an extended term. Upon qualifying for benefits, some or all of a borrower's student loan debt is forgiven or paid on his or her behalf.

A key distinction among these types of programs is whether the availability of benefits is incorporated into the loan terms and conditions and thus considered an entitlement to qualified borrowers, or whether

---

* This is an edited, reformatted and augmented version of Congressional Research Service, Publication No. R43571, dated November 20, 2018.

benefits are made available to qualified borrowers at the discretion of the entity administering the program and subject to the availability of funds. For the purposes of this chapter, the former types of programs are referred to as *loan forgiveness* while the latter are referred to as *loan repayment*.

Loan forgiveness and loan repayment programs typically are intended to support one or more of the following goals:

- Provide a financial incentive to encourage individuals to enter public service or a particular profession, occupation, or occupational specialty.
- Provide a financial incentive to encourage individuals to remain employed in a high-need profession or occupation—often in certain locations.
- Provide debt relief to borrowers who, after repaying their student loans as a proportion of their income for an extended period of time, have not completely repaid their entire student loan debt.

The number and availability of loan forgiveness and loan repayment programs have expanded considerably since the establishment of the first major federal loan forgiveness program by the National Defense Education Act of 1958. Currently, over 50 such programs are authorized at the federal level, approximately 30 of which were operational as of October 1, 2017.

While existing loan forgiveness and loan repayment programs may support similar broader goals, there is great variety across programs in their design and scope. Some programs are widely available to all borrowers who meet program eligibility criteria. However, many programs are narrowly focused on supporting specific public service or workforce needs and are available only to individuals serving in certain occupations or working in certain geographic regions, or individuals employed by certain federal agencies. In some programs, the availability of benefits is incorporated into the terms and conditions of borrowers' loans and is more certain, but in other programs, the availability of benefits is subject to discretionary funding and award criteria. Programs are also distinguished by types of loans that qualify for forgiveness or repayment, qualifying periods of service, the amount of debt that may be discharged, and the tax treatment of discharged indebtedness.

Congress may explore whether loan forgiveness and loan repayment programs are effectively achieving policy objectives. Several issues might be examined. For instance, should multiple loan forgiveness and loan repayment programs continue to exist to provide debt relief to borrowers who engage in similar types of activities? Does the structure of some programs lead to a financial windfall for borrowers who engage in the same type of activity they might otherwise have in the absence of program benefits? Are programs appropriately targeted? Is sufficient information available to assess whether existing programs are effectively achieving their intended purposes?

BACKGROUND AND HISTORY OF LOAN FORGIVENESS AND LOAN REPAYMENT PROGRAMS

Federal student loan programs that make available loan forgiveness or repayment in return for service in certain professions or occupations have existed since the enactment of the National Defense Education Act of 1958 (NDEA; P.L. 85-864), which authorized the National Defense Student Loan (NDSL) program. In recognition of the high costs to individuals of borrowing to finance postsecondary education expenses and to address identified needs for individuals to perform certain types of service or work in certain occupations, an array of student loan forgiveness and repayment programs have been enacted. These programs offer borrowers a means to have all or part of their student loan debt forgiven or repaid in return for work or service in specific fields or professions or for satisfying certain conditions relating to borrower debt and income. Throughout the years, various federal loan forgiveness and loan repayment programs have been created, and presently, over 50 such programs are authorized, approximately 30 of which were operational as of October 1, 2017.

Loan forgiveness (sometimes also referred to as cancellation or discharge) programs and loan repayment programs are characterized by the federal government's forgiving, canceling, or discharging all or a portion of an individual's total student loan indebtedness or making loan payments on a borrower's behalf, upon the individual satisfying certain requirements. Loan forgiveness and loan repayment benefits are often contingent upon a borrower completing a period of employment in public service or in certain other occupations. Increasingly, however, loan forgiveness benefits have begun to be offered as a component of certain income-driven student loan repayment plans. While the various programs operate somewhat differently, they are generally intended to support at least one of the following goals:

- Provide a financial incentive to encourage individuals to enter public service or a particular profession, occupation, or occupational specialty.
- Provide a financial incentive to encourage individuals to remain employed in a high-need profession or occupation—often in certain locations.
- Provide debt relief to borrowers who, after repaying their student loans as a proportion of their income for an extended period of time, have not completely repaid their entire student loan debt.

These types of loan forgiveness and loan repayment benefits provide debt relief to borrowers of federal student loans who make an active choice to enter public service or obtain employment in particular professions, occupations, or specialties, or to repay their loans according to an income-driven repayment (IDR) plan. Other forms of debt relief also may be available to borrowers who experience certain unfortunate circumstances. These forms of debt relief—which are beyond the scope of this chapter—include loan discharge for borrowers who become totally and permanently disabled, loan discharge upon death of the individual on whose behalf a loan was made, discharge for closure of the borrower's school, discharge for false certification of student eligibility, discharge for loans made without the borrower's authorization, discharge for unpaid refunds by a school following the borrower's withdrawal from school, discharge upon the successful assertion of a defense to repayment, and discharge in bankruptcy.[1]

---

[1] For additional information on these forms of debt relief, see U.S. Department of Education, Federal Student Aid, "How to Repay Your Loans: Forgiveness, Cancellation, and Discharge," https://studentaid.ed.gov/repay-loans/ forgiveness-cancellation.

Early Student Loan Forgiveness and Repayment Programs

One of the earliest federal student loan programs that made loan forgiveness available to borrowers was the NDSL program, authorized under the NDEA in 1958. The NDSL program was established, in part, as a response to the Union of Soviet Socialist Republics' 1957 launch of the Sputnik satellite.[2] Many Members of Congress viewed this as an issue of national security, as they believed this event illustrated that the United States was falling behind in technological developments.

To address this perceived national security issue, Congress decided to target and fund improvements in education programs because national security required "the fullest development of mental resources and technical skills of its young men and women."[3] The establishment of the NDSL program made low-interest loans available to college students to help them pursue their studies. Also as part of the NDSL program, Congress authorized a student loan forgiveness component, which was intended to increase the number and quality of teachers in U.S. schools.[4]

Specifically, students who taught full-time in a public elementary or secondary school were eligible to have up to half of their student loans cancelled.[5]

Over the years, the NDSL loan forgiveness provisions were amended, with the teacher loan forgiveness benefits targeted at individuals who were either teaching in elementary or secondary schools at which low-income students made up more than 30% of the enrollment or were teaching students with disabilities full-time. Loan forgiveness benefits were also expanded to be available to individuals serving in a Head Start program and those serving in an area of hostility while in the Armed Forces. Through these provisions, qualified borrowers became eligible to have a

---

[2] C. Ronald Kimberling, "Federal Student Aid: A History and Critical Analysis," in *The Academy in Crisis: The Political Economy of Higher Education*, ed. John W. Sommer (Oakland: The Independent Institute, 1995), pp. 69-70.

[3] P.L. 85-864 §101.

[4] U.S. Congress, Senate Committee on Labor and Public Welfare, *National Defense Education Act of 1958*, Report to accompany S. 4237, 85th Cong., 2nd sess., August 8, 1958, Report No. 2242, p. 10.

[5] P.L. 85-864 §205(b)(3).

portion of their loans canceled based on the number of years of public service completed.[6]

The NDSL program was incorporated into the Higher Education Act of 1965 (HEA; P.L. 89-329) through the Education Amendments of 1972 (P.L. 92-318) and was later renamed the Federal Perkins Loan Program[7] by amendments made through the Higher Education Amendments of 1986 (P.L. 99-498).

Subsequent to the enactment of the NDEA, other federal student loan forgiveness and repayment programs were established to target borrowers who entered other professions and worked in high- need areas. For instance, in 1965, a loan forgiveness component modeled after the NDSL was incorporated into the Health Professions Student Loan Program (HPSLP), authorized under the Public Health Service Act (PHSA; P.L. 89-290). Under this program, borrowers who practiced medicine in locations with a health manpower shortage (as defined) could have up to 50% of their loans forgiven.[8] Following these early student loan repayment and forgiveness programs, many additional programs were enacted and currently over 50 such programs exist.

OVERVIEW OF FEDERAL LOAN FORGIVENESS AND LOAN REPAYMENT PROGRAMS

This chapter identifies and describes federal student loan forgiveness and loan repayment programs that are currently authorized by federal law. It provides brief, summary descriptions of identified programs. These program descriptions are intended to provide policymakers with general

---

[6] For instance, individuals teaching students with disabilities full-time were eligible to have 100% of their loans forgiven, while individuals serving in the armed services in an area of hostility were eligible to have 50% of their loans forgiven. CRS Report CD832039, *The Experience with Loan Forgiveness and Service Payback in Federal and State Student Aid Programs*, archived, available to congressional clients upon request.

[7] For additional information on the Federal Perkins Loan program, see CRS Report RL31618, *Campus-Based Student Financial Aid Programs under the Higher Education Act*.

[8] CRS Report LB2301, *The Experience with Loan Forgiveness and Service Payback in Federal and State Student Aid Programs*, archived, available to congressional clients upon request.

information about the purpose of existing programs and how they are designed to operate. The program descriptions are not intended to be comprehensive in nature. Readers interested in comprehensive details about a particular program are encouraged to refer to additional resources, including federal statutes, regulations, and agency guidance. Citations are provided for the various programs identified in this chapter.

Over 50 federal student loan forgiveness and repayment programs are currently authorized under federal law. Although each program is designed to operate somewhat differently, they are all intended to provide student loan debt relief to borrowers who perform specified types of service, enter into and remain employed in certain professions, serve in certain locations, or repay their loans according to an income-driven repayment plan for an extended period of time.

Each of the various programs has unique characteristics and may be distinguished by features such as differing borrower eligibility criteria, benefit amounts, the means through which benefits are provided, or how the program is funded. In this overview, several parameters are identified and used to broadly characterize various aspects of the currently authorized programs. As some of the terms commonly used to identify the benefits offered through these programs (e.g., loan forgiveness, cancellation, or repayment) are often used inconsistently from program to program, this chapter's use of a consistent set of parameters to characterize various aspects of the programs facilitates the description and examination of some of the similarities and differences between the various programs.

Distinction among Loan Forgiveness and Loan Repayment Programs

In employment-focused loan forgiveness and loan repayment programs, a borrower typically must work or serve in a certain function, profession, or geographic location for a specified period of time to qualify for benefits. Under repayment plan-based loan forgiveness, a borrower typically must repay according to an income-driven repayment plan for a specified period of time to qualify for benefits. At the end of the specified term, some or all of the individual's qualifying student loan debt is forgiven or repaid on his or her behalf. The individual is thus relieved of responsibility for repaying that portion of his or her student loan debt. One of the most important distinctions among these types of programs is whether the availability of benefits is incorporated into the loan terms and conditions and is thus considered an entitlement to qualified borrowers or whether benefits are made available to qualified borrowers at the discretion of the entity administering the program and whether the benefits are subject to the availability of funds. For the purposes of this chapter, the former types of programs are referred to as *loan forgiveness* while the latter are referred to as *loan repayment*.

In general, loan forgiveness benefits are broadly available to borrowers of qualified loans. The availability of these benefits is expressed to borrowers in their loan documents, such as the master promissory note and the borrower's rights and responsibilities statement.[9] A borrower who satisfies the loan forgiveness program's eligibility criteria, as set forth in the loan terms and conditions, is entitled to the loan forgiveness benefits. Benefits that are entitlements to qualified borrowers are generally funded through mandatory appropriations and accounted for as part of federal student loan subsidy costs, which are discussed in detail later in the section titled "Cost of Loan Forgiveness and Loan Repayment Programs." There are two broad categories of loan forgiveness benefits: loan forgiveness for public service employment and loan forgiveness following income-driven repayment.

Loan repayment programs also provide debt relief to borrowers for service in a specific function, profession, or location. However, in contrast to employment-focused loan forgiveness programs, the entity that administers a loan repayment program typically either directly repays some or all of the qualified borrower's student loan debt on his or her behalf or provides funding to a separate entity for purposes of implementing a loan

---

[9] Some loan forgiveness programs have been established and made available to individuals who have already borrowed their loans. The resulting change to the terms and conditions of an existing loan program is referred to as a loan modification.

repayment program and making such payments. Loan repayment benefits are generally offered through programs that are separate or distinct from the program through which a federal student loan is made. In many instances, these programs are designed to address broad employment needs or shortages (e.g., within a specific occupation or geographic location), while other such programs are intended to help individual federal agencies recruit and retain qualified employees, often serving as an additional form of compensation to targeted employees, who may be harder to recruit or retain. Both types of loan repayment benefits are generally available to a limited number of qualified borrowers. Typically, loan repayment benefits are discretionary and their availability is subject to the appropriation of funds. A related distinguishing characteristic of the types of debt relief programs examined in this chapter is the extent to which an individual may incur a federal income tax liability based on receipt of the program's benefit. In general, debt forgiven under an employment-focused loan forgiveness program is excluded from a borrower's gross income for federal income tax purposes, and therefore, the borrower would not be responsible for paying the federal income tax liability associated with the forgiveness benefit received.[10] On the other hand, debt forgiven following income-driven repayment or repaid for public service employment is often included in a borrower's gross income for federal income tax purposes, and therefore, the borrower would be responsible for paying the income tax liability associated with the forgiveness or repayment benefit received.[11]

The text box below provides a summary of some of the distinguishing features of the three categories of debt relief programs examined in this chapter: programs that provide loan forgiveness for public service employment, programs that provide loan forgiveness following income-driven repayment, and programs that provide loan repayment for public service employment.

---

[10] IRC §108(f).

[11] For additional information on the federal income tax treatment of discharged student loans, see U.S. Congress, Senate Committee on the Budget, *Tax Expenditures: Compendium of Background Material on Individual Provisions*, committee print, prepared by the Congressional Research Service, 114th Cong., 2nd sess., December 2016, S.Prt. 114-31 (Washington: GPO, 2017), pp. 695-700.

**Distinguishing Features of Loan Forgiveness and
Loan Repayment Programs**

Loan forgiveness for public service employment

- Provides debt relief for borrowers employed in specific occupations, for specific employers, or in public service
- Benefits are potentially available to an open-ended number of qualified borrowers
- Availability of benefits is generally incorporated into the terms and conditions of certain federal student loans
- Benefits are considered an entitlement to qualified borrowers
- Funding for benefits is typically incorporated into loan subsidy costs
- Forgiven debt is generally excluded from the borrower's gross income for federal income tax purposes

Loan forgiveness following income-driven repayment

- Provides debt relief for borrowers who, after repaying their student loans as a proportion of their income for an extended period of time, have not repaid their entire student loan debt
- Benefits are potentially available to an open-ended number of qualified borrowers
- Availability of benefits is generally incorporated into the terms and conditions of certain federal student loans
- Benefits are considered an entitlement to qualified borrowers
- Funding for benefits is typically incorporated into loan subsidy costs
- Forgiven debt often may be included as part of the borrower's gross income for federal income tax purposes

Loan repayment for public service employment

- Provides debt relief for borrowers employed in specific occupations, for specific employers, or in public service
- Benefits are generally available to a limited number of qualified borrowers, subject to the appropriation of funds
- Program-specific benefits may be designed to address broad employment needs or shortages in a specific occupation or geographic location, or may be offered by government agencies to support the recruitment and retention of qualified employees
- Benefits are not considered an entitlement to qualified borrowers
- Funding for benefits is typically provided through discretionary appropriations
- Repaid debt is generally included as part of the borrower's income for federal income tax purposes

Loans Eligible for Forgiveness or Repayment

There are three broad categories of loans that may be eligible for inclusion in federal loan forgiveness and loan repayment programs:

1) Federal student loans made through programs authorized by Title IV of the Higher Education Act (HEA) and administered by the U.S. Department of Education (ED), Office of Federal Student Aid (FSA).
2) Student loans made through programs authorized by Title VII and Title VIII of the Public Health Service Act (PHSA) and administered by the U.S. Department of Health and Human Services (HHS), Health Resources and Services Administration (HRSA).
3) Private (nonfederal) education loans.

For most federal loan forgiveness and loan repayment programs, eligible loans include only federal student loans made through HEA or PHSA programs; however, for a small number of programs, eligible loans also include private education loans. Brief summaries of student loan types that may be eligible for loan forgiveness or loan repayment are provided below.

HEA Federal Student Loan Programs

At present, federal student loans are being made only through one HEA, Title IV federal student aid program—the Direct Loan program authorized under Part D of Title IV. However, federal student loans were previously also made through two other HEA programs. Until June 30, 2010, federal student loans were also made through the Federal Family Education Loan (FFEL) program, a guaranteed loan program, authorized under Part B of Title IV.[12] FFEL program loans were made with terms and conditions that were substantially similar to those of loans offered through

---

[12] Prior to the establishment of the FFEL program, federal student loans had been made through other loan programs authorized under Part B of Title IV.

the Direct Loan program.[13] Until September 30, 2017, federal student loans had been made through the Federal Perkins Loan program, which was authorized under Part E of Title IV.

In the Direct Loan program, loans are made by the government with federal capital. ED administers the program, and activities such as loan origination, servicing, and collection are performed by federal contractors. In the FFEL program, loans were made by nonfederal lenders with nonfederal capital. These entities were responsible for originating, holding, and servicing these loans. Nonprofit guaranty agencies administer federal loan insurance and process loan forgiveness benefits. During the period when the FFEL and Direct Loan programs both operated, one set of loan types was made through the FFEL program and another similar set of loan types was made through the Direct Loan program. While these two sets of loan types had borrower terms and conditions that were quite similar, some of the ways in which they differed pertained to availability of loan forgiveness benefits. Where applicable, differences in the availability of loan forgiveness benefits are noted in the discussion that follows.[14]

In the Perkins Loan program, loans were made by institutions of higher education (IHEs) with a combination of capital provided by the federal government and capital provided by the institution. In the Perkins Loan program, the institution served as the lender and remain responsible for originating and servicing Perkins Loans and for processing loan cancelation benefits.[15]

---

[13] The authority to make new loans through the FFEL program was terminated by the SAFRA Act, Title II of the Health Care and Education Reconciliation Act of 2010 (HCERA; P.L. 111-152). For additional information on the SAFRA Act, see CRS Report R41127, *The SAFRA Act: Education Programs in the FY2010 Budget Reconciliation*, archived, available to congressional clients upon request.

[14] For detailed information on the loan types made through the Direct Loan and FFEL programs, see CRS Report R40122, *Federal Student Loans Made Under the Federal Family Education Loan Program and the William D. Ford Federal Direct Loan Program: Terms and Conditions for Borrowers*.

[15] For additional information on the Federal Perkins Loan program in general, see CRS Report RL31618, *Campus- Based Student Financial Aid Programs Under the Higher Education Act*.

The following loan types comprise the primary types of loans that are currently being made—or were made in recent years—through HEA, Title IV federal student loan programs.

Subsidized Loans

In the Direct Loan program, Direct Subsidized Loans are available only to undergraduate students who demonstrate financial need.[16] The federal government "subsidizes" these loans by not assessing interest charges while the borrower is enrolled in an eligible academic program on at least a half-time basis, during a six-month grace period prior the loan entering repayment status,[17] and during periods of authorized deferment. Prior to July 1, 2012, Direct Subsidized Loans were also available to graduate and professional students.[18] Borrowing limits restrict the amounts that students may borrow during a given academic year and in the aggregate over multiple years. In FY2017, 6.2 million Direct Subsidized Loans, totaling $21.5 billion, were made.[19]

Unsubsidized Loans

Direct Unsubsidized Loans are available to undergraduate, graduate, and professional students. Students are not required to demonstrate financial need to be eligible to borrow these loans.[20] As a non-need-based

---

[16] Prior to July 1, 2010, loans with substantially similar terms and conditions as Direct Subsidized Loans—Subsidized Stafford Loans—were made through the FFEL program. For the remainder of this chapter, Direct Subsidized Loans and FFEL Subsidized Stafford Loans are referred to jointly as *Subsidized Loans*; however, in instances where loan forgiveness or loan repayment benefits are only available to borrowers of one loan type, this distinction is noted.

[17] The interest subsidy during the six-month grace period does not apply to Direct Subsidized Loans for which the first disbursement was made from July 1, 2012, through June 30, 2014.

[18] The authority to make Subsidized Loans to graduate and professional students was eliminated under the Budget Control Act of 2011 (BCA; P.L. 112-25). For additional information on changes made to the Direct Loan program by the BCA, see CRS Report R41965, *The Budget Control Act of 2011*.

[19] U.S. Department of Education, *FY 2019 Department of Education Justifications of Appropriation Estimates to the Congress*, Volume II, Student Loans Overview, p. Q-24.

[20] Prior to July 1, 2010, loans with substantially similar terms and conditions—Unsubsidized Stafford Loans—were made through the FFEL program. For the remainder of this report, Direct Unsubsidized Loans and FFEL Unsubsidized Stafford Loans are referred to jointly as Unsubsidized Loans; however, in instances where loan forgiveness or loan repayment benefits are only available to borrowers of one loan type, this distinction is noted.

loan, loan proceeds may be used to finance portions of a student's cost of attendance (COA) that would otherwise be expected to be met by the student's expected family contribution (EFC) toward postsecondary education expenses. For these loans, the borrower is responsible for paying all the interest that accrues on the loan from the time it is disbursed, although interest payments may be deferred until the loan enters repayment status. Unsubsidized Loan borrowing is also limited by annual and aggregate borrowing limits. In FY2017, 8.1 million Direct Unsubsidized Loans, totaling $49.8 billion, were made.[21]

PLUS Loans

Direct PLUS Loans are available to the parents of undergraduate students who are dependent on them for financial support, as well as to graduate and professional students.[22] Like Unsubsidized Loans, these are non-need-based loans and may be used to finance postsecondary education expenses that would otherwise be expected to be met by a student's EFC. There are no explicit limits to the amount an individual may borrow in PLUS Loans. Rather, each year, an individual may borrow up to the amount that the COA of the student on whose behalf the loan is made is greater than his or her estimated financial assistance (EFA) from other sources (e.g., Pell Grants, Subsidized Loans, Unsubsidized Loans, private scholarships, etc.). In FY2017, 0.9 million Direct PLUS Loans, totaling $12.5 billion, were made to parents of undergraduate students and 0.6 million Direct PLUS Loans, totaling $9.9 billion, were made to graduate and professional students.[23]

---

[21] U.S. Department of Education, *FY 2019 Department of Education Justifications of Appropriation Estimates to the Congress*, Volume II, Student Loans Overview, p. Q-24.
[22] When first established, PLUS Loans were referred to as Parent Loans for Undergraduate Students. Prior to July 1, 2010, PLUS Loans were made through the FFEL program with terms and conditions that were mostly similar to Direct PLUS Loans. For the remainder of this report, Direct PLUS Loans and FFEL PLUS Loans are referred to jointly as *PLUS Loans*; however, in instances where loan forgiveness or loan repayment benefits are only available to borrowers of one loan type, this distinction is noted.
[23] U.S. Department of Education, *FY 2019 Department of Education Justifications of Appropriation Estimates to the Congress*, Volume II, Student Loans Overview, p. Q-24.

Consolidation Loans

Direct Consolidation Loans allow borrowers with existing federal student loans to combine their loan obligations into a single loan and to extend their repayment period.

Consolidation Loans must include at least one loan made through either the Direct Loan or the FFEL program. In addition, Consolidation Loans may include loans made through the federal student loan programs authorized or previously authorized under Title IV of the HEA[24] and loans made through the following programs authorized under Title VII and Title VIII of the PHSA (described below):

- Health Professions Student Loans (HPSL)
- Loans for Disadvantaged Students (LDS)
- Nursing Student Loans (NSL)
- Health Education Assistance Loans (HEAL)

That borrowers may incorporate different loan types into a Consolidation Loan is particularly relevant in the examination of loan forgiveness and loan repayment programs. This characteristic of Consolidation Loans facilitates the extension of certain loan forgiveness and loan repayment benefits to borrowers of loans originally made without those benefits upon such loans being incorporated into a Consolidation Loan.

The Direct Consolidation Loans currently being made are fixed rate loans for which the interest rate is based on the weighted average interest rate of the loans being consolidated, rounded up to the nearest higher one-eighth of 1%.[25] In FY2017, 0.9 million Direct Consolidation Loans, totaling $48.8 billion, were made.[26]

---

[24] These loan types (some of which are no longer being disbursed) are Federal Perkins Loans, Guaranteed Student Loans, Federal Insured Student Loans (FISL), National Direct Student Loans, National Defense Student Loans, Supplemental Loans for Students (SLS), and Auxiliary Loans to Assist Students (ALAS).

[25] Prior to July 1, 2010, Consolidation Loans were made through both the Direct Loan and FFEL programs. The terms and conditions applicable to a Consolidation Loan depend on when the loan was made. Prior to July 1, 2006, there were notable differences between the terms and conditions of Direct Consolidation Loans and those of FFEL Consolidation Loans.

Perkins Loans

Perkins Loans were available to undergraduate and graduate and professional students. IHEs were required to make Perkins Loans reasonably available to all eligible students, with priority given to students with exceptional financial need.[27] Interest on Perkins Loans is fixed at 5% per year,[28] and interest does not accrue prior to a borrower's beginning repayment or during periods of authorized deferment. Borrowers who are engaged in certain types of public service may have a portion of their Perkins Loans cancelled for each complete year of service. In FY2017, approximately 253,000 Perkins Loans, totaling $782,230 million, were made.[29]

Health Resources and Services Administration Loan Programs

HRSA, within HHS, makes student loans to specific health professions students through five loan programs authorized under Title VII and Title VIII of the PHSA. Collectively these programs made 20,849 loans in academic year 2016-2017 for a total of approximately $162.8 million.[30] The five programs are described below.[31]

However, for loans made after July 1, 2006, the terms and conditions of loans made under both programs are substantially similar. For the remainder of this report, Direct Consolidation Loans and FFEL Consolidation Loans are referred to jointly as *Consolidation Loans*; however, in instances where loan forgiveness or loan repayment benefits are only available to borrowers of one loan type, this distinction is noted.

[26] U.S. Department of Education, *FY 2019 Department of Education Justifications of Appropriation Estimates to the Congress*, Volume II, Student Loans Overview, p. Q-24.

[27] Authorization to make new Perkins Loans to eligible students expired September 30, 2017. Borrowers of Perkins Loan remain responsible for making payments on their loans.

[28] Older Perkins Loans, which may remain outstanding, were made with other interest rates (i.e., 3% or 4%), depending on when the loan was made.

[29] U.S. Department of Education, *FY 2018 Department of Education Justifications of Appropriation Estimates to the Congress*, Volume II, Student Financial Assistance, p. O-39.

[30] Email Communication, Health Resources and Services Administration, Office of Legislation, August 15, 2018. The amount loaned under the Nurse Faculty Loan Program exceeded the program's annual appropriation because the loaned amount included non-federal matching funds and loan funds that were recouped from individuals.

[31] For additional information on PHSA loans, see U.S. Department of Health and Human Services, Health Resources and Services Administration, "Loans & Scholarships," at https://bhw.hrsa.gov/loansscholarships; for information on the Nurse Faculty Loan Program, see U.S. Department of Health and Human Services, Health Resources and Services Administration, "Nurse Faculty Loan Program (NFLP)," at http://bhpr.hrsa.gov/nursing/grants/nflp.html.

Health Professions Student Loans

This program provides low interest rate loans to full-time students who are pursuing degrees in dentistry, optometry, pharmacy, podiatric medicine, or veterinary medicine. The program is administered by schools that select participants who are citizens, nationals, or lawful permanent residents of the United States and financially needy.[32] For academic year 2016-2017, HRSA estimated that it made 6,842 loans, totaling $64.2 million.[33]

Primary Care Loans

This program provides 5% fixed interest rate loans to full-time students who are pursuing degrees in allopathic or osteopathic medicine. The program is administered by individual medical schools that select participants who are citizens, nationals, or lawful permanent residents of the United States and financially needy. In exchange for receiving a primary care loan, students must complete a residency in a primary care field (family medicine, internal medicine, pediatrics, preventive medicine, osteopathic general practice or combined programs in internal medicine and pediatrics) and practice in a primary care field for 10 years. Loan recipients who fail to meet the service requirements must repay their primary care loans at a higher interest rate of 7%.[34] For academic year 2016-2017, HRSA estimated that it made 252 loans, totaling $17.8 million.[35]

Loans for Disadvantaged Students

This program provides need-based, low interest rate loans to students from disadvantaged backgrounds—defined as coming from a background

---

[32] U.S. Department of Health and Human Services, Health Resources and Services Administration, "School-Based Scholarships and Loans," at https://bhw.hrsa.gov/loans scholarships/schoolbasedloans.

[33] Email Communication, Health Resources and Services Administration, Office of Legislation, August 15, 2018.

[34] U.S. Department of Health and Human Services, Health Resources and Services Administration, "School-Based Scholarships and Loans," at https://bhw.hrsa.gov/loans scholarships/schoolbasedloans.

[35] Email Communication, Health Resources and Services Administration, Office of Legislation, August 15, 2018.

that has inhibited the individual from pursuing a health professional degree or coming from a low-income background based on the family's income— who are pursuing degrees in allopathic or osteopathic medicine, optometry, podiatry, pharmacy, or veterinary medicine. The program is administered by individual schools that select students who are citizens, nationals, or lawful permanent residents of the United States.[36] For academic year 2016-2017, HRSA estimated that it made 1,619 loans, totaling $21.7 million.[37]

Nursing Student Loans

This program provides low interest rate loans to students who are pursuing studies that lead to a diploma, associate, baccalaureate, or graduate degree in nursing. The program is administered by nursing schools that select participants who are citizens, nationals, or lawful permanent residents of the United States and financially needy.[38] For academic year 2016-2017, HRSA estimated that it made 10,138 loans, totaling $31.8 million.[39]

Nurse Faculty Loans

This program provides loans to registered nurses who are completing their graduate studies necessary to become qualified nursing school faculty. The program is administered by individual nursing schools that offer eligible advanced masters or doctoral degree nursing programs. Nursing schools select participants for loans and may also offer loan forgiveness (see "Nursing Faculty Loan Repayment Program" in Appendix

---

[36] U.S. Department of Health and Human Services, Health Resources and Services Administration, "Loans for Disadvantaged Students," at http://www.hrsa.gov/loanscholar ships/loans/disadvantaged.html.

[37] Email Communication, Health Resources and Services Administration, Office of Legislation, August 15, 2018.

[38] U.S. Department of Health and Human Services, Health Resources and Services Administration, "School-Based Scholarships and Loans," at https://bhw.hrsa.gov/ loansscholarships/schoolbasedloans.

[39] Email Communication, Health Resources and Services Administration, Office of Legislation, August 15, 2018.

A).[40] For academic year 2016-2017, HRSA estimated that it made 1,998 loans, totaling $27.3million.[41]

Health Education Assistance Loan (HEAL) Program Loans

A sixth program, the Health Education Assistance Loans (HEAL) program, authorized in Title VII, Part A-I of the PHSA, no longer makes new loans, but the program continues to receive an appropriation to administer outstanding loans.[42] HEAL program loans were gradually phased out between 1995 and 1999 but were available to students to support their pursuit of degrees in allopathic and osteopathic medicine, dentistry, veterinary medicine, optometry, podiatry, public health, pharmacy, chiropractic, and graduate programs in health administration, clinical psychology, and allied health professions. Although the authority to make new HEAL program loans has been terminated, borrowers of these loans remain responsible for making payments on their loans.

Private Education Loans

In addition to the student loans made through the federal student loan programs identified above, student loans are also made by a variety of nonfederal entities. The most common of these are student loans made by private financial institutions (e.g., banks, credit unions), student loans made through state-supported loan programs, and loans made by IHEs. These types of loans are sometimes referred to as private student loans or alternative loans. The terms and conditions of private education loans are specified by the entity responsible for making these loans. While private education loans are not made through federal loan programs, a small

---

[40] U.S. Department of Health and Human Services, Health Resources and Services Administration, "School-Based Scholarships and Loans," at https://bhw.hrsa.gov/loans scholarships/schoolbasedloans.

[41] Email communication, Health Resources and Services Administration, Office of Legislation, August 15, 2018. The amount loaned under the Nurse Faculty Loan Program exceeded the program's annual appropriation because the loaned amount included non-federal matching funds and loan funds that were recouped from individuals.

[42] Authority for the administration of the HEAL program was transferred to the Department of Education under the Consolidated Appropriations Act, 2014 (P.L. 113-76).

number of federal loan repayment programs make benefits available to borrowers of some types of these loans.

LOAN FORGIVENESS AND LOAN REPAYMENT PROGRAM COMPONENTS

All student loan forgiveness and loan repayment programs provide some form of debt relief to borrowers who satisfy certain eligibility criteria. While these programs all support the broad common purpose of providing borrowers with debt relief, they are distinguished by unique program characteristics and features. This section of the report first outlines the three categories of debt relief programs discussed above (see "Distinction among Loan Forgiveness and Loan Repayment Programs") and the qualifying criteria for borrowers associated with these three broad categories. It then identifies a number of program components or parameters that are used to characterize or classify the various programs and to facilitate the examination of and comparison between the various programs using a common terminology. Major program components examined include types of qualifying service, the consideration of borrower economic circumstances, amounts and timing of debt relief, and exclusions or limitations on benefits. For program-specific details on the programs discussed in this section, see Appendix A.

This section presents the primary categories of debt relief programs largely in order of their potential scope of availability to borrowers. First, the loan forgiveness entitlement programs are presented, as they are potentially the largest in scale, with programs providing loan forgiveness for public service presented first and then programs providing loan forgiveness as a component of income-driven repayment plans.[43] Programs

---

[43] Programs providing loan forgiveness following income-dependent repayment have the potential to be larger in scale than programs providing loan forgiveness for public service because their availability is not contingent on an individual's completion of a specific service requirement. They are presented second in this discussion, as their availability has only recently expanded as a new variation of federal loan forgiveness benefits that

providing loan repayment for broad public service or employment needs are then presented, because their availability to borrowers is generally limited to a discrete number of individuals and they are smaller in scale than programs providing loan forgiveness. Finally, programs providing loan repayment for public service in government employment are presented, as they are generally more narrowly targeted to meet agency-specific recruitment and retention needs and are likely the smallest in scale of the loan repayment and forgiveness programs.

Availability of Loan Forgiveness for Public Service Employment

As described above, loan forgiveness for public service employment provides debt relief to qualified borrowers employed in certain occupations, for specific employers, or in public service. These benefits are considered entitlements and are written into the terms and conditions of widely available federal student loans (e.g., Direct Subsidized Loans and Direct Unsubsidized Loans and Perkins Loans). They are potentially available to an open-ended number of qualified borrowers.

Table 1 provides a summary of the various loan forgiveness for public service employment programs offered. It highlights whether forgiveness benefits are available to borrowers who are employed with a single specified employer, one of multiple eligible employers, or if there is no specific employer requirement. It also highlights whether benefits are available to borrowers who are employed in a single specified occupation, one of multiple eligible occupations; or if there is no specific occupation requirement. Finally, it highlights whether a borrower must qualify based, in part, on their economic circumstances during repayment (i.e., whether the program has an eligibility component that assesses the borrower's income). The table also provides details on the operational status of the program. Programs are listed in descending order of their size to reflect the

---

traditionally were available only after an individual's completion of specified types of public service.

scale of benefits that have been or are estimated to be made available to borrowers.

Table 1. Loan Forgiveness for Public Service Employment Programs Program Requirements and Details

Program	Eligible Employer(s)	Eligible Occupations	Income Component (Y/N)	Operational Notes
Direct Loan Public Service Loan Forgiveness	Multiple	Multiple	N	Currently active[b]; individuals were first eligible to receive benefits on October 1, 2017
Stafford Loan Forgiveness for Teachers	Multiple	Single	N	Currently active[b]
Federal Perkins Loan Cancellation	Multiple	Multiple	N	Currently active[b]

Source: CRS analysis of applicable statutory provisions in the Higher Education Act.

[a] To maximize the amount of loan forgiveness benefits realized under this program, borrowers must pay less than the amount they would pay under the Standard Repayment Plan with a 10-year repayment period. In practice, this means borrowers must qualify for reduced payments under one of the income-driven repayment plans; borrowers typically qualify for reduced payments by demonstrating a partial financial hardship. Thus, although the terms of the Public Service Loan Forgiveness program do not specify that the realization of benefits is income-driven, in practice it is often the case.

[b] A program is considered to have been active if, since October 1, 2017, borrowers have been eligible to qualify for or begin qualifying for loan forgiveness benefits under the program.

Table 1 illustrates that although loan forgiveness benefits are entitlements that are potentially available to a wide array of borrowers, to qualify for benefits borrowers must still meet specific eligibility criteria, including completing a specific type of service or entering into a particular occupation or profession.

All three programs are widely available to individuals serving as teachers, while Federal Perkins Loan Cancellation is available to individuals who also serve in other specific public service occupations, such as law enforcement personnel and public defenders, and Direct Loan Public Service Loan Forgiveness is available to an even broader array of individuals who are employed full-time in public service, which includes employment in federal, state, local, or tribal government agencies, and certain nonprofit organizations. Additionally, borrowers of loans made under these programs must serve for a minimum period of time. For these loan forgiveness programs, service commitments generally last between 1 year (for partial benefits) and 10 years.

Availability of Loan Forgiveness Following Income-Driven Repayment

Loan forgiveness following income-driven repayment provides debt relief to borrowers who repay their federal student loans as a proportion of their income for an extended period of time but who have not repaid their entire student loan debt. These benefits are considered entitlements and are written into the terms and conditions of widely available federal student loans (e.g., Direct Subsidized Loans and Direct Unsubsidized Loans). These repayment plans are potentially available to an open-ended number of qualified borrowers; however, they are distinct from those programs that target public service employment.

Table 2 provides a summary of the various loan forgiveness programs that provide debt relief to individuals following income-driven repayment and provides details on the operational status of each program. The table is organized according to the date on which borrowers first became eligible to repay under each plan. Unlike the loan forgiveness programs presented in Table 1, these programs are not grouped by the potential scope of availability to borrowers and financial resources used to provide benefits, because numerous factors and borrower characteristics may affect program participation, which makes it difficult to estimate the potential scope of each program.

Table 2 illustrates that the various programs that provide loan forgiveness following income- driven repayment are widely available to a potentially open-ended number of borrowers who meet income-driven qualifications. Unlike loan forgiveness or repayment programs that seek to encourage borrowers to enter into certain service or occupational commitments, no such employer-specific or occupational or service requirements exist for these programs. Rather, under each of the above programs, borrowers generally must make monthly payments towards their qualifying federal student loans for a specified period of time (between 20 and 25 years). The amount of monthly payments is determined based on factors including the amount of the student loan debt, family size, and adjusted gross income; monthly payments are capped at a percentage of a borrower's discretionary income (between 10% and 20%) or other income-driven criteria. At the end of each program's repayment period, the outstanding balance of a borrower's loans is then forgiven and they are no longer responsible for payments on their loans.

**Table 2. Loan Forgiveness Following Income-Driven
Repayment Programs (Program Requirements and Details)**

Program	Income-Driven (Y/N)	Operational Notes
Income-Contingent Repayment Plan	Y	Borrowers became eligible to repay under this plan on July 1, 1994
Income-Based Repayment Plan for Pre-July 1, 2014, Borrowers	Y	Borrowers became eligible to repay under this plan after July 1, 2009
Pay-As-You-Earn	Y	Borrowers became eligible to repay under this plan on December 21, 2012
Income-Based Repayment Plan for New Borrowers on or after July 1, 2014	Y	Borrowers became eligible to repay under this plan after July 1, 2014
Revised Pay-As-You-Earn	Y	Borrowers became eligible to repay under this plan on December 17, 2015

Source: CRS analysis of relevant statutory and regulatory provisions.

Availability of Loan Repayment for Public Service Employment

Loan repayment for public service employment provides debt relief benefits to borrowers employed in specific occupations, for specific employers, or in public service. Some of these program benefits are often used to meet broad employment needs or shortages (e.g., within specific occupations or geographic locations), while others are intended to help individual government agencies recruit and retain qualified employees and often serve as additional compensation, similar to benefits offered by private employers. Both types of loan repayment for public service employment are generally available to a limited number of qualified borrowers, subject to the appropriation of program funds; they are not considered entitlements to qualified borrowers.

Loan Repayment Programs Addressing Broad Employment Needs or Shortages

Loan repayment programs addressing broad employment needs or shortages are generally available to a limited number of qualified borrowers and subject to the appropriation of program funds. These programs are smaller in scale, when considering their availability to borrowers, than are the previously discussed loan forgiveness programs.

Table 3 provides a summary of the various loan repayment programs offered for the purposes of meeting broad employment needs or shortages. It highlights whether repayment benefits are available to borrowers who are employed with a single specified employer, one of multiple eligible employers, or if no particular employer is specified. It also highlights whether benefits are available to borrowers who are employed in a single specified occupation, one of multiple eligible occupations; or if there is no specific occupational requirement. Finally, it highlights whether borrowers must qualify based, in part, on their economic circumstances (i.e., whether the program has an eligibility component that assesses the borrower's income).

The table is organized by operational status of each program, and within each operational subheading, programs are grouped by administering department or agency. Unlike the loan forgiveness programs presented in Table 1, these programs are not grouped by the potential scope of availability to borrowers and financial resources used to provide benefits, because such data are inconsistently available across programs.

**Table 3. Loan Repayment for Public Service Employment
Programs Addressing Broad Employment Needs or Shortages
(Program Requirements and Details)**

Program	Eligible Employers(s)	Eligible Occupation(s)[a]	Income Component (Y/N)
Currently Active Programs[b]			
Veterinary Medicine LRP	Multiple	Single	N
Indian Health Service LRP	Multiple	Single	N
National Health Service Corps LRP	Multiple	Single	N
National Health Service Corps Students to Service LRP	Multiple	Single	N
National Health Service Corps State LRP	Multiple	Single	N
Loan Repayments for Health Professional School Faculty	Multiple	Single	N
General, Pediatric, and Public Health Dentistry Faculty Loan Repayment	Multiple	Single	N
Nursing Education LRP (NURSE Corps)	Multiple	Single	N
Nurse Faculty LRP	Multiple	Single	N
National Institutes of Health Extramural Loan Repayment Programs	Multiple	Multiple	Y
John R. Justice Loan Repayment for Prosecutors and Public Defenders	Multiple	Single	N
Previously Active Programs			
Civil Legal Assistance Attorney LRP[c]	Multiple	Single	N
Public Health Workforce LRP[c]	Multiple	Single	N
Never Active Programs[d]			
Substance Use Disorder Treatment Loan Repayment Program	Multiple	Single	N
Loan Forgiveness for Service in Areas of National Need[e]	Multiple	Multiple	N
Pediatric Subspecialist LRP	Multiple	Single	N
Nursing Workforce Development Student Loans: Loan Cancellation[e]	Multiple	Single	N
Nursing Workforce Development Student Loans: Loan Repayments[f]	n/a	n/a	Y
Eligible Individual Student Loan Repayment	Multiple	Single	N

Source: CRS analysis of relevant statutory and regulatory provisions and additional resources.

Notes: The acronym "LRP" means "loan repayment program."

[a.] In this table, the term "eligible occupation(s)" is broadly used to indicate eligible types of employment or service that are significantly similar in nature or purpose, even if tasks performed as part of the employment or service may vary somewhat among employment opportunities.

For example, some programs are available to healthcare occupations, and individuals employed in such occupations may be physicians, nurses, and other types of healthcare providers.

b. A program is considered to have been active if, since October 1, 2017, borrowers have been eligible to qualify for or begin qualifying for loan repayment benefits under the program.

c. Appropriations have not been provided since FY2010.

d. A program is considered never to have been active if it has been authorized but has not yet received appropriations.

e. Despite the program's name, this is classified as loan repayment program, because benefits are contingent on discretionary appropriations.

f. This program is only available to individuals who withdraw from nursing programs. They must have been unable to complete their studies, be in exceptionally needy circumstances, and have not resumed their studies within two years after they withdrew.

Table 3 illustrates the variety of employment needs these broad-based loan repayment programs are currently intended to meet. In total, there are 19 such programs, and 15 of these programs are targeted, at least in part, to health-related occupations. Of these health-related occupations programs, eight are intended to specifically address health care provider shortages and four are intended to meet health care faculty needs. Other occupations specifically targeted by loan repayment programs to meet broad employment needs include legal occupations and large animal veterinarians who provide emergency services.

In most of the programs detailed in Table 3, borrowers need not fulfill their service obligations with a single individual employer. Rather, they may fulfill their service by working for multiple employers within the broader class of employers.[44] Some of these programs, however, require borrowers to serve in specific geographic locations, typically underserved rural or disadvantaged areas.[45]

Finally, like the loan forgiveness programs, borrowers participating in loan repayment programs must serve for a minimum period of time. For such programs, service commitments generally last between one and five years.

---

[44] See, for example, "National Institutes of Health Extramural Loan Repayment Program: Health Disparities Research" in Appendix A.
[45] See, for example, "National Health Service Corps Loan Forgiveness Program" in Appendix A.

*Loan Repayment Programs to Recruit and Retain Federal
Government Employees*

Loan repayment programs to recruit and retain federal government
employees are generally narrowly targeted to meet agency-specific
recruitment and retention needs and are potentially the smallest in scale of
the loan repayment and forgiveness programs. Although, for many of these
programs, information on the programs' scale (e.g., number of benefit
recipients and amount of benefits received) is not readily available, the
Office of Personnel Management annually reports on the number of
agencies participating in, the number of beneficiaries from, and the amount
of benefits received from the Government Employee Student Loan
Repayment Program.[46]

Table 4 provides a summary of the various loan repayment programs
offered for the purposes of individual federal agencies' recruiting and
retaining qualified employees. It highlights whether repayment benefits are
available only to borrowers who are employed by a single government
agency or if benefits may be offered by federal government employers. It
also highlights whether benefits are available only to borrowers who are
employed in a single specified occupation, one of multiple eligible
occupations; or if no occupational requirement is specified. In addition, it
highlights whether borrowers must qualify based, in part, on their
economic circumstances (i.e., whether the program has an eligibility
component that assesses the borrower's income).

The table is organized by operational status of each program, and
within each operational subheading, programs are grouped by
administering department or agency. Unlike the loan forgiveness programs
presented in Table 1, these programs are not grouped by the potential
scope of availability to borrowers and financial resources used to provide
benefits, because such data are inconsistently available across programs.

---

[46] See Office of Personnel Management, *Federal Student Loan Repayment Program: Calendar Year 2016*, February 2018.

Table 4. Loan Repayment for Public Service Employment
in the Federal Government (Program Requirements and Details)

Program	Eligible Employer(s)	Eligible Occupation(s)[a]	Income Component (Y/N)
Currently Active Programs[b]			
LRP for Senate Employees	Multiple[c]	Multiple	N
LRP for House Employees	Multiple[d]	Multiple	N
Congressional Budget Office LRP	Single	Multiple	N
Government Employee Student LRP	Multiple	Multiple	N
Defense Acquisition Workforce LRP	Single	Multiple	N
Armed Forces LRP: Enlisted Members on Active Duty in Specified Military Specialties	Single	Multiple	N
LRP: Members of the Selected Reserve	Single	Multiple	N
LRP: Health Professions Officers Serving in the Selected Reserve with Wartime Critical Medical Skill Shortages	Single	Single	N
LRP: Chaplains Serving in the Selected Reserve	Single	Single	N
Education Debt Reduction Program	Single	Multiple	N
National Institutes of Health Intramural LRP	Single	Multiple	Y
National and Community Service Grant program, Educational Award	Single	Multiple	N
Previously Active Programs			
Capitol Police LRP[e]	Single	Multiple	N
Centers for Disease Control and Prevention/Agency for Toxic Substances and Disease Registry Educational Loan Repayment Program[f]	Multiple	Multiple	Y
Never Active Programs[g]			
Indian Health Service: Mental Health Prevention and Treatment LRP	Multiple	Multiple	N
Loan Repayment Program for Clinical Researchers from Disadvantaged Backgrounds	Single	Single	Y
Program for the Repayment of Educational Loans	Single	Single	N
Veterans Affairs Specialty Education Loan Repayment Program	Single	Single	N

Table 4. (Continued)

Program	Eligible Employer(s)	Eligible Occupation(s)[a]	Income Component (Y/N)
Program Information Unavailable[h]			
Armed Forces National Call to Service	Single	Multiple	N
LRP: Commissioned Officers in Specified Health Professions	Single	Single	N
Armed Forces Student Loan Interest Payment Program for Members on Active Duty	Single	Multiple	N
Coast Guard LRP	Single	Multiple	N
Federal Food, Drug, and Cosmetic Act LRP	Single	Single	Y
National Indian Forest Resources Management Postgraduation Recruitment Assumption of Student Loans	Single	Multiple	N
American Indian Agricultural Resource Management Postgraduation Recruitment Assumption of Student Loans	Multiple	Multiple	N

Source: CRS analysis of relevant statutory and regulatory provisions and additional resources.

Notes: The acronym "LRP" means "loan repayment program."

[a] In this table, the term "eligible occupation(s)" is broadly used to indicate eligible types of employment or service that are significantly similar in nature or purpose, even if tasks performed as part of the employment or service may vary somewhat among employment opportunities. For example, some programs are available to healthcare occupations, and individuals employed in such occupations may be physicians, nurses, and other types of healthcare providers.

[b] A program is considered to have been active if, since October 1, 2017 borrowers have been eligible to qualify for loan forgiveness benefits under the program.

[c] Individuals working for U.S. Senate offices are employed by individual Member or committee offices that may offer loan repayment benefits at their discretion.

[d] Individuals working for U.S. House of Representatives offices are employed by individual Member or committee offices that may offer loan repayment benefits at their discretion.

[e] Appropriations have not been provided since FY2010.

[f] Program authorization expired in FY2002.

[g] A program is considered never to have been active if it has been authorized but has not yet received appropriations.

[h] Neither appropriations figures nor information on the availability of benefits to borrowers is available for FY2017. Because such information is unavailable, CRS is unable to determine whether these programs were active as of FY2017.

Table 4 shows the array of loan repayment programs operated by federal agencies as a means of recruiting and retaining qualified employees. There are 25 such programs, and of these programs, 8 are designed specifically to recruit and retain members of the Armed Forces, with many of the other programs available at federal agencies to varying degrees.

The programs detailed in Table 4 vary as to whether benefits are available to any employee within an agency or only to employees in specific occupations at the agency. Several programs are generally open to any agency employee,[47] while others are available to employees employed in fields or occupations designated by the administering agency as hard-to-fill or in-need,[48] and yet others are available to agency employees who are employed in certain fields or occupations.[49]

Finally, like the loan repayment programs designed to meet broad employment needs or shortages, borrowers participating in loan repayment programs must serve for a minimum period of time. For such programs, service commitments generally are between one and five years.

Borrower's Economic Circumstances

Individuals' economic circumstances may affect eligibility, with several loan forgiveness and loan repayment programs using a borrower's economic circumstances as a criterion to qualify for benefits. There are two primary ways that individuals may qualify for benefits based on their economic circumstances. Some programs allow individuals to qualify for benefits based on their economic circumstances at the time they borrow, while other programs allow individuals to qualify for benefits based on their economic circumstances during the repayment period. In some

---

[47] See, for example, "Congressional Budget Office Student Loan Repayment" in Appendix A.
[48] See, for example, "Armed Forces Educational Loan Repayment Program: Enlisted Members on Active Duty in Specified Military Specialties" in Appendix A.
[49] See, for example, "Defense Acquisition Workforce Student Loan Repayment Program" in Appendix A.

programs, the borrower's economic circumstance is one factor that is considered alongside others, such as qualifying types of service.

Typically, for programs that extend debt relief to borrowers based on their economic circumstances, individuals may be eligible to receive program benefits if they are from a disadvantaged background (based on family economic circumstances)[50] or if their expected monthly loan payment exceeds a certain percentage of their income.[51]

Amount and Timing of Benefits

Programs can also be categorized by the amount of loan forgiveness or loan repayment benefits provided and the schedule for providing those benefits to qualified borrowers. There are three primary methods used to determine the amount of benefits an individual is eligible to receive and when those benefits are realized. Generally, programs forgive the entire outstanding balance of a borrower's loans or repay either a flat dollar amount specified in the authorizing statute or a percentage of the outstanding loan.

Several programs offer to forgive the entire amount of an individual's outstanding student loans. Typically, in these programs, a borrower is required to make a certain number of payments towards the balance of their student loans, and at the end of a specified period of time, the remaining balance of their outstanding loans is forgiven.[52]

A second way in which benefits may be awarded is by an employer paying repayment benefits in the form of a flat dollar amount, usually either paid as a lump sum or in a series of regular payments (e.g., monthly, yearly).[53] Alternatively, some programs may offer varying flat rates that

[50] See, for example, "National Institutes of Health Loan Repayment Program for Clinical Researchers from Disadvantaged Backgrounds" in Appendix A.
[51] See, for example, "Income-Based Repayment plan for pre-July 1, 2014 borrowers" in Appendix A.
[52] See, for example, "Direct Loan Public Service Loan Forgiveness" in Appendix A.
[53] See, for example, "Government Employee Student Loan Repayment Program" in Appendix A.

are available to individuals depending on the specific type of service performed.[54]

Finally, some programs pay a percentage of an individual's outstanding loans,[55] with a handful offering borrowers the greater of a certain percentage of a borrower's outstanding loans or a flat dollar amount or an amount equal to a percentage of their outstanding loans.[56]

Exclusions and Limitations

Many loan forgiveness and loan repayment programs contain provisions that may restrict or limit the availability of benefits in certain circumstances. In general, borrowers who have defaulted on their loans are ineligible for loan forgiveness or loan repayment benefits. Certain programs contain restrictions that prohibit borrowers from also receiving benefits under certain other federal student loan forgiveness or loan repayment programs for the same qualifying service. In some programs, borrowers must be U.S. citizens or nationals to be eligible for benefits. In programs that provide loan repayment benefits concurrent with or prior to the completion of the qualifying service, borrowers may be financially penalized if they do not complete their term of service.

Prohibition of Double Benefits
Many federal loan forgiveness and loan repayment programs prohibit individuals from benefitting from multiple programs for completion of the same service. For instance, the Stafford Loan Forgiveness for Teachers program will not make benefits available to individuals for the same service used to qualify for benefits under the Public Service Loan Forgiveness (PSLF) program, the Loan Forgiveness for Service in Areas of National Need program, or for AmeriCorps Education Awards.[57]

---

[54] See, for example, "Stafford Loan Forgiveness for Teachers" in Appendix A.
[55] See, for example, "Federal Perkins Loan Cancellation" in Appendix A.
[56] See, for example, "Armed Forces Educational Loan Repayment Program: Enlisted Members on Active Duty in Specific Military Specialties" in Appendix A.
[57] 20 U.S.C. §1078-10(g)(2).

Alternatively, in some programs, individuals are ineligible for benefits if they are already receiving benefits under another program, but they may become eligible for program benefits once their obligation under the first program is completed.[58]

Citizenship and Immigration Status

Some programs specifically require that participants be U.S. citizens, nationals, or legal permanent residents.[59] Many programs, on the other hand, do not expressly state such a requirement, but these programs may nonetheless only be available to these groups of individuals based on the type of loan eligible for forgiveness or repayment. For example, federal student loans made under the Higher Education Act (HEA), Title IV programs (e.g., FFEL program loans, Direct Loan program loans, and Perkins Loans) are only available to U.S. citizens, nationals, legal permanent residents, and other specified "eligible noncitizens."[60] Thus, the availability of programs that provide loan forgiveness or loan repayment benefits only for these types of loans (e.g., the PSLF program, which is only available for Direct Loan program loans) is restricted based on a borrower's citizenship and immigration status at the time the loans were obtained.[61]

Defaulted Loans

Depending on the program, the availability of loan forgiveness and loan repayment benefits may be restricted for borrowers who have defaulted on their loans. In some programs, the availability of benefits for

---

[58] See, for example, "National Institutions of Health Extramural Loan Repayment Program: Health Disparities Research" in Appendix A.

[59] See, for example, "Indian Health Service Loan Repayment Program" in Appendix A.

[60] Those noncitizens eligible to receive federal student financial aid are: U.S. nationals (including natives of American Samoa and Swains Island); permanent U.S. residents with a green card; individuals with an I-94 Arrival/Departure Record designated showing "refugee," "asylum granted," "Cuban-Haitian Entrant (Status Pending)," "Conditional Entrant" (valid only if issued before April 1, 1980), or "Parolee"; individuals with a T-visa or a T-1 visa; and a "battered immigrant-qualified alien" who is a victim of abuse by their citizen or permanent resident spouse or is a child of a person designated as a battered immigrant-qualified alien. Department of Education, Federal Student Aid, "Many non-U.S. citizens qualify for federal student aid," http://studentaid.ed.gov/eligibility/non-us-citizens.

[61] 20 U.S.C. §1087e(m)(1).

borrowers whose loans are in default status depends on certain characteristics of the defaulted loans. For instance, in the Direct Loan Stafford Loan Forgiveness for Teachers program, borrowers are generally ineligible for teacher loan forgiveness on defaulted loans, however, loan forgiveness may be granted to borrowers who have made satisfactory repayment arrangements for their loans. While in the Perkins Loan Cancellation program, borrowers of defaulted loans whose loans have not been accelerated[62] may qualify for loan forgiveness on the same terms as borrowers who have not defaulted, and borrowers of defaulted loans whose loans have been accelerated may qualify for loan forgiveness based on service performed prior to, but not after, the date of acceleration.

Clawback Provisions

Provisions that require recipients of loan forgiveness or loan repayment benefits to pay back the amount of the benefits they received if they fail to complete their service obligations may be referred to as clawback provisions. Such provisions are common in federal loan forgiveness and loan repayment programs. Some clawback provisions only require participants to repay an amount equal to the unearned or disallowed portion of their benefits,[63] while others may require participants to repay an amount equal to the benefit received, plus interest.[64] Moreover, in some programs, clawback provisions may also require beneficiaries to pay punitive fees, in addition to amounts equal to the unearned portion of their benefits.[65] Finally, many programs exempt borrowers from liability for unearned benefits if they become disabled, or upon death.[66]

---

[62] When a loan is accelerated, the institution that made the loan may demand immediate repayment of the entire loan, including any late charges, collection costs, and accrued interest. (34 C.F.R. §674.31(b)(8)).

[63] See, for example, "Armed Forces Educational Loan Repayment Program: Enlisted Members on Active Duty in Specified Military Specialties" in Appendix A.

[64] See, for example, "Indian Health Service Loan Repayment Program" in Appendix A.

[65] See, for example, "National Health Service Corps Loan Repayment Program" in Appendix A.

[66] See, for example, "John R. Justice (JRJ) Loan Repayment for Prosecutors and Public Defenders Program" in Appendix A and 42 U.S.C. §3797cc-21(d)(1)(D).

Tax Treatment of Loan Forgiveness and Repayment Benefits

In general, student loan debt (and other types of debt) that is forgiven or repaid on a borrower's behalf is included as part of the individual's gross income for the purposes of federal income taxation under the Internal Revenue Code (IRC).[67] However, in certain instances, student loan forgiveness and loan repayment benefits may be excluded from gross income and, therefore, exempt from income tax liability.

Some programs' authorizing statutes specifically state that loan forgiveness or loan repayment under those programs will be excluded from an individual's gross income for purposes of taxation. For instance, the HEA specifies that any part of a Federal Perkins Loan that is forgiven is excluded from gross income.[68]

For programs without authorizing statutes that specifically exclude loan forgiveness or loan repayment benefits from gross income, benefits may still be excluded if certain conditions in IRC Section 108(f) are met. The loans that are repaid or forgiven must have been borrowed to assist an individual in attending a qualified educational institution and must contain terms providing that some or all of the loan balance will be cancelled for work for a specified amount of time in certain professions or occupations and for any broad class of employers.[69] The loan must also have been made by specified types of lenders, including the federal and state governments.

Additionally, IRC Section 108(f)(4) provides exclusions for the National Health Service Corps Loan Repayment program (NHSCLRP) and

---

[67] IRC §61(a)(12).

[68] 20 U.S.C. §1087ee(a)(5).

[69] Loans made under the FFEL, Direct Loan, and Perkins Loan programs all contain terms that provide that if borrowers work for a specified amount of time in certain professions, for certain broad classes of employers, some or all of the debt may be cancelled. Borrowers may also refinance existing loans borrowed from *any* lender by obtaining new loans from qualifying educational or other tax-exempt organizations in order to participate in a public service program offered by that organization. The public service program must be designed to encourage individuals to serve in specific occupations and in which the services performed are under the direction of a governmental or tax-exempt organization. If borrowers refinance their loans in this way, any loan forgiveness or repayment benefits received may be excluded from gross income.

state programs eligible to receive funds under the Public Health Service Act (PHSA).[70]

In general, if loan forgiveness or repayment benefits are not specifically excluded from income by statute or if the requirements of IRC Section 108(f)(4)[71] are not met, individuals are responsible for paying any income tax liability associated with the loan forgiveness or loan repayment benefits received. However, at least eight loan forgiveness and loan repayment programs provide supplemental funds to borrowers to offset any tax liability incurred as a result of the discharge of their loans.[72]

Many recipients of loan forgiveness and loan repayment benefits can avoid being subject to thousands of dollars in taxation if their benefits are excluded from gross income. At the same time, the Joint Committee on Taxation estimated that approximately $200 million of revenue was lost in FY2017 due to the exclusion from taxation of income attributable to the forgiveness and repayment of student loan debt.[73]

EFFECTS OF LOAN FORGIVENESS AND LOAN REPAYMENT PROGRAMS

Researchers debate whether providing loan repayment or forgiveness benefits is an effective way to encourage borrowers to enter specific professional or occupational fields, serve in specific geographic areas, or

---

[70] For additional information on the federal income tax treatment of discharged student loans, see U.S. Congress, Senate Committee on the Budget, *Tax Expenditures: Compendium of Background Material on Individual Provisions*, committee print, prepared by the Congressional Research Service, 114th Cong., 2nd sess., December 2016, S.Prt. 114-31 (Washington: GPO, 2017), pp. 695-700.

[71] Federal tax law provides other exclusions from gross income that may be relevant to borrowers whose student loans are discharged. For instance, a borrower may exclude discharged debt from gross income if he or she is insolvent at the time of loan discharge. IRC §108(a)(1).

[72] See, for example, "NIH Extramural Loan Repayment Program: Health Disparities Research," in Appendix A.

[73] Joint Committee on Taxation, Estimates of Federal Tax Expenditures for Fiscal Years 2017-20121, JCX-34-18, <ay25, 2018, p. 40, https://www.jct.gov/publications.html?func=download&id=5095&chk=5095&no_html=1.

enter into government service. In general, three main issues are explored when determining the effect of these programs:

1) Whether individuals would enter into and/or remain in these fields or positions without the prospect of loan forgiveness or loan repayment.
2) Whether student loan debt is the only or the most substantial impediment to entering into and/or remaining in these fields or positions.
3) Whether the prospect of debt relief through loan repayment or loan forgiveness programs encourages students to finance a larger portion of their postsecondary education expenses with student loans than they otherwise would have without such prospects.

These issues largely focus on the individuals who receive loan forgiveness or loan repayment benefits,[74] but another aspect of effectiveness to consider is the cost of these programs to the federal government relative to the benefits received. The analysis below first discusses program effectiveness as it relates to individuals and is then followed by a discussion of the costs that the federal government incurs when operating loan forgiveness and loan repayment programs.

Influence of Loan Repayment and Forgiveness Programs on Employment Choices

In assessing the influence of a loan forgiveness or loan repayment program on an individual's employment choice, one issue to consider is whether, in the absence of such a program, the recipient would have engaged in the qualifying service. Information on the influence of such

---

[74] The majority of research has examined loan repayment programs. In general, loan forgiveness programs occur after an individual has completed a period of service, thereby, rewarding an individual for choosing a specific occupation. This differs from loan repayment programs that provide repayment during or shortly after an individual is working in a specific occupation or geographic location.

programs might be gleaned from an examination that compares the career paths of individuals who have access to loan forgiveness or loan repayment benefits with the career paths of otherwise similarly situated individuals without such access. These types of evaluations generally have not been conducted for federal loan forgiveness and loan repayment programs. However, some data from one federal program may be instructive.

The National Institutes of Health (NIH) examined the career trajectories of loan repayment recipients in its Intramural Research Program (IRP) and compared them with similar individuals who did not receive loan repayment under the IRP. The purposes of the IRP's loan repayment component is to encourage individuals to complete medical research at the NIH and to encourage qualified health professionals to continue careers in medical research in general (e.g., at a university). The NIH found that individuals receiving loan repayment benefits were more likely to continue conducting medical research at the NIH than those who did not. Likewise, individuals who received loan repayment benefits but then left the NIH were more likely to continue a career as a medical researcher than those who did not.[75] This study suggests that the program may be meeting its stated goals.

While the NIH study indicates that its loan repayment program may be meeting its stated goals, the loan repayment program is unlikely the sole reason for at least some of the individuals to remain in the NIH's targeted positions. Other research has found that some individuals would have entered certain fields or taken certain positions in the absence of loan repayments for a variety of other reasons. If this were true, then the program would not have been necessary and, therefore, might be considered ineffective. For example, a loan repayment program may be an effective incentive when jobs are plentiful for recent graduates who are weighing multiple employment opportunities but may be unnecessary when there are fewer employment opportunities. In relatively recent years,

[75] Steven Glazerman and Neil Seftor, *The NIH Intramural Research Loan Repayment Program: Career Outcomes of Participants and Nonparticipants*, Mathematica Policy Research, Inc., Final Report, Washington, DC, November 30, 2005, http://www.lrp.nih.gov/pdf/Intramural_LRP_Outcomes_Evaluation.pdf (hereinafter Glazerman, *NIH Intramural Research Loan Repayment Program*).

for instance, law school graduates have had fewer employment opportunities[76] and may take a public interest or government job because of more limited private sector opportunities. Finally, individuals who accept loan repayment for a specific job might have taken the same job without loan repayment benefits. For example, one study found that healthcare providers who practice in rural areas would have done so without receiving a loan repayment award.[77]

Although in some cases loan forgiveness or loan repayment programs may appear to be unnecessary, in some instances there is evidence showing that participants would likely not have taken a particular position but for loan repayment. For example, the NIH examined its IRP loan repayment program and found that most loan repayment award recipients had competing job offers and stated that the potential for loan repayment was an attractive benefit that was unique to the NIH employment. This was particularly true for physicians who often had competing job offers at higher salaries. Physicians who received loan repayment benefits were also more likely to remain in research at the NIH, which demonstrates that loan repayment may be an important recruitment and retention tool.[78]

Other federal agencies have found that loan repayment programs are effective at recruiting and maintaining staff, but there are indications that some aspects of a program's design may undermine its effectiveness.[79] For example, discretionary programs may have their funding reduced or cut altogether, thus making the availability of loan repayment benefits to individuals uncertain. The effectiveness of these programs as a recruitment incentive may be hard to determine because job applicants do not know

---

[76] National Association for Legal Career Professionals, *Class of 2011 Has Lowest Employment Rate Since Class of 1994*, NALP Bulletin, July 2012, http://www.nalp.org/0712research.

[77] D.M. Renner et al., "The Influence of Loan Repayment on Rural Healthcare Provider Recruitment and Retention in Colorado," *Rural and Remote Health*, vol. 10, no. 1605 (September 4, 2010).

[78] Glazerman, *NIH Intramural Research Loan Repayment Program.*

[79] U.S. Government Accountability Office, *Federal Student Loan Repayment Program: OPM Could Build on Its Efforts to Help Agencies Administer the Program and Measure Results*, 05-762, July 22, 2005.

whether they will receive a loan repayment award until after having accepted a job.[80]

Additionally, loan repayment award amounts may not be a sufficient incentive for individuals to enter into and remain in certain professions. Some researchers have theorized that loan repayment programs may be more likely to be successful in meeting recruitment and retention needs if the financial benefits are sufficiently meaningful to offset a reasonable share of the costs associated with borrowing to pursue a postsecondary education.[81]

Similarly, in some circumstances, while the dollar amount of loan repayment benefits may be perceived as sufficient, additional program design elements such as an individual's responsibility to pay federal income taxes associated with receiving a loan payment may make the benefit less attractive for an individual. Specifically, under the Government Employee Student Loan Repayment Program (GESLRP), participants are responsible for the tax liability, which some agencies estimate can account for 39% of the loan repayment amount. Some agencies suggest that this makes the program less attractive to participants than it would be if benefits were excluded from taxation.[82]

Another consideration is the short-term nature of many of these programs (e.g., providing loan repayment benefits in exchange for a two-year employment commitment), which may contribute to turnover, as individuals may decide to change jobs once they have realized the full benefit of a program. This could possibly lead to a less stable workforce for employers. For example, some researchers have found that individuals

---

[80] Glazerman, *NIH Intramural Research Loan Repayment Program.*

[81] Anna Podolsky and Tara Kini, *How Effective Are Loan Forgiveness and Service Scholarships for Recruiting Teachers?*, Learning Policy Institute, Policy Brief, April 2016, p. 7. See also, Department of Justice, Bureau of Justice Assistance, *John R. Justice Loan Repayment Program: Impact Report*, December 14, 2016, p. 4, https://www.bja.gov/ publications/JRJ-Impact-Report-122016.pdf.

[82] U.S. Government Accountability Office, *Federal Student Loan Repayment Program: OPM Could Build on Its Efforts to Help Agencies Administer the Program and Measure Results*, 05-762, July 22, 2005, p. 22.

who have a service obligation have shorter tenures in a particular position than do individuals who do not have service obligations.[83]

Influence of Student Debt on Employment Choices

A second issue regarding the assessment of loan forgiveness and loan repayment programs is whether individuals would otherwise enter a certain field or take a specific job but for their student loan debt. Loan forgiveness and loan repayment programs are predicated on the assumption that student loan debt is a large factor in making employment decisions. However, researchers have found that career choices are more complex; that debt, in some instances, may have little or no effect on career or job choices; and that a number of other deterrents may reduce student interest in a specific field or may make students less likely to seek employment in certain geographic areas.[84] For example, the National Health Service Corps Loan Repayment Program (NHSCLRP) provides loan repayment benefits to physicians (among other health professionals) who enter primary care and practice in specific geographic areas. Although lower levels of compensation are one deterrent that keep physicians from entering primary care medicine, physicians might not enter these fields for other reasons as well. For instance, a physician may prefer to focus in a specialty or may not want to assume the increased administrative duties that primary care physicians incur.[85] Moreover, others have found that debt levels may play a greater role in career decisions for certain racial and ethnic groups.[86]

---

[83] Till Barnighausen and David E. Bloom, "Financial Incentives for Return of Service in Underserved Areas: A Systematic Review," *BMC Health Services Research*, vol. 9, no. 86 (May 29, 2009).

[84] Robert L. Phillips Jr. et al., *Specialty and Geographic Distribution of the Physician Workforce: What Influences Medical Student and Resident Choices?*, Robert Graham Center and Josiah B. Macy Foundation, Washington, DC, March 2, 2009, http://www.graham-center.org/online/etc/medialib/graham/documents/publications/mongraphs-books/2009/rgcmo-specialty-geographic.Par.0001.File.tmp/Specialty-geography-compressed.pdf.

[85] U.S. Government Accountability Office, Graduate Medical Education: Trends in Training and Student Debt, 09-438R, May 4, 2009, http://www.gao.gov/new.items/d09438r.pdf.

[86] The Committee on Legal Education and Admission to the Bar, "Law School Debt and the Practice of Law," *The Record of the Association of the City of New York*, 2003.

Because it may be difficult or undesirable to target programs by racial and ethnic group, loan forgiveness and loan repayment programs may be available to individuals for whom debt is not a factor in career choice.

A related critique of loan forgiveness and loan repayment programs is that despite these programs' providing a financial inducement for individuals to enter a specific field that is relatively lower paying (e.g., primary care medicine versus a specialty field), the amount received is generally far less than the overall lifetime earnings gap. One study estimated that over a lifetime, the average primary care physician earns $3.5 million less than a specialty physician.[87]

Given that borrowers are unlikely to have $3.5 million in student loan debt, loan repayments cannot fully make up for the lower lifetime earnings from entering primary care.

Other research has found that high levels of debt do influence job choice. For example, in a literature review of the influence of law school debt on legal practice, the author found that high levels of law school debt often make it more likely for recent graduates to work at large law firms, where they are likely to earn more.[88] Similarly, when examining the career trajectories of undergraduates, researchers have found that undergraduate students with higher debt levels are more likely to choose higher salary jobs and less likely to enter education-related fields, work for a government agency, or work at a nonprofit organization—all job choices that traditionally are associated with a lower income than their private sector counterparts.[89] Some studies, however, have found that law school debt levels may play a secondary role in an individual's determination of which occupations to enter after graduation, while demographic

---

[87] The Council on Graduate Medical Education, Twentieth Report, Advancing Primary Care, Rockville, MD, December 2010.

[88] Erica Field, "Educational Debt Burden and Career Choice: Evidence from a Financial Aid Experiment at NYU Law School," *American Economic Journal: Applied Economics*, vol. 1, no. 1 (January 2009), pp. 1-21. This study also examined how the design of a law school's loan repayment program also influenced its effectiveness. Specifically, the author found that scholarship programs were more effective for encouraging students to enter public interest law when compared to loan repayment programs.

[89] Jesse Rothstein and Cecilia Elena Rouse, "Constrained After College: Student Loans and Early Career Occupational Choices," *Journal of Public Economics,* 95(1-2) (February 2011), pp. 149-163.

characteristics may be a more dominant factor in the decision-making process (similar to the finding noted above that there is racial and ethnic variation in the importance of debt on career trajectories). This may indicate that loan repayment programs have little or no effect on the career choice of law school graduates.[90]

Influence of Loan Repayment and Forgiveness Programs on Student Debt

A third issue regarding the effects of student loan forgiveness and loan repayment programs is whether the prospect of debt relief through loan repayment or loan forgiveness programs encourages students to finance a larger portion of their postsecondary education expenses with student loans than they otherwise would have without such prospects. This issue has been specifically raised with regard to those programs—the various income-driven repayment (IDR) plans and PSLF—that provide an open-ended amount of student loan debt relief after borrowers make student loan payments that are capped at a smaller portion of their discretionary income for a limited duration (e.g., 20 years).

Under the IDR plans, monthly payments are tied to income, not amount owed, and individuals may receive forgiveness of their entire outstanding balance of loan principal and interest after certain conditions are met. Monthly payments are limited to a portion (e.g., 10%, 15%) of discretionary income and maximum repayment periods are shorter than may otherwise be necessary to repay the entirety of the debt. Some argue that tying monthly payments to income and not debt in this way may "render the size of the debt irrelevant" to a borrower and may encourage student over-borrowing.[91] In addition, some hypothesize that the lack of student incentive to limit borrowing also may make some students less

---

[90] The Committee on Legal Education and Admission to the Bar, "Law School Debt and the Practice of Law," *The Record of the Association of the City of New York*, 2003.

[91] See, for example, Brian Z. Tamanaha, "The Problems with Income Based Repayment, and the Charge of Elitism: Responses to Schrag and Chambliss," *The Georgetown Journal of Legal Ethics*, vol. 26 (2013), pp. 532-534.

sensitive to the price of education.[92] Similar arguments have been made about the PSLF program, under which individuals may gain the largest amount of forgiveness benefit by repaying their loans under an IDR plan for 10 years while working in public service.[93]

COST OF LOAN FORGIVENESS AND LOAN REPAYMENT PROGRAMS

The granting of loan forgiveness and loan repayment benefits to borrowers results in costs to the federal government. The nature of the costs that are incurred by the government depends on the structure of the applicable program through which these benefits are made available. There are three categories of costs that typically may be associated with loan forgiveness and loan repayment programs: loan subsidy costs, appropriated program costs, and administrative costs.

Loan Subsidy Costs

Loan forgiveness programs typically make available benefits that are incorporated into the terms and conditions of loans that are made through the federal student loan programs, most of which are classified as federal credit programs for federal budgeting purposes. Federal credit consists of federal direct loans and federal loan guarantees.[94] The William D. Ford Federal Direct Loan program is a direct loan program, and the Federal Family Education Loan (FFEL) program is a guaranteed loan program.

---

[92] See, for example, ibid. See also John R. Brooks, "Income-Driven Repayment and the Public Financing of Higher Education," *Georgetown Law Journal*, vol. 108 (2016), pp. 283-284.

[93] See, for example, Jason Delisle and Alexander Holt, *Zero Marginal Cost: Measuring Subsidies for Graduate Education in the Public Service Loan Forgiveness Program*, New America, September 2014.

[94] In a federal direct loan program, the federal government directly lends federal funds to a borrower. In a federal loan guarantee program, the federal government guarantees lenders against loss through borrower default, death, permanent disability, or, in limited circumstances, bankruptcy.

Loan subsidy costs for these programs are funded through mandatory indefinite appropriations. According to requirements of the Federal Credit Reform Act of 1990 (FCRA),[95] the budgetary costs of direct loans and loan guarantees are measured on the basis of their estimated long-term costs to the government on a net present value basis, and these costs are attributable to the fiscal year during which a direct loan obligation or guaranteed loan commitment is made (as opposed to the year during which the cash flows associated with these benefits occur). The federal budget reflects the unreimbursed costs of making or guaranteeing loans—the subsidy cost of loans (discussed below) and administrative costs (which are expressed separately on a cash basis, and discussed in a following section).[96]

The loan subsidy cost is the estimated present value of the cash flows from the government (excluding administrative expenses), less the estimated present value of the cash flows to the government, resulting from a direct loan or loan guarantee, and discounted to the time when the loan is disbursed. A positive loan subsidy cost means that there is a cost to the government of providing the loan subsidy to borrowers. A negative loan subsidy cost means that the government earns a positive return from the extension of credit to borrowers. With regard to loan forgiveness benefits that are incorporated into the terms and conditions of direct loan or guaranteed loan programs, the availability (and eventual granting) of these benefits alters the expected cash flows of the program and results in an increase in loan subsidy costs.[97]

For example, in the Direct Loan program, Stafford Loan Forgiveness to Teachers is a benefit that is made available to qualified borrowers. When borrowers qualify for loan forgiveness under the program, a portion

---

[95] Title V of P.L. 101-508.

[96] For additional background on federal credit programs, see CRS Report R42632, *Budgetary Treatment of Federal Credit (Direct Loans and Loan Guarantees): Concepts, History, and Issues for Congress*; and Office of Management and Budget, Budget of the United States Government, Fiscal Year 2019, Analytical Perspectives, "Budget Concepts and Budget Process: Federal Credit," pp. 91-92, https://www.whitehouse.gov/wp-content/uploads/2018/02/ap_8_concepts-fy2019.pdf.

[97] Loan subsidy costs are estimated for each cohort of loans and these rates are reestimated annually while loans in the cohort are still outstanding. A final accounting of loan subsidies is not available until loans in the cohort are no longer outstanding.

of each borrower's loan balance (e.g., $5,000, $17,500) is discharged by the government. As a consequence, these borrowers are relieved of responsibility for repaying some portion of their loans and the cash flows to the government associated with these loans are reduced. This results in an increase in loan subsidy costs for the program. While these loan forgiveness benefits may not be provided until many years after a loan is made, the estimated cost of providing these loan forgiveness benefits is accounted for in the loan subsidy costs for the fiscal year during which the loan was originally made. Other examples of this type of program include the Public Service Loan Forgiveness (PSLF) program and loan forgiveness following completion of the maximum repayment period (e.g., 20 years, 25 years) in the income-based repayment (IBR) plan and the income-contingent repayment (ICR) plan.

Appropriated Program Costs

In loan repayment programs, the direct costs of borrower benefits are not incorporated into the subsidy rates of the federal credit programs through which the federal student loans were made, but rather are funded through the appropriation of funds for the fiscal year during which the loan repayment benefits are made available. (However, the early repayment of a loan may also have an effect on loan subsidy costs.) Funding may be provided through either discretionary or mandatory appropriations. For these types of programs, benefits are available to borrowers only in years for which appropriations have been made and only to the extent that the availability of funds allows. Thus, for these types of programs, sufficient funding might not be available to extend benefits to all borrowers who satisfy the eligibility criteria for loan repayment benefits. Examples of programs funded through discretionary appropriations include the Government Employee Student Loan Repayment (GESLR) program and the John R. Justice (JRJ) Loan Repayment for Prosecutors and Public Defenders Program. An example of a program funded through mandatory appropriations is the National Health Service Corps Loan Repayment program (NHSCLRP).[98]

The manner of providing funding for Perkins Loan Cancellation benefits is unique. The availability of Perkins Loan Cancellation benefits is specified in the terms and conditions of Perkins Loans and all borrowers who satisfy program eligibility criteria must be granted loan forgiveness by the institution that made the Perkins Loan. However, whereas most loan forgiveness program benefits are components of federal credit programs, the Perkins Loan program is not a federal credit program. Funding for reimbursement from the federal government to institutions for Perkins Loan Cancellation benefits is authorized to be made available through discretionary appropriations. While funding was last appropriated for Perkins Loan Cancellation reimbursements in FY2009, qualified borrowers have continued to have their loans canceled despite no funding being appropriated. Since the Perkins Loan program is a revolving loan fund program, institutions that have canceled Perkins Loans for eligible borrowers have absorbed the costs of loan cancellation without having these costs reimbursed by the federal government. ED currently maintains a record of reimbursement amounts institutions would be eligible to receive should funding be appropriated.[99]

Administrative Costs

Whereas most of the costs associated with loan forgiveness and loan repayment programs may be considered programmatic costs and are either incorporated into loan subsidy rates or are funded on a fiscal year basis through discretionary or mandatory appropriations for the applicable program, the costs of administering these programs are generally

---

[98] The National Health Service Corps Loan Repayment Program had been a discretionary program prior to its receiving mandatory funding beginning in FY2011. Between FY2012 and FY2017, the program was funded exclusively with mandatory funding; however, in FY2018 the program received both mandatory and discretionary funds. See CRS Report R44970, *The National Health Service Corps*.

[99] U.S. Department of Education, Office of Federal Student Aid, Electronic Announcement, "2016-2017 Federal Perkins Loan Service Cancellation Reimbursement," May 4, 2018.

accounted for and funded separately. For loan forgiveness benefits that are offered through federal credit programs, in accordance with requirements of the FCRA, administrative costs are accounted for separately on a cash basis and are funded through annual appropriations. Loan repayment programs are administered by numerous agencies and there is variation across programs in how administrative costs are funded. For ED programs administered by Federal Student Aid, discretionary appropriations are provided for federal student aid administration.

Estimated and Actual Costs for Loan Forgiveness and Loan Repayment Programs

Limited information is available on the actual costs to the government of loan forgiveness and loan repayment programs. For some programs— particularly many loan forgiveness programs—the only information available on program costs are estimates of the dollar amount or number of loans projected to be forgiven in future years, because borrowers have not yet become eligible to realize these benefits. For other programs— primarily loan repayment programs—information is often available on items such as the total amount of benefits provided or the number of borrowers who received benefits in a given fiscal year. Cost estimates for loan forgiveness programs in which benefits have not yet been realized are discussed below. For a limited set of programs in which benefits have been awarded to borrowers, and where relevant data are available, data on the amount of debt relief provided and the number of recipients is presented in Appendix A on a program-by-program basis.

Cost Estimates for Selected Loan Forgiveness Programs

For the Direct Loan Public Service Loan Forgiveness program, in a 2008 notice of proposed rulemaking (NPRM) to implement changes made by the College Cost Reduction and Access Act of 2007 (P.L. 110-84), ED estimated a cost to the government of $1.5 billion over the five-year period of FY2008-FY2012, with $1.2 billion of that amount being associated with loans made prior to FY2008.[100] (For federal credit programs, costs are associated with the cohort year in which a loan is made, as opposed to the year in which benefits are realized.) ED did not provide estimates of the number of borrowers expected to receive loan forgiveness benefits.[101]

For the Revised Pay-As-You-Earn (REPAYE) repayment plan, in the 2015 Final Regulation, ED estimated that for the cohorts of borrowers from 1994 to 2025, a total of approximately 6 million borrowers will be eligible for REPAYE, and of those, approximately 2 million borrowers would choose to enroll in the plan.[102] It also estimated that the availability of the REPAYE plan would cost approximately $15.4 billion.[103]

For the Pay-As-You-Earn (PAYE) repayment plan, in a 2012 NPRM, ED estimated a cost to the government of $2.1 billion over the 10-year period of FY2012-FY2021. In arriving at this figure, ED estimated that approximately 1.67 million borrowers would elect to repay their loans according to the PAYE plan.[104] Of these borrowers, ED estimated that approximately 400,000 would receive loan forgiveness through either public service loan forgiveness or after 20 years of repayment according to the PAYE plan.[105] On a per-borrower basis, ED estimated that the average original loan balance of borrowers receiving loan forgiveness would be $39,500 and that, because many borrowers would pay only interest and no

---

[100] U.S. Department of Education, "Federal Perkins Loan Program, Federal Family Education Loan Program, and William D. Ford Federal Direct Loan Program; Proposed Rule," 73 *Federal Register* 127, July 1, 2008, p. 37709.

[101] ED reports that as of June 30, 2018, 96 borrowers have received a total of $5.52 million in PSLF program benefits. U.S. Department of Education, Office of Federal Student Aid, "Public Service Loan Forgiveness Data," PSLF Report, https://studentaid.ed.gov/sa/about/data-center/student/loan-forgiveness/pslf-data, accessed October 24, 2018.

[102] ED reports that as of March 31, 2018, approximately 2.17 million borrowers, with outstanding loans totaling $199.0 billion, are enrolled in the REPAYE repayment plan. U.S. Department of Education, Office of Federal Student Aid Data Center, "Portfolio by Repayment Plan (DL, FFEL, ED-Held FFEL, and ED-owned)."

[103] U.S. Department of Education, Office of Postsecondary Education, "Student Assistance General Provisions, Federal Family Education Loan Program, and William D. Ford Federal Loan Program," 80 *Federal Register* 67229, October 30, 2015.

[104] ED reports that as of March 31, 2018, approximately 1.22 million borrowers, with outstanding loans totaling $72.5 billion, are enrolled in the PAYE repayment plan. U.S. Department of Education, Office of Federal Student Aid Data Center, "Portfolio by Repayment Plan (DL, FFEL, ED-Held FFEL, and ED-owned)."

[105] U.S. Department of Education, "Federal Perkins Loan Program, Federal Family Education Loan Program, and William D. Ford Federal Direct Loan Program; Proposed Rule," 77 *Federal Register* 137, July 17, 2012, p. 42121.

principal on their loans under the PAYE plan, these borrowers would have an average of $41,000 in loans forgiven.[106] In the same 2012 NPRM, ED estimated that approximately 1 million borrowers from the 2014-2021 cohorts would elect to repay their loans according to the IBR plan for post-July 1, 2014 borrowers, but it did not provide estimations on how many individuals might realize forgiveness benefits under the plan.[107]

Finally, for the IBR plan for pre-July 1, 2014, borrowers, ED estimated in its 2008 NPRM that 126,000 borrowers from the FY2009 loan cohort would repay their loans according to IBR, and that 44,000 of such borrowers would have at least some portion of their student loan debt forgiven after 25 years. For the FY2012 cohort, ED estimated that 146,000 borrowers would repay according to the IBR plan, and that 52,000 of these borrowers would have some portion of their debt forgiven after 25 years.[108]

Given that many of these loan forgiveness benefits are relatively new, and that both loan forgiveness receipt and benefit amounts are contingent upon borrower repayment behavior and/or labor market experiences over a sustained period of time, it is likely difficult to precisely estimate loan forgiveness benefits in the aggregate.

ISSUES FOR CONGRESS

Congress may explore whether existing policy on the availability of federal student loan forgiveness and loan repayment programs is optimal or whether changes should be made. Several issues related to loan forgiveness and loan repayment policy might be examined. For instance, should multiple programs make available loan forgiveness or loan repayment benefits for borrowers who engage in similar types of activities? Does the structure of some loan forgiveness or loan repayment programs lead to a financial windfall for borrowers who engage in the same type of activity they otherwise would have even if debt relief were not available? Is

---

[106] Ibid., p. 42122.
[107] Ibid.
[108] Ibid., p. 33709.

sufficient information available to assess whether existing programs are effectively achieving their intended purposes?

Overlapping of Benefits across Programs

Programs may be considered to overlap if multiple programs have the same or substantially similar goals and activities. There are two primary ways that student loan forgiveness and repayment programs can be considered overlapping. First, the same borrower could receive benefits from two different programs for the same service performed. Second, multiple programs may be available to the same group of individuals and may serve the same purpose, such that the federal government could be spending money on administrative costs for both programs when only one may be sufficient.

Individuals potentially may be able to qualify for benefits under multiple programs. Although some programs (e.g., Stafford Loan Forgiveness for Teachers) specifically state that recipients are not allowed to receive benefits under that and certain other programs for the same qualifying service, other programs do not contain such restrictions. Without such limitations, recipients may be able to receive benefits from multiple sources for the same service performed. For instance, an individual working in a federal agency may be eligible to receive up to $10,000 per year in loan repayment benefits (and up to $60,000 in total) under the Government Employee Student Loan Repayment program (GESLRP), while concurrently qualifying for forgiveness of the remainder of their student loan debt after 10 years of service with a federal agency and 120 concurrent monthly loan payments under the Public Service Loan Forgiveness program (PSLF).[109] If the individual applied the benefits received under the GESLRP towards the 120 monthly payments necessary to qualify for loan forgiveness under the PSLF, he or she potentially would

---

[109] 5 U.S.C. §5379; 20 U.S.C. §1087e(m).

be receiving benefits under two programs for the same federal government service.[110]

Another way in which programs can overlap is that multiple programs may be available to the same groups of individuals. Here, the federal government may be funding administrative costs for two separate programs that are serving the same purpose or same group of people. The Nursing Education Loan Repayment Program (NELRP), for instance, provides repayment benefits to, among others, individuals who serve as nurse faculty at accredited nursing schools.[111] The Nursing Faculty Loan Repayment Program (NFLRP) is available to individuals who serve as nurse faculty at accredited nursing schools.[112] Both programs are intended to increase the number of qualified nursing faculty,[113] and both programs are administered by the Department of Health and Human Services, Health Resources and Services Administration (HRSA). However, under the NFLRP, the HRSA grants money to nursing schools that establish their own loan repayment programs and then choose which individuals may receive benefits. These programs may be creating an administrative burden on the HRSA if it is responsible for administering both the NELRP and also granting money to the NFLRP when both programs are available to the same group of individuals and are intended to serve the same purpose.

Congress may consider combining, altering, or abolishing programs that either make available double benefits to individuals for the same service or that are available to the same group of individuals and intended to serve the same purpose.

---

[110] In such a case, individuals are not making a profit. Rather, they are having more of their loans paid off than is typically expected as a part of these programs.

[111] 42 U.S.C. §297n.

[112] 42 U.S.C. §297n-1.

[113] In addition, it is possible that there is significant overlap among individuals eligible for these programs and individuals eligible for PSLF, as the types of employment eligible for PSLF are quire broad. This potential overlap in eligibility likely exists in PSLF and other federal student loan repayment and loan forgiveness programs.

Debt Relief or Windfall?

Many loan forgiveness and repayment programs are intended to encourage individuals to enter into specified jobs, careers, or public service that may otherwise be undesirable or hard-to-fill. While this may be an effective way of recruiting and retaining some individuals who might not have otherwise considered entering such fields, these programs could be providing windfalls for other individuals who would have entered the field regardless of benefit availability.

For instance, there are no limits on the amounts that may be forgiven under certain loan forgiveness plans (e.g., the Direct Loan Public Service Loan Forgiveness program and loan forgiveness following income-driven repayment). Notably, the Direct Loan Public Service Loan Forgiveness program operates in conjunction with the income-driven repayment plans. Some concerns have been raised that certain characteristics of these programs, combined with the large amounts that individuals may borrow— particularly amounts borrowed under non-need-based PLUS Loans made to graduate and professional students—may create situations in which individuals may borrow larger amounts than they otherwise would, knowing that the possibility exists for loan forgiveness.[114] Congress may consider whether limits should be established on amounts that may be forgiven under certain loan forgiveness programs.[115]

Some research indicates that some individuals may take certain positions or enter into certain fields in the absence of loan forgiveness for a variety of other reasons.[116] If the goal of loan forgiveness and loan repayment programs is to immediately place individuals in or attract highly skilled employees to specified occupations or service and they are already

---

[114] Jason Delisle and Alex Holt, "Safety Net or Windfall? Examining Changes to Income-Based Repayment for Federal Student Loans," New America Foundation, October 2012.

[115] For example, in his FY2015 Budget, President Obama has proposed capping the amount that may be forgiven under the Direct Loan Public Service Loan Forgiveness program at $57,500. (See U.S. Department of Education, *FY 2015 Department of Education Justifications of Appropriation Estimates to the Congress*, Student Loans Overview, p. S-15).

[116] See the section of this report titled "Influence of Loan Repayment and Forgiveness Programs on Employment Choices."

seeking employment within such fields, then the programs may be considered ineffective, as they may not have played a role in individual employment decisions. However, if the goal of these programs is to create pipelines for future careers or retain highly skilled employees, then the programs may be somewhat effective, as some reports indicate that loan repayment programs do play at least some role in an individual's choice in staying in a specific job or career.[117]

To tailor loan repayment programs to more specific needs, Congress may consider implementing more sensitive funding controls, such as more narrowly defining the circumstances in which individuals could become eligible for repayment benefits, rather than giving administering agencies broad discretion in implementation. Alternatively, since many programs are funded through discretionary appropriations, Congress could also direct the use of funds through language included in appropriations measures.

Data on Program Outcomes and Effectiveness

In general, insufficient data are available on federal loan forgiveness and loan repayment programs to assess their effectiveness in achieving program objectives. For many programs, only a limited amount of programmatic data is available. For others, data will only become available once borrowers apply for and receive benefits. Since, for some programs, the period to qualify for benefits spans many years and no benefits have yet been awarded, limited or no programmatic data are available. For example, in the PSLF program, borrowers must remain employed in a public service job for 10 years while making 120 monthly payments on their loans. Borrowers first became eligible to apply for forgiveness benefits under this program on October 1, 2017; therefore, little is known about the forgiveness benefits received under the program based on the

[117] Office of Personnel Management, *Federal Student Loan Repayment Program Calendar Year 2016*, February 2018, pp. 7-8, https://www.opm.gov/policy-data-oversight/pay-leave/student-loan-repayment/reports/2016.pdf. (hereinafter OPM, *Federal Student LRP*); Glazerman, *NIH Intramural Research Loan Repayment Program*.

experience of actual cohorts of borrowers. In addition, projecting future participation is difficult because borrowers may, but are not required to, document their employment in public service jobs on PSLF Employment Certification Forms filed with the Department of Education (ED).

Thus, information available for this program may provide a snapshot of interest in PSLF, but little more.[118] Loan forgiveness is also available for borrowers who repay according to the income- driven repayment plans (e.g., income-based repayment (ICR) plan and income-based repayment (IBR) plan) for extended periods (e.g., 25 or 20 years). However, these programs also have not been in existence long enough for borrowers to qualify for forgiveness benefits.

For many programs, longitudinal data are not collected on participants beyond what is necessary for program administration. Thus, while data may be available to verify that a borrower remained employed in a targeted position long enough to qualify for benefits, it may be difficult to determine whether a beneficiary remained in his or her position after the qualifying period of employment ended. Where data are collected and available, the data may provide information on program outcomes, but may be of limited use in assessing program effects. While improved data collection and reporting may be resource intensive, the improved availability of information may be necessary for determining program effects and whether program design changes could improve effective-ness.[119]

Qualifying Loan Types and Amounts

There is variation from program to program in the types and amounts of student loan debt that may qualify for debt relief. For some programs, debt relief is limited to specific loan types (e.g., Perkins Loan

---

[118] For additional information on PSLF, see CRS Report R45389, *The Public Service Loan Forgiveness Program: Selected Issues.*

[119] It would take evaluation, however, to assess what would have happened in the absence of the availability of benefits.

cancellation), or to specific amounts (e.g., $5,000 or $17,500 for Stafford Teacher Loan Forgiveness). While for other programs, debt relief is available for multiple loan types (e.g., John R. Justice (JRJ) Loan Repayment), or with few limitations on maximum amounts (e.g., PSLF and loan forgiveness following IBR).

Consideration might be given to whether additional limitations should be imposed on the types and amounts of student loan debt that qualifies under loan forgiveness and loan repayment programs. For instance, in recent years, amounts that students may borrow in non-need-based loan aid have increased substantially—particularly due to PLUS Loans being made available to graduate and professional student borrowers.[120] In addition, concerns have been raised that the availability of some student loan repayment or forgiveness programs may provide incentives to students to over-borrow more than they would have in the absence of such programs.[121] Should individuals continue to be permitted to borrow non-need-based federal student loans to finance expenses that, according to federal need analysis rules, would otherwise be met by their expected family contribution (EFC), and then have a substantial portion of that amount discharged through federal student loan forgiveness or loan repayment programs? Should limits be established on the amount or type of student loan debt that may qualify for debt relief?

Variability of Selection Criteria among Administering Agencies

Selection criteria among agencies administering student loan repayment programs can vary greatly.[122] For example, the GESLRP

---

[120] Unlike Direct Subsidized Loans to undergraduate students and Direct Unsubsidized Loans to undergraduate, graduate, and professional students, there are no aggregate borrowing limits on Direct PLUS Loans to graduate and professional students.

[121] See, for example, Jason Delisle and Alexander Holt, *Zero Marginal Cost: Measuring Subsidies for Graduate Education in the Public Service Loan Forgiveness Program*, New America, September 2014.

[122] For a table summarizing how many of the federal agencies administer their programs, see, U.S. Government Accountability Office, *Federal Student Loan Repayment Program: OPM*

permits federal agencies to administer their own student loan repayment programs so long as they meet basic statutory requirements. Because of this, selection criteria may be unpredictable throughout the federal government, and in some cases, agencies may not administer a repayment program at all. In calendar year (CY) 2016, of the many federal agencies, 34 agencies provided employees with loan repayment benefits under the GESLRP.[123]

Under the GESLRP, all participants must sign a service agreement to serve in the paying agency for at least three years and they must reimburse a paying agency for any benefits received if they do not complete their service. Also, participants cannot be employees in the excepted service due to their position being confidential, policy-determining, policy-making, or policy-advocating in nature.[124] Beyond these limitations, however, agencies can otherwise determine to whom benefits are given. The Department of Defense, for example, uses its program extensively to recruit employees in nursing, engineering, and contracting positions.[125] The U.S. Department of State, on the other hand, provides benefits only to individuals who have a loan balance of at least $5,000.[126]

Although individual agencies can tailor their specific loan repayment program to meet their unique needs, these variations throughout a single government-wide program can make eligibility requirements difficult for participants to discern. If the goal of the program is to attract qualified individuals to work in the federal government, the GESLRP may only attract individuals to work in a limited number of agencies that administer the program.[127]

Could Build on Its Efforts to Help Agencies Administer the Program and Measure Results, 05-762, July 22, 2005, p. 16, Table 1, http://www.gao.gov/assets/250/247197.pdf.

[123] OPM, *Federal Student LRP*, p. 4.

[124] 5 U.S.C. §5379(a)(2).

[125] OPM, *Federal Student LRP*, p. 6.

[126] Ibid.

[127] Moreover, because each agency's funding levels differ and the GESLRP is a discretionary program that may have its funding reduced or cut altogether, the availability of benefits to individuals among agencies may be uncertain, and applicants may not know whether they will receive benefits until after accepting a job. Glazerman, *NIH Intramural Research Loan Repayment Program.*

APPENDIX A. PROGRAM-SPECIFIC DETAILS

The following appendix provides program-specific details about each program included in this chapter's analysis. Efforts were made to present the information in a relatively consistent manner; however, the programs are sufficiently different that information varies in scope and level of detail.

For each program, the following information, where available, is provided:

- statutory and regulatory citations,
- the federal administering agency and (where appropriate) the specific office within that agency,
- the program's purpose,
- types of loans eligible for forgiveness or repayment,
- qualifying service required of program participants,
- maximum amount of benefits program participants can receive,
- restrictions on eligibility for program benefits,
- requirements for program participants after receipt of all or part of a program's benefits,
- federal income tax treatment of benefits,
- budgetary classification of the program's spending,
- annual amounts appropriated in FY2013-FY2017,
- annual amount of loans discharged or repaid in FY2013-FY2017,
- annual number of program beneficiaries in FY2013-FY2017, and
- citations to relevant CRS reports and additional resources.

Information was derived from statutes, regulations, agency websites, or other authoritative sources.

Only selected information that is relevant to the overall analysis of this chapter is included in these program descriptions. Programs are described as they exist as of the date of this chapter. For complete information about a particular program of interest, readers are referred to the legal citations provided, the federal administering agency, or the identified CRS report. A notation of "N/A" indicates that criteria are not applicable to a specific program. Abbreviations used throughout this appendix include Federal Family Education Loan (FFEL) program and the Public Health Service Act (PHSA).

The various programs are presented in the same order as discussed earlier in this chapter. Loan forgiveness programs for public service are presented first. These are followed by programs that offer forgiveness following income-driven repayment. Next, loan repayment programs for public service addressing broad employment needs or shortages are presented. Loan repayment programs for public service employment in the federal government are presented last.

Loan Forgiveness for Public Service Employment Programs

The loan forgiveness programs presented in this section provide debt relief to qualified borrowers employed in certain occupations, for specific employers, or in public service. These benefits are considered entitlements and are written into the terms and conditions of widely available federal student loans. They are potentially available to an open-ended number of qualified borrowers and are presented first in this appendix, as they have a potentially large scope of availability to borrowers.

Direct Loan Public Service Loan Forgiveness (PSLF) Program

- Authority: Statute: HEA, Title IV, §455(m); 20 U.S.C. §1087e(m). Regulations: 34 C.F.R. §§685.212(i) & 685.219.
- Federal administering agency: U.S. Department of Education, Federal Student Aid.
- Purpose or description of program: To provide student loan forgiveness for the balance of any principal and interest that remains due on the Direct Loan program loans of borrowers who, after October 1, 2007, have made 120 full, scheduled, monthly

payments (10 years) on those loans, according to certain repayment plans, while concurrently employed full-time in public service.

- Eligible loan types: Direct Loan program Subsidized Loans, Unsubsidized Loans, Graduate PLUS Loans, and Consolidation Loans.

- Qualifying service or other activity: To qualify for loan forgiveness, borrowers must be employed full-time in public service, which includes employment in public service organizations and service in AmeriCorps or the Peace Corps. Public service organizations are federal, state, local, or tribal government agencies, organizations, or entities; tribal colleges and universities; public child or family service agencies; nonprofit organizations that are tax-exempt under IRC §501(c)(3); and private nonprofit organizations (other than labor unions or partisan political organizations). An eligible public service organization must provide any of the following public services: emergency management, military service, public safety, law enforcement, public interest law services, early childhood education, public service for individuals with disabilities and the elderly, public health, public education, public library services, and school library or other school- based services.

- Maximum benefit amount: The maximum amount that may be forgiven is any loan balance that remains after 120 qualifying monthly payments have been made on the loan.

- Restrictions on eligibility: Borrowers must make 120 separate, full, on-time, scheduled monthly payments within 15 days of the due date. Each of the payments must be made according to either the income-based repayment (IBR) plan, the income-contingent (ICR) plan, the Pay-As-You-Earn (PAYE) plan, the Revised Pay-As-You-Earn (REPAYE) plan, a standard repayment plan with a 10-year repayment period, or another Direct Loan program repayment plan if the payment amounts are equal to or greater than the amount that would be required according to a standard repayment plan with a 10-year repayment period. Borrowers must be employed (or serving) full- time in public service at the time each of the required 120 payments are made, at the time the application for forgiveness is made, and at the time forgiveness is granted. Borrowers' loans may not be in default. Any time spent participating in religious instruction, worship services, or proselytizing may not be included as part of full-time public service at a nonprofit organization.

- Post-award conditions: N/A
- Federal tax treatment: The amount of student loans forgiven is excluded from gross income.
- Budgetary classification and funding: Mandatory. Amounts provided for loan forgiveness are incorporated into student loan subsidy costs.
- Amounts discharged or repaid: N/A. Borrowers first became eligible for loan forgiveness in October 2017.
- Annual number of beneficiaries: N/A. Borrowers first became eligible for loan forgiveness in October 2017.
- Additional resources: U.S. Department of Education, Federal Student Aid, "Public Service Loan Forgiveness," https://student aid.ed.gov/sa/repay-loans/forgiveness-cancellation/public-service.

Stafford Loan Forgiveness for Teachers

- Authority: Statute: HEA, Title IV, §§428J and 460; 20 U.S.C. §§1078-10 and 1087j. Regulations: 34 C.F.R. §§682.216, 685.212(h), and 685.217.
- Federal administering agency: U.S. Department of Education, Federal Student Aid.
- Purpose of program: To encourage individuals to enter into and continue in the teaching profession.

- Eligible loan types: FFEL and Direct Loan program Subsidized Loans, Unsubsidized Loans, and Consolidation Loans to the extent used to repay a Subsidized Loan or an Unsubsidized Loan.

- Qualifying service or other activity: To qualify for loan repayment benefits, a borrower must serve as a full-time teacher for at least five consecutive complete academic years in a designated public nonprofit school, a private nonprofit school, or a public education service agency (ESA) that serves children from low-income families. For teaching service in a school, at least one of the five school years must be after the 1997-1998 school year, and for teaching service in an ESA, a portion of the five school years must be after the 2007-2008 school year. A borrower whose five- year service periods began on or after October 30, 2004, must be a "highly qualified teacher," as defined under the Elementary and Secondary Education Act (ESEA) of 1965, as amended, for the full five years of service.

- Maximum benefit amount: Up to $5,000, in general, and up to $17,500 for special education teachers and secondary school teachers of mathematics or science. Forbearance from making loan payments may be granted during the five-year service period.

- Restrictions on eligibility: Repayment benefits are available to borrowers who had no outstanding balance on any federal student loan made through a program authorized under Title IV of the HEA on October 1, 1998, or as of the date the borrower first borrowed such a loan after October 1, 1998. Loans must have been obtained prior to the end of the five consecutive complete academic years of teaching service and may not be in default. Loan forgiveness may not be provided for the same service used to qualify for benefits under the Direct Loan Public Service Loan Forgiveness (PSLF) program, the Loan Forgiveness for Service in Areas of National Need program, or AmeriCorps education awards.

- Post-award conditions: N/A

- Federal tax treatment: The amount of student loans forgiven is excluded from gross income.
- Budgetary classification and funding: Mandatory. Amounts provided for loan forgiveness are incorporated into student loan subsidy costs.
- Amounts discharged or repaid: FFEL program loans: FY2013: $179.6 million; FY2014: $177.6 million; FY2015: $154.8 million; FY2016: $133.4 million; FY2017: $120.5 million.
- Direct Loan program loans: FY2013: $106.8 million; FY2014: $144.7 million; FY2015: $170.2 million; FY2016: $187.0 million; FY2017: $230.9 million.
- Annual number of beneficiaries: FFEL program loans: FY2013: 22,038; FY2014: 22,569; FY2015: 19,860; FY2016: 18,153; FY2017: 17,342.
- Direct Loan program loans: FY2013: 12,951; FY2014: 16,822; FY2015: 18, 646; FY2016: 20,286; FY2017: 24,955.
- Additional resources: U.S. Department of Education, Federal Student Aid, "Teacher Loan Forgiveness," https://studentaid.ed.gov/sa/repay-loans/forgiveness-cancellation/teacher.

Federal Perkins Loan Cancellation

- Authority: Statute: HEA, Title IV, §465; 20 U.S.C. §1087ee. Regulations: 34 C.F.R. §674, Part D.
- Federal administering agency: U.S. Department of Education, Federal Student Aid.
- Purpose of program: To provide loan forgiveness benefits to borrowers of Perkins Loans for each complete year that they are employed or serve full-time in certain public service occupations.
- Eligible loan types: Federal Perkins Loans.
- Qualifying service or other activity: To qualify for cancellation benefits, borrowers must be employed or serve full-time in the following categories of occupations: teachers in low-income

schools; staff in Head Start and other state-licensed preschool programs; special education teachers; members of the Armed Forces who serve in areas of hostilities; Peace Corps or AmeriCorps VISTA volunteers; law enforcement personnel and public defenders; teachers of mathematics, science, foreign languages, bilingual education, or other shortage subject areas; nurses and medical technicians; providers of social services to high-risk children; fire fighters; faculty members at Tribal Colleges and Universities; librarians with master's degrees in library science; and speech language pathologists who have a master's degree and who work exclusively with Elementary and Secondary Education Act, Title I-A schools.

- Maximum benefit amount: Perkins Loan cancellation is based on both the number of years of service a borrower has completed and a rate of cancellation applicable to each particular type of service. For most types of service, up to 100% of a borrower's loan balance may be cancelled according to the following schedule: 15% of the outstanding loan balance is cancelled for each of the 1st and 2nd years of service; 20% is cancelled for each of the 3rd and 4th years of service; and the remaining 30% is cancelled for the 5th year of service. For service as Peace Corps and AmeriCorps VISTA volunteers, loan cancellation is provided at these rates for up to only four years of service (for a maximum of 70%). For work in Head Start and other state-licensed preschool programs, loan cancellation is provided at the rate of 15% per year for up to five years of service (for a maximum of 75%). Perkins Loan borrowers are also granted deferment from making payments on their loans (during which interest does not accrue) while performing service that qualifies for loan cancellation.

- Restrictions on eligibility: Perkins Loans may not be cancelled for service performed prior to the loan being disbursed nor during the enrollment period covered by the loan. A complete year of service consists of 12 consecutive months of service, except for teaching service where a full academic year is considered a complete year of service. Loans to be canceled may not be in default. Loan cancellation may not be provided for the same service used to qualify for AmeriCorps education awards.

- Post-award conditions: N/A
- Federal tax treatment: The amount of student loans cancelled is excluded from gross income
- Budgetary classification and funding: The Secretary is required—to the extent feasible—to reimburse institutions of higher education for Perkins Loans that are cancelled for borrowers engaged in public service, however, funding for Perkins Loan cancellations is classified as discretionary for congressional budget purposes. Funds have not been appropriated for Perkins Loan cancellations since FY2009.
- Amounts discharged or repaid: Information currently unavailable to CRS.
- Annual number of beneficiaries: Information currently unavailable to CRS.
- Additional resources: U.S. Department of Education, Federal Student Aid, 2015-2016 Federal Student Aid Handbook, Volume 6. Chapter 4—Perkins Repayment Plans, Forbearance, Deferment, Discharge and Cancellation, http://ifap.ed.gov/fsahandbook/attachments/1516FSAHbkVol6Ch4.pdf.

Loan Forgiveness Following Income-Driven Repayment Programs

Loan forgiveness following income-driven repayment provides debt relief to borrowers who repay their federal student loans as a proportion of their income for an extended period of time but who have not repaid their entire student loan debt. These benefits are considered entitlements and are written into the terms and conditions of widely available federal student loans. They are potentially available to an open-ended number of qualified borrowers, but they are not intended to meet the traditional purpose of encouraging participation in specific occupations or service for which other federal loan forgiveness and repayment programs are intended.

Income-Contingent Repayment (ICR)

- Authority: Statute: HEA, Title IV, §455(d)(1)(D) & (e); 20 U.S.C. §1087e(d)(1)(D) & (e).
- Regulations: 34 C.F.R. §685.208(k) and 685.209.
- Federal administering agency: U.S. Department of Education, Federal Student Aid.
- Purpose or description of program: To provide borrowers of Direct Loan program loans the opportunity to make payment amounts that are determined according to a formula that establishes maximum payment amounts based on their Direct Loan program federal student loan debt, family size, and adjusted gross income (AGI), with any loan balance remaining after 25 years of ICR repayment being forgiven.
- Eligible loan types: Direct Loan program Subsidized Loans, Unsubsidized Loans, PLUS Loans, and Consolidation Loans (except PLUS Consolidation Loans). Consolidation Loans may include Direct Loan program PLUS Loans made to parent borrowers (if the loans were consolidated on or after July 1, 2006) and FFEL program loans.
- Qualifying service or other activity: To qualify for forgiveness benefits, borrowers must make payments towards their outstanding loans for the equivalent of 25 years. The qualifying 25-year repayment period includes periods during which payments were made according to the ICR REPAYE, PAYE, or IBR plans; an extended repayment plan of not more than 12 years for borrowers who entered repayment before October 1, 2007; standard repayment plans that have a 10-year amortization, periods after October 1, 2007, in any repayment plan in amounts not less than the amount required according to a standard repayment plan with a 10-year amortization, and periods of economic hardship deferment.

Monthly payments are generally capped at 20% of a borrower's discretionary income.

- Maximum benefit amount: There is no maximum benefit amount. Any loan balance that remains after 25 years of qualifying repayment is forgiven.
- Restrictions on eligibility: Borrowers may not be in default on their loans. During periods of repayment according to the REPAYE, PAYE, ICR, or IBR plans, borrowers must annually provide the Secretary with documentation of their AGI (e.g., a copy of their federal tax return) and family size.
- Post-award conditions: N/A
- Federal tax treatment: The amount of student loans forgiven is included in gross income, and borrowers are responsible for any tax obligation that results from the forgiveness of any student loan debt that remains after 25 years of repayment according to the ICR plan.
- Budgetary classification and funding: Mandatory. Amounts provided for loan forgiveness are incorporated into student loan subsidy costs.
- Amounts discharged or repaid: N/A. Borrowers have not yet been able to qualify for loan forgiveness by repaying loans according to the ICR plan for 25 years.
- Annual number of beneficiaries: N/A. Borrowers have not yet been able to qualify for loan forgiveness by repaying loans according to the ICR plan for 25 years.
- Additional Resources: U.S. Department of Education, Federal Student Aid, "Income-Driven Plans," https://studentaid.ed.gov/sa/repay-loans/understand/plans/income-driven#icr.

Income-Based Repayment (IBR) Plan for Pre-July 1, 2014, Borrowers

- Authority: Statute: HEA, Title IV, §493C; 20 U.S.C. §1098e. Regulations: 34 C.F.R. §§682.215 and 685.221.

- Federal administering agency: U.S. Department of Education, Federal Student Aid.
- Purpose or description of program: To provide borrowers of Direct Loan and FFEL program loans the opportunity to make payment amounts that are determined according to a formula that establishes maximum payment amounts based on their eligible federal student loan debt, family size, and adjusted gross income (AGI), with any loan balance that remains after 25 years of IBR repayment being forgiven.
- Eligible loan types: Direct Loan and FFEL program Subsidized Loans, Unsubsidized Loans, PLUS Loans made to graduate and professional students, and Consolidation Loans (except Consolidation Loans that repaid a Parent PLUS Loan).
- Qualifying service or other activity: To qualify for forgiveness benefits, borrowers must make payments towards their outstanding loans for the equivalent of 25 years. The qualifying 25-year repayment period includes periods during which payments were made according to the IBR, REPAYE, PAYE, or ICR plans; a standard repayment plan with a 10-year amortization based on the loan amount at the time the borrower selected the IBR plan; or any repayment plan in amounts not less than the amount required according to a standard repayment plan with a 10-year amortization and periods of economic hardship. Monthly payments are capped at 15% of a borrower's discretionary income.
- Maximum benefit amount: There is no maximum benefit amount. Any loan balance that remains after 25 years of qualifying repayment is forgiven.
- Restrictions on eligibility: Borrowers may not be in default on their loans. During periods of repayment according to the IBR, REPAYE, PAYE, or ICR plans, borrowers must annually provide the Secretary or their loan holder with documentation of their AGI (e.g., a copy of their federal tax return) and family size.
- Post-award conditions: N/A

- Federal tax treatment: The amount of loans forgiven is included in gross income, and borrowers are responsible for any tax obligation that results from the forgiveness of any student loan debt that remains after 25 years of repayment according to the IBR plan.
- Budgetary classification and funding: Mandatory. Amounts provided for IBR loan forgiveness are incorporated into student loan subsidy costs.
- Amounts discharged or repaid: N/A. Borrowers have not yet been able to qualify for loan forgiveness by repaying loans according to the IBR plan for 25 years.
- Annual number of beneficiaries: N/A. Borrowers have not yet been able to qualify for loan forgiveness by repaying loans according to the IBR plan for 25 years.
- Additional resources: U.S. Department of Education, Federal Student Aid, "Income-Driven Plans," https://studentaid.ed.gov/sa/repay-loans/understand/plans/income-driven#ibr-pay-as-you-earn.

Pay-as-You-Earn (PAYE) Repayment Plan

- Authority: Statute: HEA, Title IV, §455(d)(1)(D) & (e); 20 U.S.C. §1087e(d)(1)(D) & (e).
- Regulations: 34 C.F.R. §§685.208(k) and 685.209.
- Federal administering agency: U.S. Department of Education, Federal Student Aid.
- Purpose of program: To provide certain borrowers of Direct Loan program loans the opportunity to make payment amounts that are determined according to a formula that establishes maximum payment amounts based on their Direct Loan program federal student loan debt, family size, and adjusted gross income (AGI), with any loan balance remaining after 20 years of PAYE repayment being forgiven.

- Eligible loan types: Direct Loan program Subsidized Loans, Unsubsidized Loans, Graduate PLUS Loans, and Consolidation Loans (other than Consolidation Loans used to repay Parent PLUS Loans).

- Qualifying service or other activity: To qualify for forgiveness benefits, borrowers must make payments towards their outstanding loans for the equivalent of 20 years after October 1, 2007. The 20-year repayment period that qualifies borrowers for loan forgiveness under the PAYE plan includes periods during which payments were made according to the PAYE, REPAYE, IBR, or ICR plans; a standard repayment plan with a 10-year amortization for the amount of the borrower's loans that were outstanding at the time the borrower selected the PAYE repayment plans; or any repayment plan in amounts not less than the amount required according to a standard repayment plan with a 10-year amortization, and periods of economic hardship. Monthly payments are capped at 10% of a borrower's discretionary income.

- Maximum benefit amount: There is no maximum benefit amount. Any loan balance that remains after 20 years of qualifying repayment is forgiven.

- Restrictions on eligibility: Repayment according to the PAYE plan is limited to individuals who had no outstanding loan balance on any DL or FFEL program loans on either October 1, 2007, or on the date they first borrowed after that date, and who on or after October 1, 2011, received a Direct Loan program loan disbursement or applied for and obtained a Direct Loan program Consolidation Loan. Eligibility to begin repaying according to the PAYE plan is limited to borrowers whose student loan payments exceed 10% of their discretionary income. Borrowers may not be in default on their loans. During periods of repayment according to the PAYE, REPAYE, IBR, or ICR plans, borrowers must annually provide the Secretary with documentation of their AGI (e.g., a copy of their federal tax return) and family size.

- Post-award conditions: N/A

- Federal tax treatment: The amount of student loans forgiven is included in gross income, and borrowers are responsible for any tax obligation that results from the forgiveness of any student loan debt that remains after 20 years of repayment according to the PAYE plan.
- Budgetary classification and funding: Mandatory. Amounts provided for loan forgiveness are incorporated into student loan subsidy costs.
- Amounts discharged or repaid: N/A. Borrowers have not yet been able to qualify for loan forgiveness by repaying loans according to the PAYE plan for 20 years.
- Annual Number of beneficiaries: N/A. Borrowers have not yet been able to qualify for loan forgiveness by repaying loans according to the PAYE plan for 20 years.
- Additional resources: U.S. Department of Education, Federal Student Aid, "Income-Driven Plans," https://studentaid.ed.gov/sa/repay-loans/understand/plans/income-driven#ibr-pay-as-you- earn. 77 Federal Register 212, November 1, 2012, pp. 66088-66147, http://www.gpo.gov/fdsys/pkg/FR-2012-11-01/pdf/2012-26348.pdf.

Income-Based Repayment (IBR) Plan for New Borrowers on or after July 1, 2014

- Authority: Statute: HEA, Title IV, §493C; 20 U.S.C. §1098e. Regulations: 34 C.F.R. §682.215 and 685.221.
- Federal administering agency: U.S. Department of Education, Federal Student Aid.
- Purpose or description of program: The program will provide borrowers of Direct Loan program loans the opportunity to make payment amounts that are determined according to a formula that establishes maximum payment amounts based on their eligible federal student loan debt, family size, and adjusted gross income (AGI). Payments are capped at 10% of discretionary income. Any

loan balance that remains after 20 years of IBR repayment will be forgiven.

- Eligible loan types: Direct Loan program Subsidized Loans, Unsubsidized Loans, PLUS Loans made to graduate and professional students, and Consolidation Loans (except Consolidation Loans that repay a PLUS Loan made to a parent borrower).

- Qualifying service or other activity: To qualify for repayment benefits, borrowers must make payments towards their outstanding loans for the equivalent of 20 years. The qualifying 20-year repayment period includes periods during which payments are made according to the IBR, REPAYE, PAYE, or ICR plans; a standard repayment plan with a 10-year amortization based on the loan amount at the time the borrower selected the IBR plan; or any repayment plan in amounts not less than the amount required according to a standard repayment plan with a 10-year amortization, and periods of economic hardship. Monthly payments are capped at 10% of a borrower's discretionary income.

- Maximum benefit amount: There is no maximum benefit amount. Any loan balance that remains after 20 years of qualifying repayment will be forgiven.

- Restrictions on eligibility: Borrowers may not be in default on their loans. During periods of repayment according to the IBR, REPAYE, PAYE, or ICR plans, borrowers must annually provide the Secretary or their loan holder with documentation of their AGI (e.g., a copy of their federal tax return) and family size.

- Post-award conditions: N/A

- Federal tax treatment: Recipients are responsible for any tax obligation that results from the forgiveness of any student loan debt that remains after 20 years of repayment according to the IBR plan.

- Budgetary classification and funding: Mandatory. Amounts provided for IBR loan forgiveness are incorporated into student loan subsidy costs.

- Amounts discharged or repaid: N/A. The program will only be available to individuals who have no outstanding balance of Direct Loan or FFEL program loans on July 1, 2014, or when they first borrow a Direct Loan program loan after July 1, 2014.
- Annual number of beneficiaries: N/A. The program will only be available to individuals who have no outstanding balance of Direct Loan or FFEL program loans on July 1, 2014, or when they first borrow a Direct Loan program loan after July 1, 2014.
- Additional resources: U.S. Department of Education, Federal Student Aid, "Income-Driven Plans," https://studentaid.ed.gov/sa/repay-loans/understand/plans/income-driven#ibr-pay-as-you- earn.

Revised Pay-as-You-Earn (REPAYE) Repayment Plan

- Authority: Statute: HEA, Title IV, §455(d)(1)(D) & (e); 20 U.S.C. §1087e(d)(1)(D) & (e).
- Regulations: 34 C.F.R. §§685.208(k) & 685.209.
- Federal administering agency: U.S. Department of Education, Federal Student Aid.
- Purpose of program: To provide certain borrowers of Direct Loan program loans the opportunity to make payment amounts that are determined according to a formula that establishes maximum payment amounts based on their Direct Loan program federal student loan debt, family size, and adjusted gross income (AGI), with any loan balance remaining after 20 years of repayment for borrowers with only undergraduate loans and after 25 years of repayment for borrowers with at least one graduate or professional loan being forgiven.
- Eligible loan types: Direct Loan program Subsidized Loans, Unsubsidized Loans, Graduate PLUS Loans, and Consolidation Loans (other than Consolidation Loans used to repay parent PLUS Loans).

- Qualifying service or other activity: To qualify for forgiveness benefits, borrowers with only outstanding loans borrowed as an undergraduate student must make payments toward their outstanding loans for the equivalent of 20 years; borrowers with any outstanding loans borrowed as a graduate or professional school student must make payments towards their outstanding loans for the equivalent of 25 years. The 20- and 25-year periods that qualify borrowers for loan forgiveness under the REPAYE plan include periods during which payments were made according to the REPAYE, PAYE, IBR, or ICR plans; a standard repayment plan with a 10-year amortization; or any repayment plan in amounts not less than the amount required according to a standard repayment plan with a 10-year amortization, and periods of economic hardship. Monthly payments are capped at 10% of a borrower's discretionary income.
- Maximum benefit amount: None. Any loan balance that remains after 20 years of qualifying repayment for borrowers with only undergraduate debt or after 25 years of qualifying repayment for borrowers with graduate or professional school debt will be forgiven.
- Restrictions on eligibility: Borrowers may not be in default on their loans. During periods of repayment according to the REPAYE, PAYE, IBR, or ICR plans, borrowers must annually provide the Secretary or their loan holder with documentation of their AGI (e.g., a copy of their federal tax return) and family size.
- Post-award conditions: N/A
- Federal tax treatment: Recipients are responsible for any tax obligation that results from the forgiveness of any student loan debt that remains after 20 or 25 years of repayment according to the REPAYE plan, as appropriate.
- Budgetary classification and funding: Mandatory. Amounts provided for REPAYE loan forgiveness are incorporated into student loan subsidy costs.

- Amounts discharged or repaid: N/A. Borrowers have not yet been able to qualify for loan forgiveness by repaying loans according to the REPAYE plan for 20 or 25 years, as appropriate.
- Annual number of beneficiaries: N/A. Borrowers have not yet been able to qualify for loan forgiveness by repaying loans according to the REPAYE plan for 20 or 25 years, as appropriate.
- Additional resources: U.S. Department of Education, Federal Student Aid, "Income-Driven Plans," https://studentaid.ed.gov/sa/repay-loans/understand/plans/income-driven#repaye. 80
- Federal Register 210, October 30, 2015, pp. 67204-67242, https://www.federalregister.gov/articles/2015/10/30/2015-27143/student-assistance-general-provisions-federal-family-education-loan-program-and-william-d-ford.

Loan Repayment for Public Service Employment Programs Supportive of Broad Employment Needs or Shortages

Loan repayment programs addressing broad employment needs or shortages are presented third in this appendix, as they are generally available to a limited number of qualified borrowers and subject to the appropriation of program funds, thus, they are likely to be smaller in scale than most, if not all, of the previously presented loan forgiveness programs.

Veterinary Medicine Loan Repayment Program

- Authority: Statute: National Agricultural Research, Extension, and Teaching Policy Act of 1977, as amended, §1415A; 7 U.S.C. §3151a. Regulations: 7 C.F.R. §3431.1 et seq.
- Federal administering agency: U.S. Department of Agriculture (USDA), National Institute of Food and Agriculture (NIFA).

- Purpose of program: To provide loan repayment for large animal veterinarians who provide short-term services in designated shortage areas during emergency situations.

- Eligible loan types: Any loan used to pay all or part of the cost of tuition and reasonable educational and living expenses to attend an accredited college of veterinary medicine, resulting in a Doctor of Veterinary Medicine or an equivalent (this may include FFEL and Direct Loan program Subsidized Loans, Unsubsidized Loans, PLUS Loans, and Consolidation Loans; Perkins Loans; and private education loans).

- Qualifying service or other activity: To qualify for repayment benefits, borrowers must be large animal veterinarians who provide short-term services to the federal government in designated shortage areas during emergency situations. Borrowers must complete a maximum of 60 days of service per year for a minimum of three years and can agree to complete additional years of service.

- Maximum benefit amount: $25,000 per year. Borrowers also receive salary and travel expenses during the time they are providing emergency services.

- Restrictions on eligibility: Repayment benefits are awarded on a competitive basis, and borrowers must be nominated by State Animal Health Officials.

- Post-award conditions: Individuals who breach their program contract are liable for an amount equal to the sum of: (1) the amount of loan repayments paid to the participant for a period of service not completed; (2) $7,500 multiplied by the months of service not completed; and (3) the interest on the sum of (1) and (2) calculated at the maximum prevailing rate—as determined by the Treasury—from the date of the contract breach.

- Federal tax treatment: Borrowers can receive an additional 39% of the total loan repayment amount for income tax liability.

- Budgetary classification and funding: Discretionary. Previous amounts appropriated, FY2013: $4.4 million; FY2014: $4.8

million; FY2015: $5.0 million; FY2016: information currently unavailable to CRS; FY2017: information currently unavailable to CRS.

- Annual amounts discharged or repaid: FY2013: $3.8 million; FY2014: $4.4 million; FY2015: $4.5 million; FY2016: $4.4 million; FY2017: information currently unavailable to CRS.
- Annual number of beneficiaries: FY2013: 36 new awards and 11 award renewals; FY2014: 39 new awards and 13 award renewals; FY2015: 44 new awards and 5 award renewals; FY2016: 49;
- FY2017: 49. Information on whether awards made in FY2016 and FY2017 were new or renewals is currently unavailable to CRS.
- Additional resources: U.S. Department of Agriculture, National Institute of Food and Agriculture, FY2010 Annual Report, http://www.nifa.usda.gov/nea/animals/in_focus/an_health_if_vmlr p_repts_stats.html; U.S. Department of Agriculture, National Institute of Food and Agriculture, FY2011 Annual Report, http://www.nifa.usda.gov/nea/ animals/in_focus/an_health_if_vmlrp_repts_stats.html;   USDA, NIFA Sample Veterinary Medicine Loan Repayment Program Contract,   OMB   No.   0524-0047,   http://www.nifa.usda.gov/ nea/animals/pdfs/vmlrp_nifa_12_contract_sample.pdf;   and   U.S. Department of Agriculture, National Institute of Food and Agriculture, FY2018 Request for Applications, https://nifa.usda. gov/sites/default/files/ resource/2018-VMLRP-RFA.pdf.

Indian Health Service Loan Repayment Program

- Authority: Statute: Indian Health Care Improvement Act, Title I, §108; 25 U.S.C. §§1616a &1616a-1. Regulations: None.
- Federal administering agency: U.S. Department of Health and Human Services (HHS), Indian Health Service (IHS).
- Purpose of program: To assure an adequate supply of health professionals necessary to maintain accreditation of, and provide

health care services to Indians through Indian health programs ("Indian health programs" refers to facilities operated by the IHS, an Indian Tribe, a Tribal Organization, or an Urban Indian Organization).

- Eligible loan types: Government and private loans obtained for tuition, other educational expenses, and reasonable living expenses for undergraduate education, graduate education, or both.

- Qualifying service or other activity: To qualify for repayment benefits, borrowers must hold a degree in and be licensed in an eligible health profession, be enrolled in their final year of a health profession program at an accredited institution, or be enrolled in an approved graduate training program in a health profession. Eligible health professions are identified by the HHS Secretary. Borrowers must complete at least two years of service and can agree to complete additional years of service.

- Maximum benefit amount: Up to $35,000 per year (generally, IHS makes annual awards of $20,000 per year).

- Restrictions on eligibility: Repayment benefits are awarded on a competitive basis. Priority is given to American Indians and Alaska Natives, IHS scholarship recipients, current employees, certain health professions, and borrowers serving at the Indian Health Programs with the greatest shortages. Repayment benefits are limited to U.S. citizens or nationals. Borrowers must be eligible to hold an appointment as a commissioned officer in the Regular or Reserve Corps of the Public Health Service, be eligible for selection for a civilian service position in the Regular or Reserve Corps of the Public Health Service, and must meet the standards for civil service employment in the IHS or be employed in an Indian health program. Individuals may not have a service obligation under another program.

- Post-award conditions: Borrowers must pay an amount equal to three times the loan repayments made on their behalf, plus interest, if they fail to complete their service commitment. The amount to be repaid is adjusted to account for any period of the service commitment that was completed.

- Federal tax treatment: IHS makes additional payments, up to $5,000 per year, for any loan repayments that result in borrowers' income tax liability.
- Budgetary classification and funding: Discretionary. The program is permanently authorized. Previous amounts appropriated include amounts appropriated for all IHS health professions programs. FY2013: $34.1 million; FY2014: $33.5 million; FY2015: $48.3 million; FY2016: information currently unavailable to CRS; FY2017: information currently unavailable to CRS.
- Annual amounts discharged or repaid: FY2013: information currently unavailable to CRS; FY2014: $17.6 million; FY2015: $30.0 million; FY2016: $48.3 million; FY2017: $49.3 million.
- Annual number of beneficiaries: FY2013: 520 new awards and 290 contract extensions; FY2014: 379 new awards and 311 contract extensions; FY2015: 437 new awards and 395 contract extensions; FY2016: 437 new awards and 379 contract extensions; FY2017: 434 new awards and 396 contract extensions.
- Additional resources: U.S. Department of Health and Human Services, Indian Health Service, "IHS Loan Repayment Program Overview," http://www.ihs.gov/loanrepayment/; various years of the Department of Health and Human Services, Justification of Estimates for Appropriations Committees.

National Health Service Corps Loan Repayment Program

- Authority: Statute: PHSA, Title III, §§331-336, 338B-338E; 42 U.S.C. §§254d-254f, 254l-1, 254m, 254n, 254o. Regulations: 42 C.F.R. §62.21 et seq.
- Federal administering agency: U.S. Department of Health and Human Services, Health Resources and Services Administration (HRSA).

- Purpose of program: To eliminate health manpower shortages in health professional shortage areas (HPSAs).

- Eligible loan types: Government and private loans obtained for tuition, other educational expenses, and reasonable living expenses for undergraduate education, graduate education, or both. PLUS loans made to parents are ineligible.

- Qualifying service or other activity: To qualify for repayment benefits, borrowers must serve as a health professional in a HPSA as designated by HRSA. Borrowers must complete at least two years of service. Borrowers can enter into additional one year service agreements, for up to a total of six years of service (i.e., six years of loan repayment).

- Maximum benefit amount: Up to $60,000 per year or $240,000 in total. Loan repayment amounts vary by the HPSA score of the location where the borrowers are fulfilling their National Health Service Corps (NHSC) service commitment; borrowers serving at sites with lower HPSA scores (i.e., sites with less severe shortages) receive $40,000 per year. Clinicians may receive half of the typical amounts in return for half-time service (e.g., $30,000 or $20,000 per year in return for a two-year half-time commitment). For FY2018, the NHSC received funding to support Opioid and Substance Use Disorder Treatment. Under this expansion, qualified providers may receive up to $75,000 in total loan repayment for a three-year service commitment.

- Restrictions on eligibility: Repayment benefits are awarded on a competitive basis, and awards may be based on the demonstrated interest of an applicant and other factors determined to be relevant. Repayment benefits are limited to U.S. citizens or nationals who are trained as, or in their last year of training to become, primary care physicians, dentists, primary care certified nurse practitioners, certified nurse midwives, primary care physician assistants, registered dental hygienists, health service psychologists, licensed clinical social workers, psychiatric nurse specialists, marriage and family therapists, or licensed professional counselors. For FY2018, additional providers are eligible for the NHSC program expansion for Opioid and Substance Use Disorder Treatment. These providers include physician assistants who are eligible to administer Medication Assisted Treatment and substance use disorder counselors.

- Post-award conditions: Borrowers must pay an amount equal to the sum of: (1) the amount of loan repayments paid to them for a period of service not completed; (2) $7,500 multiplied by the months of service not completed; and (3) the interest on the sum of (1) and (2) calculated at the maximum prevailing rate—as determined by the Treasury—from the date of the contract breach if they do not complete their service commitment.
- Federal tax treatment: The amount of student loan repayments received is excluded from gross income if the loan meets certain conditions.
- Budgetary classification and funding: Mandatory from FY2011 through FY2019 because of funds appropriated in the Affordable Care Act (P.L. 111-148, as amended) and subsequent extensions included in P.L. 114-10 and P.L. 115-123 and discretionary thereafter. Previous amounts appropriated, FY2013: $169.7 million; FY2014: $156.2 million; FY2015: $159.2 million; FY2016: $172.0 million; FY2017: $167.7 million.
- Annual amount discharged or repaid: Information currently unavailable to CRS.
- Annual number of beneficiaries: FY2013: 2,106 new loan repayment awards and 2,399 continuations; FY2014: 2,775 new loan repayment awards and 2,105 continuations; FY2015: 2,934 new awards and 1,841 continuations; FY2016: 3,079 new and 2,259 continuations; FY2017: 2,554 new and 2,259 continuations.
- Additional resources: Health Resources and Services Administration, "National Health Service Corps Loan Repayment Program," https://nhsc.hrsa.gov/loanrepayment/loanrepayment program.html; various years of the Department of Health and

Human Services, Health Resources and Services Administration, Justification of Estimates for Appropriations Committees.

National Health Service Corps Students to Service Loan Repayment Program

- Authority: Statute: PHSA, Title III, §§331-336, 338B-338E; 42 U.S.C. 254d-254f, 254l-1, 254m, 254n, 254o. Regulations: 42 C.F.R. §62.21 et seq.
- Federal administering agency: U.S. Department of Health and Human Services, Health Resources and Services Administration.
- Purpose of program: To eliminate health manpower shortages in health professional shortage areas (HPSAs).
- Eligible loan types: Government and private loans obtained for tuition and other educational expenses and reasonable living expenses for undergraduate education, graduate education, or both. PLUS loans made to parents are ineligible.
- Qualifying service or other activity: To qualify for repayment benefits, borrowers must practice full- or part-time primary care (internal medicine, family practice, pediatrics, obstetrics and gynecology, or geriatrics) at an approved site in a HPSA. Borrowers must complete three years of service.
- Maximum benefit amount: Up to $40,000 per year or $120,000 total; a half-time option is available in exchange for a six-year service commitment.
- Restrictions on eligibility: Repayment benefits are awarded on a competitive basis, and if there are more applicants than available funds, priority is given to applicants from disadvantaged backgrounds. Repayment benefits are available only to full-time medical students, who are U.S. citizens or U.S. nationals, in their last year of medical school. Borrowers must be planning to complete a residency in a primary care field (internal medicine, family practice, pediatrics, obstetrics and gynecology, or geriatrics).

- Post-award conditions: Borrowers must pay an amount equal to the sum of: (1) the amount of loan repayments paid to them for a period of service not completed; (2) $7,500 multiplied by the months of service not completed; and (3) the interest on the sum of (1) and (2) calculated at the maximum prevailing rate—as determined by the Treasury—from the date of the contract breach if they do not complete their service commitment.
- Federal tax treatment: The amount of student loan repayments received is excluded from gross income if the loan meets certain conditions.
- Budgetary classification and funding: Mandatory from FY2011 through FY2015 because of funds appropriated in the Affordable Care Act (P.L. 111-148, as amended) and discretionary thereafter. Previous amounts appropriated, FY2014: $9.3 million; FY2015: $11.5 million; FY2016: $14.0 million; FY2017: $15.1 million.
- Annual amounts discharged or repaid: Information currently unavailable to CRS.
- Annual number of beneficiaries: FY2013: 78; FY2014: 87; FY2015: 96; FY2016: 92; FY2017: 175.

National Health Service Corps State Loan Repayment Program

- Authority: Statute: PHSA, Title III, §338I; 42 U.S.C. §254q-1. Regulations: 42 C.F.R. §62.51 et seq.
- Federal administering agency: U.S. Department of Health and Human Services, Health Resources and Services Administration.
- Purpose of program: To increase the availability of primary care services in state-designated shortage areas.
- Eligible loan types: Government and private loans obtained for tuition, other educational expenses, and reasonable living expenses for undergraduate education, graduate education, or both.
- Qualifying service or other activity: To qualify for repayment benefits, borrowers must be health professionals who provide

health services in a state-designated shortage area. Matching grants are provided to states operating National Health Service Corps student loan repayment programs (NHSCSLRPs). Service requirements and eligible health professions vary by state.

- Maximum benefit amount: Amounts available vary by state. Amounts in excess of the amount provided to NHSC health professionals (NHSCLRP) must be awarded using state funds.
- Restrictions on eligibility: Loan repayment awards criteria vary by state.
- Post-award conditions: Borrowers must repay the relevant state if they do not complete their service commitment. States are required to have penalties in place for a breach; specific penalties vary by state.
- Federal tax treatment: The amount of student loan repayments received is excluded from gross income if the loan meets certain conditions.
- Budgetary classification and funding: Mandatory from FY2011 through FY2015 because of funds appropriated in the Affordable Care Act (P.L. 111-148, as amended) and discretionary thereafter. Previous amounts appropriated, FY2013: $9.4 million; FY2014: $12.7 million; FY2015: $12.7 million; FY2016: $13.0 million; FY2017: $15 million.
- Annual amounts discharged or repaid: Information currently unavailable to CRS.
- Annual number of beneficiaries: FY2013: 447; FY2014: 464; FY2015: 620; FY2016: 634; FY2017: 535.
- Additional resources: NHSC, "State Loan Repayment," http://nhsc.hrsa.gov/loanrepayment/stateloanrepaymentprogram/index.html, and various years of the Department of Health and Human Services, Health Resources and Services Administration, Justification of Estimates for Appropriations Committees.

Loan Repayments for Health Professional School Faculty

- Authority: Statute: PHSA, Title VII, §738(a); 42 U.S.C. §293b. Regulations: None.
- Federal administering agency: U.S. Department of Health and Human Services, Health Resources and Services Administration.
- Purpose of program: To provide loan repayment benefits to borrowers from disadvantaged backgrounds, based on environmental and/or economic factors, and who serve as faculty at health professions schools.
- Eligible loan types: Government and private loans obtained for tuition, other educational expenses, and reasonable living expenses for undergraduate education, graduate education, or both.
- Qualifying service or other activity: To qualify for loan repayment, borrowers must be from a disadvantaged background—based on environmental and/or economic factors—have a degree in medicine, osteopathic medicine, dentistry, nursing, or another health profession or be in the final year of study in an approved graduate training program in one of these fields and agree to serve as faculty at a school of medicine, nursing, osteopathic medicine, pharmacy, allied health, podiatric medicine, optometry, veterinary medicine, or public health, or at a school offering physician assistant education programs or graduate programs in behavioral and mental health. Borrowers must complete at least two years of service.
- Maximum benefit amount: Up to $40,000 for a two-year period or $20,000 per year.
- Restrictions on eligibility: Repayment benefits are awarded on a competitive basis. Borrowers must be U.S. citizens or nationals from disadvantaged backgrounds, based on environmental and/or economic factors.
- Post-award conditions: Borrowers are placed in default and are liable for an amount equal to the sum of the amount of loan repayments paid to them for a period of service not completed,

plus 39% of that amount (representing the amount paid/withheld for federal taxes on that amount), and $1,000 for each month of service not completed if borrowers do not complete their service commitment. Borrowers breaching their service contract are ineligible to apply for this program in the future and may also be disqualified from certain other federal programs.

- Federal tax treatment: Borrowers receive funds, up to 39% of the award amount, to offset the tax burden associated with receiving loan repayment.
- Budgetary classification and funding: Discretionary. Previous amounts appropriated, FY2013: $1.1 million; FY2014: $1.2 million; FY2015: $1.2 million; FY2016: $1.2 million; FY2017. $1.2 million.
- Annual amounts discharged or repaid: Information currently unavailable to CRS.
- Annual number of beneficiaries: FY2013: 21; FY2014: 19; FY2015: 21; FY2016: 21; FY2017: 20.
- Additional resources: U.S. Department of Health and Human Services, Health Resources and Services Administration, "Faculty Loan Repayment Program," http://www.hrsa.gov/loan scholarships/repayment/Faculty/index.html https://bhw.hrsa.gov/ loansscholarships/flrp; and various years of the Department of Health and Human Services, Health Resources and Services Administration, Justification of Estimates for Appropriations Committees.

General, Pediatric, and Public Health Dentistry Faculty Loan Repayment

- Authority: Statute: PHSA, Title VII, §748(a)(2); 42 U.S.C. §293k-2. Regulations: None.
- Federal administering agency: U.S. Department of Health and Human Services, Health Resources and Services Administration.

- Purpose of program: To provide loan repayment for general, pediatric, and public health dental faculty.
- Eligible loan types: Any outstanding student loan (this may include FFEL and Direct Loan program Subsidized Loans, Unsubsidized Loans, PLUS Loans, and Consolidation Loans; Perkins Loans; and private education loans).
- Qualifying service or other activity: Borrowers must serve as full-time faculty in general, pediatric, or public health dentistry.
- Maximum benefit amount: Borrowers receive the following loan repayment amounts for each year of service as a full-time faculty member: 10% of their student loan balance in the first year, 15% in the second year, 20% in the third year, 25% in the fourth year, and 30% in the fifth year.
- Restrictions on eligibility: Grants are awarded on a competitive basis to dental or dental hygiene schools or approved residency or advanced education programs in general, pediatric, or public health dentistry to, among other activities, award repayment benefits. Entities may partner with schools of public health.
- Post-award conditions: N/A
- Federal tax treatment: N/A
- Budgetary classification and classification: Discretionary. Previous amounts appropriated FY2013:$20.1 million; FY2014: $20.6 million; FY2015: $21.0 million; FY2016: $21.1 million; FY2017: $21.1 million. This amount represents the entire appropriation for all training in general, pediatric, and public health dentistry programs; amount includes, but is not exclusive to, loan repayment.
- Annual amounts discharged or repaid: Information currently unavailable to CRS.
- Annual number of beneficiaries: FY2013: 28; FY2014: 34; FY2015: 34; FY2016: 47; FY2017: 62.
- Additional resources: U.S. Department of Health and Human Services, Health Resources and Services Administration, "Dental

Faculty Loan Repayment Program," https://bhw.hrsa.gov/funding opportunities/?id=fffeea86-88b9-4fcb-8283-18eaba8447ec   and various years of the Department of Health and Human Services, Health Resources and Services Administration, Justification of Estimates for Appropriations Committees.

Substance Use Disorder Treatment Loan Repayment Program

- Authority: Statute: PHSA, Title VII, §781. Regulations: None.
- Federal administering agency: U.S. Department of Health and Human Services, Health Resources and Services Administration.
- Purpose of program: To provide loan repayment benefits to borrowers who are employed as substance use disorder treatment providers in mental health professional shortage areas or in areas with high rates of drug overdose deaths.
- Purpose of program: Government and private loans obtained for tuition, other educational expenses, and reasonable living expenses for undergraduate education, graduate education, or both.
- Qualifying service or other activity: To qualify for repayment benefits, borrowers must serve as substance use disorder treatment providers in either a mental health professional shortages area or in an area with high rates of drug overdose deaths. Borrowers must complete at least two years of service. Borrowers can enter into additional one-year service agreements, for up to a total of six years of service (i.e., six years of loan repayment).
- Maximum benefit amount: Up to $250,000 over a six-year period. For each year of obligated service, a borrower receives one-sixth of the principal and interest on his or her eligible loans that are outstanding as of the date that the individual began fulfilling his or her service commitment.
- Restrictions on eligibility: Loan repayment benefits may not be provided for the same service used to qualify for benefits under any federally supported loan forgiveness program, including under the National Health Service Corps (NHSC) Loan Repayment

Program, the NHSC Students to Service Loan Repayment Program, the NHSC State Loan Repayment Program, the Nursing Education Loan Repayment Program (NURSE Corps), Stafford Loan Forgiveness for Teachers, the Civil Legal Assistance Attorney Student Loan Repayment Program, and the Public Service Loan Forgiveness Program.

- Post-award conditions: The HHS Secretary is authorized to establish a formula to determine damages owed by the borrower in the event that a borrower does not complete his or her service commitment.
- Federal tax treatment: Undetermined, as the program has not yet been implemented.
- Budgetary classification and funding: Discretionary. Amounts provided are subject to annual appropriations for FY2019 through FY2023.
- Annual amounts discharged or repaid: N/A.
- Annual number of beneficiaries: N/A
- Additional resources: None.

Nursing Education Loan Repayment Program (NURSE Corps)

- Authority: Statute: PHSA Title VIII, §846(a), (b), & (c); 42 U.S.C. §297n & 297n-1.
- Regulations: 42 C.F.R. §57.312.
- Federal administering agency: U.S. Department of Health and Human Services, Health Resources and Services Administration.
- Purpose of program: To provide loan repayment benefits to borrowers who serve as nurses at health care facilities with a critical shortage of nurses or as nurse faculty at accredited schools of nursing.
- Eligible loan types: Eligible loans include those made under nursing student loan programs and any other education loan for nurse training costs (relevant loan programs are not specified).

- Qualifying service or other activity: To qualify for repayment benefits, borrowers must serve as nurses at nonprofit health care facilities with a shortage of nurses or as nurse faculty at accredited schools of nursing. Nurses at shortage facilities must have received a diploma or a baccalaureate, associate, or graduate degree in nursing in exchange for services as a nurse at a nonprofit health care facility. Nurse faculty members must have received a graduate degree. Borrowers must complete at least two years of service.

- Maximum benefit amount: Up to 85% of a borrower's loan balance may be repaid in the following installments: 30% of the principal and interest of their loan balance in exchange for one year of service; another 30% of the principal and interest in exchange for the second year of service; and 25% in exchange for a third year of service.

- Restrictions on eligibility: Repayment benefits are awarded on a competitive basis. Funding preference is giving to: (1) applicants with the greatest financial need, defined as individuals whose loans are 20% or greater of their annual base salary, and (2) individuals who either work in facilities that have the most severe nursing shortages or as nursing faculty. Awards are made first to applicants who meet the debt-to-income ratio criteria. Within this category, individuals employed at facilities that target the underserved and faculty members at nursing schools receive preference.

- Post-award conditions: Borrowers must repay the amount of all student loan payments received, plus interest, at the maximum legal prevailing rate from the date of breach if they do not complete their service commitment. Borrowers who breach a one-year continuation contract are liable to repay all loan repayments received for the third year of service (including amounts withheld for federal taxes), plus interest, at the maximum legal prevailing rate from the date of breach. Borrowers who breach either an initial or continuing loan repayment award are also permanently disqualified from receiving future awards under this or another federal loan repayment program. Borrowers who breach a loan repayment award must repay the amount owed to the federal government (including interest amount owed) within three years of the breach date. Borrowers who do not repay within the three year period may be assessed penalties.

- Federal tax treatment: The amount of student loan repayments received is included in gross income.
- Budgetary classification and funding: Discretionary. Authorization of appropriations provided for FY2003-FY2007. Previous amounts appropriated, FY2013: $78.0 million for both program scholarships and loan repayments; FY2014: $79.8 million for both program scholarships and loan repayments; FY2015: $81.8 million for both program scholarships and loan repayments; FY2016: $83.1 million for both program scholarships and loan repayments; FY2017: $87.1 million for both program scholarships and loan repayments.
- Annual amounts discharged or repaid: Information currently unavailable to CRS.
- Annual number of beneficiaries: FY2013: 580 new awards and 606 award extensions; FY2014: 667 new awards and 412 award extensions; FY2015: 674 new awards and 309 award extensions; FY2016: 518 new awards and 365 award extension; FY2017: 501 new awards and 340 extensions.
- Additional resources: U.S. Department of Health and Human Services, Health Resources and Services Administration, "NURSE Corps, Loan Repayment Program," https://bhw.hrsa.gov/loansscholarships/nursecorps; and various years of the Department of Health and Human Services, Health Resources and Services Administration, Justification of Estimates for Appropriations Committees.

Nursing Faculty Loan Repayment Program

- Authority: Statute: PHSA Title VIII, §846A; 42 U.S.C. §297n-1. Regulations: None.

- Federal administering agency: U.S. Department of Health and Human Services, Health Resources and Services Administration.
- Purpose of program: To increase the number of qualified nursing faculty.
- Eligible loan types: Government and private loans obtained for tuition, fees, books, other educational expenses, and reasonable living expenses. Eligible loans must be repayable over a 10- year period that begins 9 months after a borrower completes nursing school, and the interest rate is limited to 3% per year. Individual nursing schools operating a loan repayment fund may determine eligible loan types that meet the above criteria.
- Qualifying service or other activity: To qualify for repayment benefits, borrowers must serve as full-time faculty at accredited nursing schools.
- Maximum benefit amount: Up to 85% of a borrower's loan balance may be repaid in the following installments: 20% of their loan balance for each of three years of service and 25% of their loan balance for a fourth year of service.
- Restrictions on eligibility: Grants are awarded on a competitive basis to nursing schools to establish a loan repayment program. Individual nursing schools determine repayment recipients.
- Post-award conditions: N/A
- Federal tax treatment: The amount of student loan repayments received is included in gross income.
- Budgetary classification and funding: Discretionary. Authorization of appropriations provided for FY2010-FY2014. Previous amounts appropriated, FY2013: $23.3 million; FY2014: $24.5 million; FY2015: $26.5 million; FY2016: $26.5 million; FY2017: $26.4 million. These amounts represent the amounts awarded to schools to administer student loan funds and not the amounts used for loan repayment.
- Annual amounts discharged or repaid: Information currently unavailable to CRS.

- Annual number of beneficiaries: Information currently unavailable to CRS.
- Additional resources: U.S. Department of Health and Human Services, Health Resources and Services Administration, "Nurse Faculty Loan Program (NFLP)," https://bhw.hrsa.gov/funding opportunities/?id=92be63e6-2b39-4627-abdc-b6174968f4bb and various years of the Department of Health and Human Services, Health Resources and Services Administration, Justification of Estimates for Appropriations Committees.

National Institutes of Health Extramural Loan Repayment Programs

- Authority: Statute: PHSA, Title IV, §487B, as amended by P.L. 114-255; 42 U.S.C. §288-2.
- Regulations: 42 C.F.R. §68c.
- Federal administering agency: U.S. Department of Health and Human Services, National Institutes of Health (NIH).
- Purpose of program: To recruit highly qualified health professionals to conduct research at NIH on topics related to contraception and infertility, pediatric research (including pediatric pharmacological research), minority health disparities research, clinical research, clinical research conducted by individuals from disadvantaged backgrounds, and areas of emerging scientific or workforce needs.
- Eligible loan types: FFEL and Direct Loan program Subsidized Loans, Unsubsidized Loans, Graduate PLUS Loans, and Consolidation Loans; loans made available under PHSA Title VII-A and Title VIII-E; loans made or guaranteed by a state, the District of Columbia, the Commonwealth of Puerto Rico, or a territory or possession of the United States; loans made by academic institutions; and private education loans including MEDLOANS.
- Qualifying service or other activity: To qualify for repayment benefits, borrowers must conduct research on issues related to

contraception and/or infertility, pediatrics, minority health disparities, clinical research, or an area of emerging scientific need at an eligible institution (a domestic nonprofit foundation, a university, a professional association, another type of nonprofit institution, or a U.S. government agency (federal, state, or local)). Borrowers must hold a health professional degree (e.g., a doctoral degree in medicine, pharmacy, dentistry, optometry, osteopathic medicine, nursing, psychology, veterinary medicine) or a PhD. Borrowers must complete at least 20 hours of research per week for at least two years and can agree to complete one or two additional years of service.

- Maximum benefit amount: Up to $50,000 per year.
- Restrictions on eligibility: Repayment benefits are awarded on a competitive basis, based on NIH's research priorities. Borrowers must be U.S. citizens or nationals and may not have a federal judgment or lien against their property. Individuals must have qualifying educational debt in excess of 20% of their annual base salary. Borrowers must not have received support from any of the following programs: Physicians Shortage Area Scholarship Program, National Research Service Award Program, Public Health Service Scholarship Program, National Health Service Corps Scholarship Program, Primary Care Loan Program, Armed Forces (Army, Navy, or Air Force) Professions Scholarship Program, and the Indian Health Service Scholarship Program, but they may be eligible if they receive a deferral from their service commitment. Borrowers who have breached another NIH loan repayment contract may not receive support under this program.
- Borrowers may not concurrently receive support under an NIH intramural research program or an NIH Cancer research and training program, and they may not receive any income from a for-profit source or from private practice.
- Post-award conditions: Borrowers must pay $7,500 per month of service not completed, plus all the amounts paid on their behalf for months that were not served. Borrowers must also pay interest on

the amount owed, with interest accruing from the date of breach. The U.S. government is entitled to recover not less than $31,000. Borrowers may terminate renewal contracts at any time without penalties. Loan repayments are prorated and terminated on the date that research stops.

- Federal tax treatment: Borrowers can receive an additional 39% of the total loan repayment amount for federal income tax liability.
- Budgetary classification and funding: Discretionary. Amounts appropriated are included in individual institute's operating budgets.
- Annual amounts discharged or repaid: FY2013: $66.7 million; FY2014: $69.0 million; FY2015: $69.4 million; FY2016: $68.2 million; FY2017: $68.2 million.
- Annual number of beneficiaries: FY2013: 1,328 awards; FY2014: 71,357 awards; FY2015: 1,351 awards; FY2016: 1,325 awards; FY2017: 1,282 awards.
- Additional resources: Various years of Department of Health and Human Services, National Institutes of Health, Justification of Estimates for Congressional Committees, Office of the Director, Washington, DC and U.S. Department of Health and Human Service, National Institutes of Health, NIH Division of Loan Repayment, "LRP Dashboard," https://dashboard.lrp.nih.gov/app/#/.

John R. Justice (JRJ) Loan Repayment for Prosecutors and Public Defenders Program

- Authority: Statute: The Omnibus Crime Control and Safe Streets Act of 1968, as amended, Title I, Part JJ, §3001; 34 U.S.C. §10671. Regulations: None.
- Federal administering agency: U.S. Department of Justice, Office of Justice Programs, Bureau of Justice Assistance.

- Purpose or description of program: To encourage qualified attorneys to enter and continue employment as prosecutors and public defenders for at least 36 months.

- Eligible loan types: FFEL and Direct Loan program Subsidized Loans, Unsubsidized Loans, Graduate PLUS Loans, and Consolidation Loans (other than Consolidation Loans used to repay Parent PLUS Loans); and Perkins Loans.

- Qualifying service or other activity: To qualify for repayment benefits, borrowers must be employed as full-time prosecutors, public defenders, or federal defender attorneys. Borrowers must be attorneys who are continually licensed to practice law and must complete at least three years of service.

- Maximum benefit amount: Up to $10,000 per year and $60,000 in cumulative benefits.

- Restrictions on eligibility: Borrowers may not be in default on their loans. The program is administered as a partnership between the Bureau of Justice Assistance and state governors. Funds are awarded to states to operate loan repayment programs. In general, within each state, loan repayment benefits must be equally distributed between prosecutors and public defenders.

- Within each state, priority consideration must be given to eligible beneficiaries who have the least ability to repay their student loans. While receiving loan repayment benefits, recipients are required to continue making payments on their federal student loans. Individuals who receive benefits in one year are not guaranteed to receive benefits for any subsequent years that are covered by a service agreement. Funds for loan repayment are allocated to states in proportion to each state's share of the national population, with a minimum state allocation of $100,000.

- Post-award conditions: Borrowers must notify the state agency that administers the program if they transfer to a new position or employer, if they intend to voluntarily leave their position, or if they default on their loans. Borrowers must repay the Department of Justice for any benefits received if, prior to completing the required three-year term of service, they voluntarily separate from employment or are involuntarily separated for misconduct or unacceptable performance.

- Federal tax treatment: The amount of student loans repaid is excluded from gross income.
- Budgetary classification and funding: Discretionary. Amounts provided are subject to annual appropriations. Previous amount appropriated, FY2013: $3.72 million; FY2014: $2.0 million; FY2015: $2.0 million; FY2016: $2.0 million; FY2017: $2.0 million.
- Amounts discharged or repaid: FY2013: $3.3 million; FY2014: $1.8 million; FY2015: information currently unavailable to CRS; FY2016: information currently unavailable to CRS; FY2017: Information currently unavailable to CRS.
- Annual number of beneficiaries: FY2013: 2,194; FY2014: 1,762; FY2015: information currently unavailable to CRS; FY2016: information currently unavailable to CRS; FY2017: information currently unavailable to CRS.
- Additional resources: U.S. Department of Justice, Bureau of Justice Assistance, "John R. Justice (JRJ) Program," https://www.bja.gov/ProgramDetails.aspx?Program_ID=65; "John R. Justice (JRJ) Grant Program, FY2018 State Solicitation Frequently Asked Questions (FAQs) (Revised 4/3/2018)," https://www.bja.gov/Funding/FY18-JRJ-FAQs.pdf. Letter from U.S. Department of the Treasury, Internal Revenue Service to Rafael A. Madan, General Counsel, Department of Justice, December 31, 2012, https://www.bja.gov/Programs/IRS-JRJ-Letter.pdf. U.S. Department of Justice, Office of the Inspector General, Audit of the Office of Justice Programs Bureau of Justice Assistance John R. Justice Grant Program, Audit Report 14-23, May 2014, http://www.justice.gov/oig/reports/2014/a1423.pdf.

Civil Legal Assistance Attorney Student Loan Repayment Program

- Authority: Statute: HEA, Title IV, §428L; 20 U.S.C. §1078-12. Regulations: None.
- Federal administering agency: U.S. Department of Education, Federal Student Aid.
- Purpose of program: To encourage qualified individuals to enter into and continue employment as civil legal assistance attorneys.
- Eligible loan types: FFEL and Direct Loan program Subsidized Loans, Unsubsidized Loans, Graduate PLUS Loans, and Consolidation Loans (other than Consolidation Loans used to repay Parent PLUS Loans) and Perkins Loans.
- Qualifying service or other activity: To qualify for repayment benefits, borrowers must enter into service agreements to remain employed full-time as civil legal assistance attorneys and must be continually licensed to practice law. Borrowers must complete at least three years of service, and they subsequently can agree to complete additional year of service.
- Maximum benefit amount: Up to $6,000 per year and $40,000 cumulatively.
- Restrictions on eligibility: Loan repayment benefits are made available to borrowers on a first-come, first-served basis and are subject to the appropriation of funds for each fiscal year. Benefits are only available until funds are fully committed and the receipt of benefits in one year does not guarantee benefits for subsequent years covered by a service agreement. Loans to be repaid may not be in default. Loan forgiveness may not be provided for the same service used to qualify for benefits under the Loan Forgiveness for Service in Areas of National Need program or the Direct Loan Public Service Loan Forgiveness (PSLF) program.
- Post-award conditions: Borrowers must repay any benefits received if they voluntarily separate from employment or are involuntarily separated for misconduct before the end of the service agreement.

- Federal tax treatment: The amount of student loans repaid is excluded from gross income.
- Budgetary classification and funding: Discretionary. Authorization of appropriations provided for FY2010-FY2014. Previous amounts appropriated, FY2009: $10 million; FY2010: $5 million; no appropriations were provided for FY2011 through FY2016.
- Amounts discharged or repaid: Information currently unavailable to CRS.
- Annual number of beneficiaries: Information currently unavailable to CRS.
- Additional resources: None.

Public Health Workforce Loan Repayment Program

- Authority: Statute: PHSA §776; 42 U.S.C. §295f-1. Regulations: None.
- Federal administering agency: U.S. Department of Health and Human Services (HHS), Health Resources and Services Administration.
- Purpose of program: To assure an adequate supply of public health professionals to eliminate critical public health workforce shortages in federal, state, local, and tribal public health agencies.
- Eligible loan types: Any loan used to pay for the borrower's undergraduate or graduate education (this may include FFEL and Direct Loan program Subsidized Loans, Unsubsidized Loans, PLUS Loans, and Consolidation Loans; Perkins Loans; and private education loans).
- Qualifying service or other activity: To qualify for repayment benefits, borrowers must be employed full-time or have accepted a full-time position at a federal, state, local, or tribal public health agency or must be completing a related training fellowship. Borrowers must complete at least three years of service in a priority service area as determined by the HHS Secretary.

- Maximum benefit amount: $35,000 per year for borrowers with a student loan balance greater than $105,000 and one-third of the loan balance per year for borrowers with a lower balance.
- Restrictions on eligibility: Repayment benefits are awarded on a competitive basis. Borrowers must be U.S. citizens and must not have received benefits under the Public Service Loan Forgiveness, Stafford Loan Forgiveness for Teachers, Loan Forgiveness for Service in Areas of National Need, Civil Legal Assistance Attorneys Loan Repayment, or Perkins Loan Cancellation programs for the same service. Borrowers must have graduated in the last 10 years with a public health or health professions degree.
- Post-award conditions: Borrowers must pay an amount equal to the sum of: (1) the amount of loan repayments paid to them for a period of service not completed; (2) $7,500 multiplied by the months of service not completed; and (3) the interest on the sum of (1) and (2) calculated at the maximum prevailing rate—as determined by the Treasury—from the date of the contract breach if they do not complete their service commitment.
- Federal tax treatment: Borrowers can receive an additional 39% of the total loan repayment amount for income tax liability.
- Budgetary classification and funding: Discretionary. Funding was last appropriated in FY2010.
- Annual amounts discharged or repaid: N/A
- Annual number of beneficiaries: N/A
- Additional resources: None.

Loan Forgiveness for Service in Areas of National Need

- Authority: Statute: HEA, Title IV, §428K; 20 U.S.C. §1078-11. Regulations: None.
- Federal administering agency: U.S. Department of Education.
- Purpose or description of program: To provide loan forgiveness to borrowers who are employed full-time in an area of national need.

- Eligible loan types: FFEL and Direct Loan program Subsidized Loans, Unsubsidized Loans, Graduate PLUS Loans, and Consolidation Loans (other than Consolidation Loans used to repay Parent PLUS Loans).
- Qualifying service or other activity: To qualify for forgiveness benefits, borrowers must be employed full-time in one of the following areas of national need: early childhood educator; nurse; foreign language specialist; librarian; highly qualified teacher; child welfare worker; speech-language pathologist or audiologist; school counselor; public sector employee in public safety, emergency management, public health, or public interest legal services; nutrition professional; medical specialist; mental health professional; dentist; employee in the science, technology, engineering, and mathematics (STEM) fields; physical therapist; superintendent, principal, or other (school) administrator; occupational therapist; and allied health professional.
- Maximum benefit amount: Up to $2,000 per school year, academic year, or calendar year of full- time employment in an area of national need completed on or after August 14, 2008, and $10,000 cumulatively.
- Restrictions on eligibility: Forgiveness benefits are available to borrowers on a first-come, first- served basis. Full-time employment in an area of national need must be completed on or after August 14, 2008, and loans to be forgiven may not be in default. Loan forgiveness may not be provided for the same service used to qualify for benefits under the Stafford Loan Forgiveness for Teachers program, the Direct Loan Public Service Loan Forgiveness (PSLF) program, or the Civil Legal Assistance Attorney Student Loan Repayment Program (CLAARP).
- Post-award conditions: N/A
- Federal tax treatment: Undetermined, as the program has not yet been implemented.

- Budgetary classification and funding: Discretionary. Authorization of appropriations provided for FY2009-FY2016. Funding has never been appropriated for the program.
- Amounts discharged or repaid: N/A
- Annual number of beneficiaries: N/A
- Additional resources: None.

Pediatric Subspecialist Loan Repayment Program

- Authority: Statute: PHSA, Title VII, §775; 42 U.S.C. §295f. Regulations: None.
- Federal administering agency: U.S. Department of Health and Human Services, Health Resources and Services Administration.
- Purpose of program: To provide loan repayment to pediatric medical, surgical, and mental health subspecialists who provide care in a health professional shortage area (HPSA).
- Eligible loan types: Any loans used to pay all or part of the cost of attendance at an institution of higher education, including loans incurred for undergraduate, graduate, or graduate medical education expenses. (This may include FFEL and Direct Loan program Subsidized Loans, Unsubsidized Loans, PLUS Loans, and Consolidation Loans; Perkins Loans; and private education loans).
- Qualifying service or other activity: To qualify for loan repayment benefits, borrowers must be employed full-time as pediatric medical or surgical subspecialists or health professionals in child or adolescent mental and behavioral health care facilities. They must be employed in a HPSA or a medically underserved area. Borrowers may also be in training in one of these fields. Borrowers must complete at least two years of service, and they can agree to complete an additional year of service.
- Maximum benefit amount: Up to $35,000 per year for a minimum of two years and a maximum of three years.

- Restrictions on eligibility: U.S. citizens or legal permanent residents who are licensed to practice in one of the eligible fields or those who are enrolled in an accredited graduate program in one of these fields.
- Post-award conditions: Undetermined, as the program has not yet been implemented.
- Federal tax treatment: Undetermined, as the program has not yet been implemented.
- Budgetary classification and funding: Discretionary. This program has not yet received any appropriations.
- Annual amounts discharged or repaid: N/A
- Annual number of beneficiaries: N/A
- Additional resources: None.

Nursing Workforce Development Student Loans: Loan Cancellation

- Authority: Statute: PHSA §836(b)(3); 42 U.S.C. §297b(b)(3). Regulations: None.
- Federal administering agency: U.S. Department of Health and Human Services, Health Resources and Services Administration.
- Purpose of program: To provide loan cancellation for borrowers who are employed as professional full-time nurses (including as a teacher, administrator, supervisor, or consultant in a nursing field) in public or nonprofit private agencies, institutions, or organizations.
- Eligible loan types: Loans made to nursing students by schools from funds established under the statute (i.e., nursing education loans).
- Qualifying service or other activity: To qualify for repayment benefits, borrowers must have received their loans before September 29, 1995 and must be employed as professional full-time nurses (including as a teacher, administrator, supervisor, or

consultant in a nursing field) in a public or nonprofit private agencies, institutions, or organizations.

- Maximum benefit amount: Up to 85% of the total loan made under the statute. 15% of the loan amount is repaid for each the first three years of service and 20% is paid for the fourth and fifth years of service.
- Restrictions on eligibility: Undetermined, as the program has not yet been implemented.
- Post-award conditions: Undetermined, as the program has not yet been implemented.
- Federal tax treatment: Undetermined, as the program has not yet been implemented.
- Budgetary classification and funding: Discretionary. The program has not yet received any appropriations.
- Annual amounts discharged or repaid: N/A
- Annual number of beneficiaries: N/A
- Additional resources: None.

Nursing Workforce Development Student Loans: Loan Repayment

- Authority: Statute: PHSA §836; 42 U.S.C. §297b(i). Regulations: None.
- Federal administering agency: U.S. Department of Health and Human Services, Health Resources and Services Administration.
- Purpose of program: To provide loan repayment for nursing students who withdraw from nursing programs.
- Eligible loan types: Loans made to nursing students by schools from funds established under the statute (i.e., nursing education loans).
- Qualifying service or other activity: To qualify for repayment benefits, borrowers must have been unable to complete their studies, be in exceptionally needy circumstances, and have not

resumed their studies within two years after they withdrew from their nursing studies.

- Maximum benefit amount: Undetermined, as the program has not yet been implemented.
- Restrictions on eligibility: Undetermined, as the program has not yet been implemented.
- Post-award conditions: Undetermined, as the program has not yet been implemented.
- Federal tax treatment: Undetermined, as the program has not yet been implemented.
- Budgetary classification and funding: Discretionary. The program has not yet received any appropriations.
- Annual amounts discharged or repaid: N/A
- Annual number of beneficiaries: N/A
- Additional resources: None.

Eligible Individual Student Loan Repayment

- Authority: Statute: PHSA §847. 42 U.S.C. §297o. Regulations: None.
- Federal administering agency: U.S. Department of Health and Human Services, Health Resources and Services Administration.
- Purpose of program: To increase the number of qualified nursing faculty.
- Eligible loan types: Any loan used to pursue a nursing degree.
- Qualifying service or other activity: To qualify for loan repayment, borrowers must be licensed nurses who have completed a master's or doctoral degree program (or are currently enrolled in such a program) and agree to serve as full-time nursing faculty members. Borrowers must complete at least four years of service during a six-year period that begins either when they receive their degrees or when they into loan repayment agreements.

- Maximum benefit amount: Master's level nurses may receive up to $10,000 per year for a maximum total of $40,000. Doctoral degree nurses may receive $20,000 per year for a maximum total of $80,000. These amounts apply to FY2010 and FY2011 and are adjusted annually thereafter to account for cost-of-attendance increases.

- Restrictions on eligibility: Undetermined, as the program has not yet been implemented, but at a minimum, borrowers must be U.S. citizens, nationals, or lawful permanent residents.

- Post-award conditions: Borrowers must repay the total amount of all student loan repayments made on their behalf, plus interest calculated at the prevailing rate, if they do not complete their service agreement.

- Federal tax treatment: Undetermined, as the program has not yet been implemented.

- Budgetary classification and funding: Discretionary. Authorization of appropriations provided for FY2010-FY2014. The program has not yet received an appropriation.

- Annual amounts discharged or repaid: N/A

- Annual number of beneficiaries: N/A

- Additional resources: None.

Loan Repayment for Public Service Employment in the Federal Government

Loan repayment programs to recruit and retain federal government employees are presented last in this appendix, as they are narrowly targeted to meet agency-specific recruitment and retention needs and, in general, are likely to be smaller in scale than the other loan repayment and forgiveness programs.

Student Loan Repayment Program for Senate Employees

- Authority: Statute: Congressional Appropriations Act, 2002, Title I, §102; 2 U.S.C. §60c-5.
- Regulations: None.
- Federal administering agency: The Secretary of the Senate establishes standard procedures for program administration, and each employing office has the option of participating in the program.
- Purpose of program: To recruit or retain qualified personnel.
- Eligible loan types: FFEL and Direct Loan program Subsidized Loans, Unsubsidized Loans, PLUS Loans, and Consolidation Loans; Perkins Loans; and loans made available under PHSA Title VII-A and Title VIII-E.
- Qualifying service or other activity: To qualify for repayment benefits, borrowers must be employees of the U.S. Senate or the Office of Congressional Accessibility Service. Borrowers must agree to complete at least one year of service and can enter into additional service agreements for successive one-year increments.
- Maximum benefit amount: Up to $500 in any month and $40,000 in cumulative benefits.
- Restrictions on eligibility: Repayment benefits are only available for the amount of a borrower's outstanding debt on the date that a service agreement is executed. Borrowers' salaries cannot exceed the ES-1 Senior Executive Service level of pay, and any loan payment made in any month cannot cause a borrower's monthly salary to be greater than $1/12^{th}$ of the statutorily maximum allowed salary. Loans to be repaid may not be in default or arrears. Loan repayment to employees of the Congressional Accessibility Service may not be provided for the same service used to qualify for benefits under the Government Employee Student Loan Repayment Program. A Member of the U.S. Senate is ineligible.

- Post-award conditions: Borrowers must repay the amount of all student loan payments made on their behalf if they voluntarily separate, engage in misconduct, do not meet an acceptable level of performance, or violate a condition of a service agreement before they complete the required service period in a service agreement.
- Federal tax treatment: The amount of student loan repayments received is included in gross income.
- Budgetary classification and funding: Discretionary. Authorizations of appropriations provided for FY2002 and each year thereafter. Authorized amount for each employing office is 2% of the total amount appropriated for its administrative and clerical salaries.
- Annual amount discharged or repaid: Information currently unavailable to CRS.
- Annual number of beneficiaries: Information currently unavailable to CRS.
- Additional resources: None.

Student Loan Repayment Program for House Employees

- Authority: Statute: Consolidated Appropriations Resolution, 2003, Div. H, Title I, §105; 2 U.S.C. §60c-6. Regulations: None.
- Federal administering agency: The Committee on House Administration establishes regulations for program administration, and each employing office has the option of participating in the program.
- Purpose of program: To recruit or retain qualified personnel.
- Eligible loan types: FFEL and Direct Loan program Subsidized Loans, Unsubsidized Loans, PLUS Loans, and Consolidation Loans; Perkins Loans; and loans made available under PHSA Title VII-A and Title VIII-E.
- Qualifying service or other activity: To qualify for repayment benefits, borrowers must be employees of the U.S. House of

Representatives. Borrowers must agree to complete at least one year of service.

- Maximum benefit amount: Up to $833 in any month and $60,000 in cumulative benefits.
- Restrictions on eligibility: Repayment benefits are only available for the amount of a borrower's outstanding debt on the date that a service agreement is executed. Loans to be repaid may not be in default or arrears. A Member of the U.S. House of Representatives (including a Delegate or Resident Commissioner to the Congress) is ineligible.
- Post-award conditions: Borrowers must repay the amount of all student loan payments made on their behalf if they voluntarily separate or are involuntarily separated before they complete the required service period in the service agreement.
- Federal tax treatment: The amount of student loan repayments received is included in gross income.
- Budgetary classification and funding: Discretionary. Authorization of appropriations provided for FY2003 and each fiscal year thereafter. Authorized amounts for each employing office is 3.5% of the amount available for office salaries and operating costs.
- Annual amount discharged or repaid: Information currently unavailable to CRS.
- Annual number of beneficiaries: Information currently unavailable to CRS.
- Additional resources: U.S. House of Representatives, Student Loan Repayment Program: Overview, February 25, 2009, https://housenet.house.gov/sites/housenet.house.gov/files/documents/student_loan_program_overview.pdf.

Congressional Budget Office Student Loan Repayment

- Authority: Statute: Congressional Appropriations Act, 2002, Title I, §127; 2 U.S.C. §610. Regulations: None.

- Federal administering agency: Congressional Budget Office.
- Purpose of program: To recruit or retain qualified personnel.
- Eligible loan type: Any student loan previously taken out by a qualifying employee (this may include FFEL and Direct Loan program Subsidized Loans, Unsubsidized Loans, PLUS Loans, and Consolidation Loans; and Perkins Loans).
- Qualifying service or other activity: To qualify for repayment benefits, borrowers must be employees of the Congressional Budget Office.
- Maximum benefit amount: Up to $6,000 per year and $40,000 in cumulative benefits.
- Restrictions on eligibility: Repayment benefits are only available for the amount of a borrower's outstanding debts on the date a repayment agreement is executed.
- Post-award conditions: N/A
- Federal tax treatment: The amount of student loan repayments received is included in gross income.
- Budgetary classification and funding: Discretionary. Information on previous amounts appropriated for FY2013 through FY2014 is currently unavailable to CRS; FY2015: $18,000; FY2016: $18,000; FY2017: $18,000.
- Annual amount discharged or repaid: FY2013: $6,000; FY2014: $12,000; FY2015: $17,000; FY2016: $12,000; FY2017: $10,000.
- Annual number of beneficiaries: FY2013: 1; FY2014: 1; FY2015: 3; FY2016: 2; FY2017: 2.
- Additional resources: None.

Government Employee Student Loan Repayment Program

- Authority: Statute: National Defense Authorization Act for Fiscal Year 1991, Div. A, Title XII, §1206(b)(1); 5 U.S.C. §5379. Regulations: 5 C.F.R. §537.
- Federal administering agency: Individual executive agencies.

- Purpose of program: To recruit or retain highly qualified personnel.
- Eligible loan type: FFEL and Direct Loan program Subsidized Loans, Unsubsidized Loans, PLUS Loans, and Consolidation Loans; Perkins Loans; and loans made available under PHSA Title VII-A and PHSA Title VIII-E.
- Qualifying service or other activity: To qualify for repayment benefits, borrowers must be employees of an Executive branch agency; certain Legislative branch agencies including the Government Accountability Office, the Government Publishing Office, the Library of Congress, the Architect of the Capitol, the Botanic Garden, the Office of Congressional Accessibility; or government corporations (e.g., the Federal Deposit Insurance Corporation). Individual agencies can choose to provide repayment benefits to all employees or can target a particular occupation. Borrowers can be permanent employees; temporary employees who are serving appointments that can be converted to term or permanent appointments; term employees with at least three years left on their appointments; and employees serving in excepted appointments that can be converted to term, career, or career conditional appointments (e.g., Presidential Management Fellow, Career Intern). Borrowers must agree to complete at least three years of service.
- Maximum benefit amount: Up to $10,000 per year and $60,000 in cumulative benefits.
- Restrictions on eligibility: Repayment benefits are not available to borrowers who are employees in the excepted service because their position is confidential, policy-determining, policy-making, or policy-advocating in nature. Repayment benefits are only available for the amount of a borrower's outstanding debts on the date a repayment agreement is executed. An agency may not authorize student loan repayment benefits to recruit an individual from outside the agency who is currently in the federal service. An

individual agency may specify that only student loans made within a certain timeframe are eligible for repayment.

- Post-award conditions: Borrowers must repay employing agencies for the amount of all student loan payments made on their behalf if they voluntarily separate or are involuntarily terminated before the end of the service agreement. However, reimbursement may not be required if borrowers voluntarily enter into service with another agency.

- Federal tax treatment: The amount of student loan repayments received is included in gross income.

- Budgetary classification and funding: Discretionary. Amounts provided are subject to annual appropriations for each administering agency.

- Annual amount discharged or repaid: Beginning in calendar year 2009, the Office of Personnel Management, which is the agency responsible for reporting on the program, changed from fiscal year to calendar year reporting to synchronize and simplify agency reporting requirements. CY2013: $52.9 million; CY2014: $58.7 million; CY2015: $69.5 million; CY2016: $71.6 million; CY2017: information currently unavailable to CRS.

- Annual number of beneficiaries: CY2013: 7,314 within 31 agencies; CY2014: 8,469 within 33 agencies; CY2015: 9,610 within 32 agencies; FY2016: 9,868 within 34 agencies; CY2017: information currently unavailable to CRS.

- Additional resources: Office of Personnel Management, Federal Student Loan Repayment Program Calendar Year 2016, February 2018, https://www.opm.gov/policy-data-oversight/pay-leave/student-loan-repayment/reports/2016.pdf.

Defense Acquisition Workforce Student Loan Repayment Program

- Authority: Statute: Defense Acquisition Workforce Improvement Act, Div. A, Title XII, §1202(a); 10 U.S.C. §1745. Regulations: None.

- Federal administering agency: Department of Defense.
- Purpose of program: To recruit and retain qualified acquisition employees.
- Eligible loan type: FFEL and Direct Loan program Subsidized Loans, Unsubsidized Loans, PLUS Loans, and Consolidation Loans; Perkins Loans; and loans made available under PHSA Title VII-A and Title VIII-E.
- Qualifying service or other activity: To qualify for loan repayment benefits, borrowers must be acquisition personnel in the Department of Defense. Borrowers can be permanent employees, temporary employees who are serving appointments that can be converted to term or permanent appointments, term employees with at least three years left on their appointments, and employees serving in excepted appointments that can be converted to term, career, or career conditional appointments (e.g., Presidential Management Fellow, Career Intern). Borrowers must agree to complete at least three years of service.
- Maximum benefit amount: Up to $10,000 per year and $60,000 in cumulative benefits.
- Restrictions on eligibility: Benefits are only available for the amount of a borrower's outstanding student loan debt on the date a repayment agreement is executed.
- Post-award conditions: Borrowers must reimburse employing agencies for the amount of all student loan payments made on their behalf if they voluntarily separate or are involuntarily terminated before they complete their service.
- Federal tax treatment: The amount of student loan repayments received is included in gross income.
- Budgetary classification and funding: It appears that funds for loan repayment benefits under the Department of Defense Acquisition Workforce Student Loan Repayment Program have been made available from the Department of Defense Acquisition Workforce Development Fund (DAWDF) since DAWDF's inception in FY2008. DAWDF provides annual dedicated funding to education,

training, recruitment, retention, research, and other initiatives for the acquisition workforce and acquisition-related positions. Statute specifies three ways in which DAWDF may be funded (1) discretionary appropriations, (2) credits remitted from Department of Defense components from operation and maintenance accounts, and (3) transfers of expired funds.

- Annual amount discharged or repaid: Information currently unavailable to CRS.
- Annual number of beneficiaries: FY2013: 959; FY2014: 2,332; FY2015: 287; FY2016: 1,026; FY2017: 420.
- A 2017 report from the Government Accountability Office indicates that the Department of Defense-reported FY2016 figure may significantly underrepresent the actual number of program beneficiaries for that year. See U.S. Government Accountability Office, Defense Acquisition Workforce: DOD Has Opportunities to Further Enhance Use and Management of Development Fund, GAO-17-332, March 2017, p. 25.
- Additional resources: Department of Defense, Human Capital Initiatives, Department of Defense Acquisition Workforce Development Fund: 2017 Year-In-Review Report, March 7, 2018.

Armed Forces Educational Loan Repayment Program: Enlisted Members on Active Duty in Specified Military Specialties

- Authority: Statute: Department of Defense Authorization Act, 1986, Title VI, Part F, §671(a)(1); 10 U.S.C. §2171. Regulations: None.
- Federal administering agency: Department of Defense, applicable military branch.
- Purpose of program: To recruit individuals to serve in certain military occupational specialties.
- Eligible loan type: FFEL and Direct Loan program Subsidized Stafford Loans, Unsubsidized Stafford Loans, PLUS Loans, and

Consolidation Loans; Perkins loans; and state and private education loans.

- Qualifying service or other activity: To qualify for repayment benefits, borrowers must perform active duty in an officer program or military specialty specified by the Secretary of Defense. Borrowers must complete at least one year of service, and loan repayments are made for each complete year of service. Both officers and enlisted members on active duty are eligible.

- Maximum benefit amount: The greater of 33 1/3% of a borrower's outstanding student loan debt or $1,500 for each year of service. The Army, Army Judge Advocate General Corps, and Navy offer up to $65,000 in cumulative benefits; the Air Force offers up to $10,000 in cumulative benefits, and the Marine Corps offers up to $30,000 in cumulative benefits.

- Restrictions on eligibility: Benefits are only available for the amount of a borrower's outstanding student loan debt on the date a repayment agreement is executed; outstanding accrued interest and capitalized interest is not repaid.

- Post-award conditions: Borrowers must repay an amount equal to the unearned portion of loan repayments if they fail to complete their service.

- Federal tax treatment: The amount of student loan repayments received is included in gross income.

- Budgetary classification and funding: Discretionary. Amounts appropriated are included as part of the relevant military service component's personnel appropriation.

- Annual Amount Discharged or repaid: Army. FY2013: $114.4 million; FY2014: $56.0 million; FY2015: $44.7 million; FY2016: $21.1 million; FY2017: $6.0 million. Navy. FY2013: $14.2 million; FY2014: $11.4 million; FY2015: $4.8 million; FY2016: $3.8 million; FY2017: $4.6 million. Marine Corps. FY2013: $7.3 million; FY2014: $4.1 million; FY2015: $2.6 million; FY2016: $13,000; FY2017: $596,000. Air Force. FY2013: $4.8 million; FY2014: $4.6 million; FY2015: $3.9 million; FY2016: $2.6

million; FY2017: $320,000. Air Force, Judge Advocate General Corps. FY2013: $5.2 million; FY2014: $4.1 million; FY2015: $3.6 million; FY2016: $5.2 million; FY2017 (estimate): $3.9 million.

- Annual number of beneficiaries: Army. FY2103: 9,954; FY2014: 3,294; FY2015: 2,632; FY2016: 1,242; FY2017: 355. Navy. FY2013: 566; FY2014: 455; FY2015: 190; FY2016: 152; FY2017: 185. Marine Corps. FY2013: 729; FY2014: 406; FY2015: 280; FY2016: 1; FY2017: 20. The Air Force reports number of beneficiaries based on work years. Work year is a concept that is commonly used in budget and cost analyses and generally represents the number of hours that a full-time employee can work in a year (on average, 2,087 work hours in a calendar year). However, due to the number of hours an employee may actually have worked, information reported by the Air Force may not represent the total number of individuals who have received the program's benefits. Air Force. FY2013: 1,194 work years; FY2014: 1,521 work years; FY2015: 1,174 work years; FY2016: 777 work years; FY2017: 96 work years. Air Force, Judge Advocate General Corps. FY2013: 242 work years; FY2014: 187 work years; FY2015: 155 work years; FY2016: 238 work years; FY2017: 182 work years.

- Additional resources: Department of Defense, Individual Military Services, Congressional Budget Justifications, various years, http://comptroller.defense.gov/BudgetMaterials.aspx#detailed; National Council of Higher Education Loan Programs, Program Regulations Committee, "Matrix of Department of Defense (DOD) and Other Federal Student Loan Repayment Programs," February 2, 2012, http://c.ymcdn.com/sites/www.ncher.us/resource/ collection/F4EAF7F5-F223-4EC9-9C0E-5511898606A6/02-08-13_DOD_Repayment_Matrix.pdf.

Education Loan Repayment Program: Members of the Selected Reserve

- Authority: Statute: National Defense Authorization Act for Fiscal Year 1996, Div. A, Title XV, Subtitle G, §1079(b); 10 U.S.C. §16301. Regulations: None.
- Federal administering agency: Department of Defense, applicable military branch.
- Purpose of program: To serve as bonus pay for service in the Selected Reserve.
- Eligible loan type: FFEL and Direct Loan program Subsidized Loans, Unsubsidized Loans, PLUS Loans, and Consolidation; Perkins loans; and state and private education loans made by specified agencies.
- Qualifying service or other activity: To qualify for repayment benefits, borrowers must serve as members of the Selected Reserve of the Ready Reserve of an armed force in a reserve component, in an officer program, or in a military specialty authorized by the Secretary of Defense. Loan repayments are made for each complete year of service.
- Maximum benefit allowed: The greater of 15% of a borrower's outstanding student loans or $500 for each year of service, plus any interest that accrues during the current year. Cumulative amounts vary by military branch.
- Restrictions on eligibility: A loan must have been made before the borrower served in an armed force.
- Post-award conditions: Borrowers must repay an amount equal to the unearned portion of student loan repayment if they fail to complete their service.
- Federal tax treatment: The amount of student loan repayments received is included in gross income.
- Budgetary classification and funding: Discretionary. Amounts appropriated are included as part of the relevant military service component's personnel appropriation.

- Annual amount discharged or repaid: Army Reserve. FY2013: 16.7 million; FY2014: $8.3 million; FY2015: $8.8 million; FY2016: $7.9 million; FY2017: $0. Army National Guard. FY2013:$33.1 million; FY2014: $30.7 million; FY2015: $42.5 million; FY2016: $53.6 million; FY2017: $48.4 million. Air National Guard. FY2013: $10.8 million; FY2014: $6.1 million; FY2015: $914,000. The program for the Air National Guard was discontinued in FY2009, with all obligations completed in FY2015. Air Force Reserve: FY2013: information currently unavailable to CRS; FY2014: $350,000; FY2015: $422,000; FY2016: $630,000; FY2017: $635,000.

- Annual number of beneficiaries: Army Reserve. FY2013: 7,116; FY2014: 1,357; FY2015: 1,442; FY2016: 1,292; FY2017: 0. Army National Guard. FY2013: 15,603; FY2014: 18,234; FY2015: 18,612; FY2016: 14,136; FY2017: 21,958. Air National Guard. FY2013: 3,099; FY2014: 1,748; FY2015: 261. The program for the Air National Guard was discontinued in FY2009, with all obligations completed in FY2015. Air Force Reserve: FY2013: information currently unavailable to CRS; FY2014: 98; FY2015: 281; FY2016: 420; FY2017: 423.

- Additional resources: Department of Defense, Individual Military Services, Congressional Budget Justifications, various years, http://comptroller.defense.gov/ BudgetMaterials.aspx#detailed; National Council of Higher Education Loan Programs, Program Regulations Committee, "Matrix of Department of Defense (DOD) and Other Federal Student Loan Repayment Programs," February 2, 2012, http://c.ymcdn.com/sites/www.ncher.us/resource/collection/F4EAF7F5-F223-4EC9-9C0E-5511898606A6/02-08-13_DOD_Repayment_Matrix.pdf.

Education Loan Repayment Program: Health Professions
Officers Serving in Selected Reserve with Wartime Critical Medical
Skill Shortages

- Authority: Statute: Department of Defense Authorization Act, 1986; 10 U.S.C. §16302.
- Regulations: None.
- Federal administering agency: Department of Defense, applicable military branch. The program has been implemented by the Army Reserve, the Army National Guard, and the Air National Guard.
- Purpose of program: To provide loan repayment to health professionals who provide health care in specialties that meet identified wartime skill shortages.
- Eligible loan types: FFEL and Direct Loan program Subsidized Loans, Unsubsidized Loans, Graduate PLUS Loans, Consolidation Loans; Perkins Loans; and loans made available under PHSA Title VII-A and PHSA Title VIII-B; loans made through the Primary Care Loan Program; and commercial loans used to pursue a health profession education. Parent PLUS loans are ineligible.
- Qualifying service or other activity: To qualify for repayment benefits, borrowers must perform satisfactory service in the Selected Reserve of an armed force and be qualified or enrolled in an educational program leading to such qualifications in a health profession that the Secretary of Defense determines to be critically needed in order to meet identified wartime combat medical skills shortages. Borrowers must complete one year of service for each year of loan repayment received.
- Maximum benefit amount: Up to $60,000 per year. Annual amounts vary by military branch and health professions receiving the loan repayment benefits.
- Restrictions on eligibility: Borrowers must be commissioned officers on or before December 31, 2018. Loans to be repaid may not be in default and must be more than one year old.

- Post-award conditions: N/A
- Federal tax treatment: The amount of student loan repayments received is included in gross income.
- Budgetary classification and funding: Discretionary. Amounts appropriated are included as part of the relevant military service component's personnel appropriation.
- Annual amounts discharged or repaid: Army Reserve. FY2013: $15.6 million; FY2014: $10.9 million; FY2015: $13.0 million; FY2016: $8.3 million; FY2017: $6.7 million. Army National Guard. FY2013: $5.7 million; FY2014: $8.4 million; FY2015: $13.6 million; FY2016: $12.2 million; FY2017: $28.2 million. Navy Reserve. FY2013: $1.0 million; FY2014: $1.5 million; FY2015: $597,000; FY2016: $795,000; FY2017: $589,000. Air Force Reserve. FY2013: $3.5 million; FY2014: $3.8 million; FY2015: $3.5 million; FY2016: $3.7 million; FY2017: $3.5 million. Air National Guard. FY2013: $1.5 million; FY2014: $2.3 million; FY2015: $941,000; FY2016: $520,000; FY2017: $274,000.
- Annual number of beneficiaries: Army Reserve. FY2013: 808; FY2014: 547; FY2015: 628; FY2016: 403; FY2017: 324. Army National Guard. FY2013: 28; FY2014: 264; FY2015: 441; FY2016: 376; FY2017: 319. Navy Reserve. FY2013: 65; FY2014: 94; FY2015: 41; FY2016: 20; FY2017: 15. Air Force Reserve. FY2013: 88; FY2014: 113; FY2015: 131; FY2016: 140; FY2017: 110. Air National Guard. FY2013: 78; FY2014: 125; FY2015: 47; FY2016: 26; FY2017: 14.
- Additional resources: Department of Defense, Individual Military Services, Congressional Budget Justifications, various years, http://comptroller.defense.gov/BudgetMaterials.aspx#detailed.
Department of Defense, Instruction No. 1205.21, "Reserve Component Incentive Programs Procedures," September 20, 1999. http://www.esd.whs.mil/Portals/54/Documents/DD/issuances/dodi/120521p.pdf.

Education Loan Repayment Program: Chaplains Serving in the Selected Reserve

- Authority: Statute: National Defense Authorization Act for Fiscal Year 2006, Div. A, Title VI, Subtitle F, §§684(a), 687(c)(14); 10 U.S.C. §16303. Regulations: None.
- Federal administering agency: Department of Defense, applicable military branch.
- Purpose of program: To maintain adequate numbers of chaplains in the Selected Reserve.
- Eligible loan type: Any loan used to pay all or part of the cost of attendance at an institution of higher education (this may include FFEL and Direct Loan program Subsidized Loans, Unsubsidized Loans, PLUS Loans, and Consolidation Loans; Perkins Loans; and private education loans).
- Qualifying service or other activity: To qualify for repayment benefits, borrowers must satisfy the requirements for accessioning and commissioning of chaplains and be fully qualified for or appointed as chaplains in a reserve component. Borrowers must also enter into a written agreement with the relevant military branch and serve at least three years in the Selected Reserve.
- Maximum benefit allowed: Up to $10,000 in the first year and $20,000 in total for each three year period of obligated service.
- Restrictions on eligibility: Borrowers accessioned into the Chaplain Candidate Program cannot receive repayment benefits.
- Post-award conditions: Borrowers must repay an amount equal to the unearned portion of loan repayments if they fail to complete their service.
- Federal tax treatment: The amount of student loan repayments received is included in gross income.
- Budgetary classification and funding: Discretionary. Amounts appropriated are included as part of the relevant military service component's personnel appropriation.

- Annual amount discharged or repaid: Air National Guard, FY2013: $408,000; FY2014: $570,000; FY2015: $100,000; FY2016: $300,000; FY2017: $30,000.
- Annual number of beneficiaries: Air National Guard, FY2013: 62; FY2014: 76; FY2015: 20; FY2016: 60; FY2017: 3.
- Additional resources: Department of Defense, Individual Military Services, Congressional Budget Justifications, various years, http://comptroller.defense.gov/ BudgetMaterials.aspx#detailed.

Education Debt Reduction Program

- Authority: Statute: Caregivers and Veterans Omnibus Health Services Act of 2010, as amended, Title III, §301, P.L. 111-136; 38 U.S.C. §§7681-7683. Regulations: None.
- Federal administering agency: U.S. Department of Veterans Affairs (VA), Veterans Health Administration (VHA).
- Purpose of program: To recruit and retain qualified health professionals to serve in positions within the VHA for which recruitment or retention is difficult.
- Eligible loan types: Loans used to pay all or part of the cost of tuition and reasonable educational and living expenses to obtain a health professional degree to qualify the individual for the VHA position (this may include FFEL and Direct Loan program Subsidized Loans, Unsubsidized Loans, Graduate PLUS Loans, and Consolidation Loans; Perkins Loans; and private education loans).
- Qualifying service or other activity: To qualify for repayment benefits, borrowers must be VHA employees who provide direct patient care or services incident to direct patient care services for which the recruitment and retention of qualified health professions is difficult. Each VHA facility determines the specific qualifying positions based on available funding and critical staffing needs. Eligible borrowers include those in the following fields: audiology, dentistry, dental hygiene, nursing, occupational therapy,

optometry, medicine (including physician assistants), podiatry, physical therapy (including assistants), social work, speech pathology, radiological technology, and respiratory therapy. Borrowers must have been appointed to the VA within the six months prior and have acceptable performance ratings in their positions.

- Maximum benefit amount: Up to $200,000 over a total of five years of service, but repayment amounts may not exceed $40,000 in the fourth or fifth year of service. Borrowers may not receive annual loan repayment amounts that would exceed the amount of the principal and interest on their education or training loans.
- Restrictions on eligibility: Repayment benefits are awarded on a competitive basis, with priority given to the health professions that are most difficult positions to fill.
- Post-award conditions: N/A
- Federal tax treatment: The amount of student loan repayments received is excluded from gross income.
- Budgetary classification and funding: Discretionary. Funding for this program is derived from amounts available to the Secretary of the VHA for medical services.
- Annual amounts discharged or repaid: FY2013: $16.6 million; FY2014: $13.2 million; FY2015: $11.3 million; FY2016: 22.5 million; FY2017: $36.0 million.
- Annual number of beneficiaries: FY2013: 2,678; FY2014: information currently unavailable to CRS; FY2015: 1,110; FY2016: 1,971; FY2017: 2,302.
- Additional resources: U.S. Department of Veterans Affairs, Congressional Submission, FY2019 Funding and FY2020 Advance Appropriations Request, Volume II, Medical Programs and Information Technology Programs, Washington, DC, http://www.va.gov/budget/products.asp; and Department of Veterans Affairs, Veterans Health Administration, "Education Debt Reduction Program," https://www.vacareers.va.gov/why-choose-va/education-support.asp#.

National Institutes of Health Intramural Loan Repayment Programs

- Authority: Statute: PHSA, Title IV, §487A, as amended by P.L. 114-255; 42 U.S.C. §288-1; Regulations: None.
- Federal administering agency: U.S. Department of Health and Human Services, National Institutes of Health (NIH).
- Purpose of program: To help assure an adequate supply of qualified health professionals in general research, research on Acquired Immunodeficiency Syndrome (AIDS), clinical research conducted by individuals who are from disadvantaged backgrounds, and individuals conducting research in areas of emerging scientific or workforce need.
- Eligible loan types: FFEL and Direct Loan program Subsidized Loans, Unsubsidized Loans, Graduate PLUS Loans, and Consolidation Loans; loans made available under PHSA Title VII-A and Title VIII-E; loans made or guaranteed by a state, the District of Columbia, the Commonwealth of Puerto Rico, or a territory or possession of the United States; loans made by academic institutions; and private education loans including MEDLOANS. PLUS loans made to parents are ineligible.
- Qualifying service or other activity: To qualify for repayment benefits, borrowers must be employees of the NIH—appointed under the Federal Civil Service (Title V or Title 42) or under the Commissioned Corps of the U.S. Public Health Service—and must conduct clinical research on AIDS. Borrowers must complete at least two years of service and can agree to complete an additional year of service.
- Maximum benefit amount: Up to $50,000 per year.
- Restrictions on eligibility: Repayment benefits are awarded on a competitive basis, based on NIH's research priorities. Borrowers must be U.S. citizens or permanent legal residents and must have obtained a health professional doctoral degree (i.e., a PhD; a doctorate in medicine, osteopathic medicine, dentistry, pharmacy, veterinary medicine; or an equivalent) or a bachelor's of science in

nursing, a physician assistant degree, or an associate degree in nursing. Borrowers must have qualifying educational debt in excess of 20% of their annual NIH base salary, and borrowers with a federal judgment or lien against their property are ineligible. Borrowers must not have received support from any of the following programs: Physicians Shortage Area Scholarship Program, National Research Service Award Program, Public Health Service Scholarship Program, National Health Service Corps Scholarship Program, Primary Care Loan Program, Armed Forces (Army, Navy, or Air Force) Professions Scholarship Program, and the Indian Health Service Scholarship Program; borrowers who have received a deferral from one of these programs may be eligible.

- Post-award conditions: Borrowers must pay $7,500 per month of service not completed plus all the amounts paid on their behalf for months that were not served. Borrowers must also pay interest on the amount owed, with interest accruing from the date of breach. The U.S. government is entitled to recover not less than $31,000. Borrowers may terminate renewal contracts at any time without penalties. Loan repayments are prorated and terminated on the date that research stops.

- Federal tax treatment: Borrowers can receive an additional 39% of the total loan repayment amount for federal income tax liability.

- Budgetary classification and funding: Discretionary. FY2013: $7.0 million; FY2014: $7.1 million; FY2015: $7.1 million; FY2016: $7.4 million; FY2017: $7.4 million.

- Annual amounts discharged or repaid: FY2013: $3.2 million; FY2014: $4.1 million; FY2015: $3.5 million; FY2016: $3.8 million; FY2017: $3.1 million.

- Annual number of beneficiaries: FY2011: 1 new award and 6 renewals; FY2012: 2 new and 3 renewals; FY2013: 22 new award and 43 renewals; FY2014: 31 new awards and 49 renewals; FY2015: 32 new awards and 37 renewals; FY2016: 30 new awards and 37 renewals; FY2017: 25 new awards and 39 renewals.

- Additional resources: Various years of Department of Health and Human Services, National Institutes of Health, Justification of Estimates for Congressional Committees, Office of the Director, Washington, DC and various years of the NIH Intramural Loan Repayment Annual Report, https://www.lrp.nih.gov/data-reports#DataReportsDataBooksTile.

National and Community Service Grant Program, Use of Educational Award to Repay Outstanding Student Loans

- Authority: Statute: National and Community Service Trust Act of 1993, as amended, Title I, Subtitle A, §102(a); 42 U.S.C. §12604. Regulations: 45 C.F.R. §2526 et seq.
- Federal administering agency: Corporation for National and Community Service (the Corporation), the National Service Trust.
- Purpose of program: To encourage citizens to participate in national service programs intended to meet unmet human, educational, environmental, and public safety needs.
- Eligible loan type: FFEL and Direct Loan Subsidized Loans Unsubsidized Loans, PLUS Loans, and Consolidation Loans; Perkins loans; loans made available under PHSA Title VII-A and Title VIII-E; and any other loan determined by an institution of higher education to be necessary to cover a student's educational expenses and made, insured, guaranteed by an eligible lender.
- Qualifying service or other activity: To qualify for award benefits, borrowers must successfully complete service in either the AmeriCorps State or National, the National Civilian Community Corps (NCCC), or Volunteers in Service to America (VISTA) programs and be eligible to receive a national service educational award, summer of service educational award, or silver scholar educational award from the National Service Trust. Additionally, within the NCCC, participants may serve in FEMA Corps, which is a partnership between FEMA and the Corporation under which

participants serve solely devoted to disaster preparedness, response, and recovery.

- Maximum benefit allowed: An amount equal to the maximum Pell Grant award in effect at the beginning of the fiscal year in which the Corporation approves an individual's service position (in either AmeriCorps, NCCC, VISTA, or FEMA Corps). For national service and silver scholar educational awards, borrowers cannot receive an amount greater than two full-time education awards. Prorated awards are also available based on term of service. For instance, in FY2017 the award amounts for term of service were the following:
  o Full-time service (at least 1,700 hours of service): $5,592
  o Reduced full-time service (at least 1,200 hours of service): $4,144
  o One-year half time service (at least 900 hours of service): $2,960
  o Reduced half time (at least 675 hours of service): $2,255.24
  o Quarter time (at least 450 hours of service): $1,566.14
  o Minimum time (at least 300 hours of service): $1,252.91
- Restrictions on eligibility: In general, award recipients must use awards within seven years of the date the term of service was completed. Summer of service participants must use awards within 10 years of the date the term was completed.
- Post-award conditions: N/A
- Federal tax treatment: The amount of education awards received is included in gross income.
- Budgetary classification and funding: Discretionary. Authorization of appropriations provided for FY2010 through FY2014. Previous amounts appropriated, FY2013: $200.7 million; FY2014: $207.4 million; FY2015: $209.6 million; FY2016: $220.0 million; FY2017: $206.8 million. In addition to the Corporation's annual appropriations, CNCS is authorized to transfer additional amounts from AmeriCorps State and National Grants programs funds to support the activities of national service participants, including

educational awards. Also, as part of the FEMA Corps partnership, FEMA makes a contribution to the Trust towards participants' education awards (National Service Cost Share; NSCS).

- Annual amount discharged or repaid: Beneficiaries of the program can use their awards up to seven years after they are awarded, therefore, the dollar amount reported reflects the cumulative amount of money used by beneficiaries in a particular program year (PY). It is expected that amounts for each program year used will increase as more students use their award for tuition or loan repayment. A program year refers to service positions awarded to participants with a particular fiscal year's funds. Positions are often filled in time periods after the year in which they are awarded (e.g., money is granted to an AmeriCorps State program in FY2016, but not all positions available in the program are filled until FY2017). Education awards can be used to pay current tuition expenses and to repay student loans, therefore, the numbers reported include money expended to both pay current tuition expenses and to repay student loans. PY2013: $155.2 million; PY2014: $142.9 million; PY2015: $117.9 million; PY2016: $77.5 million; PY2017: $3.7 million.

- Annual number of beneficiaries: Because program beneficiaries have up to seven years to use an education award after it is made, the annual beneficiaries presented here reflect cumulative the number of AmeriCorps State and National, NCCC, VISTA, and FEMA Corps participants who earned education awards. The number of individuals who have earned awards is expected to increase for each program year as more individuals complete their service. PY2013: 59,643; PY2014: 58,903; PY2015: 57,216; PY2016: 56,324; PY2017: 5,242.

- Additional resources: Corporation for National & Community Service, Annual Management Report: Fiscal Year 2017, https://www.nationalservice.gov/sites/default/files/documents/CN CS-FY17-AMR-508_v2r2.pdf.

Capitol Police Student Loan Repayment

- Authority: Statute: Department of Defense Appropriations Act, 2002, Div. B, Ch. 9, §908; 2 U.S.C. §1926. Regulations: None.
- Federal administering agency: U.S. Capitol Police.
- Purpose of program: To recruit or retain qualified personnel.
- Eligible loan type: Any student loan previously taken out by a qualifying employee (this may include FFEL and Direct Loan program Subsidized Loans, Unsubsidized Loans, PLUS Loans, and Consolidation Loans; and Perkins Loans).
- Qualifying service or other activity: To qualify for repayment benefits, borrowers must be employees of the Capitol Police.
- Maximum benefit amount: Up to $40,000.
- Restrictions on eligibility: Repayment benefits are only available for the amount of a borrower's outstanding debts on the date a repayment agreement is executed.
- Post-award conditions: N/A
- Federal tax treatment: The amount of student loan repayments received is included in gross income.
- Budgetary classification and funding: Discretionary. Information on previous amounts appropriated is currently unavailable to CRS.
- Annual amount discharged or repaid: The program has not been operational since at least FY2009.
- Annual number of beneficiaries: The program has not been operational since at least FY2009.
- Additional resources: None.

Centers for Disease Control/Agency for Toxic Substances and Disease Registry Educational Loan Repayment Program

- Authority: Statute: PHSA Title III, §317F; 42 U.S.C. §247b-7. Regulations: None.

- Federal administering agency: Centers for Diseases Control and Prevention (CDC) and Agency for Toxic Substances and Disease Registry (ATSDR).
- Purpose of program: To provide loan repayment benefits for health professionals conducting prevention activities at the CDC or the ATSDR.
- Eligible loan types: Government and private loans obtained for tuition, other educational expenses, and reasonable living expenses for undergraduate education, graduate education, or both.
- Qualifying service or other activity: To qualify for repayment benefits, borrowers must be CDC or ATSDR employees serving in hard-to-fill positions. Borrowers must complete at least three years of service.
- Maximum benefit amount: Up to $35,000 per year.
- Restrictions on eligibility: Borrowers must have a substantial amount of education loans relative to income (i.e., debt is more than 20% of a borrower's annual federal salary). Borrowers must be U.S. citizens and must hold a relevant doctoral degree or its equivalent.
- Post-award conditions: Borrowers must pay an amount equal to the sum of: (1) the amount of loan repayments paid to the participant for a period of service not completed; (2) $7,500 multiplied by the months of service not completed; and (3) the interest on the sum of (1) and (2) calculated at the maximum prevailing rate—as determined by the Treasury—from the date of the contract breach if they fail to complete their service commitment.
- Federal tax treatment: Borrowers can receive an additional 39% of the total loan repayment amount for federal income tax liability.
- Budgetary classification and funding: Discretionary. Authorization expired in FY2002.
- Annual amounts discharged or repaid: N/A
- Annual number of beneficiaries: N/A

- Additional resources: The program was initiated as a pilot program, see Department of Health and Human Services, Centers for Disease Control and Prevention, "CDC/ATSDR Educational Loan Repayment Program," 66 Federal Register 54528, October 29, 2001.

Indian Health Service: Mental Health Prevention and Treatment Loan Repayment Program

- Authority: Statute: Indian Health Care Improvement Act, Title I, §209(f); 25 U.S.C. §1621h. Regulations: None.
- Federal administering agency: U.S. Department of Health and Human Services, Indian Health Service (IHS).
- Purpose of program: To recruit and retain personnel providing mental health services.
- Eligible loan types: Loans used to pursue a health profession education.
- Qualifying service or other activity: To qualify for repayment benefits, borrowers must be employees of an Indian health program ("Indian health programs" refers to facilities operated by the IHS, an Indian Tribe, a Tribal Organization, or an Urban Indian Organization). The duration of the service commitment is undetermined, as the program has not yet been implemented. Priority is given to borrowers who provide mental health services to children and adolescents with mental health problems.
- Maximum benefit amount: Undetermined, as the program has not yet been implemented.
- Restrictions on eligibility: Undetermined, as the program has not yet been implemented.
- Post-award conditions: Undetermined, as the program has not yet been implemented.
- Federal tax treatment: Undetermined, as the program has not yet been implemented.

- Budgetary classification and funding: Discretionary. The program has not yet received any appropriations.
- Annual amounts discharged or repaid: N/A
- Annual number of beneficiaries: N/A
- Additional resources: None.

Loan Repayment Program for Clinical Researchers from Disadvantaged Backgrounds

- Authority: Statute: Caregivers and Veterans Omnibus Health Services Act of 2010, Title VI, §604, P.L. 111-163; 38 U.S.C. §7681, note. Regulations: None.
- Federal administering agency: U.S. Department of Veterans Affairs, Veterans Health Administration (VHA).
- Purpose of program: To recruit qualified health professionals who are from disadvantaged backgrounds to conduct clinical research for the VHA.
- Eligible loan types: Loans used to pay all or part of the cost of tuition and reasonable educational and living expenses to obtain a health professional degree (this may include FFEL and Direct Loan program Subsidized Loans, Unsubsidized Loans, PLUS Loans, and Consolidation Loans; Perkins Loans; and private education loans).
- Qualifying service or other activity: To qualify for repayment benefits, borrowers must conduct clinical research as VHA employees and be from disadvantaged backgrounds defined by environmental or family economic circumstances.
- Maximum benefit amount: Up to $35,000 per year.
- Restrictions on eligibility: Borrowers must be U.S. citizens or permanent legal residents and must have obtained a health professional doctoral degree (i.e., a PhD or a doctorate in medicine, osteopathic medicine, dentistry, pharmacy, veterinary medicine, or an equivalent). Borrowers with a federal judgment or

lien against their property are ineligible. Borrowers must not have received support from any of the following programs: Physicians Shortage Area Scholarship Program, National Research Service Award Program, Public Health Service Scholarship Program, National Health Service Corps Scholarship Program, Primary Care Loan Program, Armed Forces (Army, Navy, or Air Force) Professions Scholarship Program, and the Indian Health Service Scholarship Program. Borrowers who have received a deferral from one of these programs may be eligible.

- Post-award conditions: Borrowers must pay $7,500 per month of service not completed, plus all the amounts paid on their behalf for the months of service that were not completed. Borrowers must also pay interest on the amount owed, with interest accruing from the date of breach. The U.S. government is entitled to recover not less than $31,000. Borrowers may terminate renewal contracts at any time without penalties. Loan repayments are prorated and terminated on the date that research stops.
- Federal tax treatment: Borrowers can receive an additional 39% of the total loan repayment amount for income tax liability.
- Budgetary classification and funding: Discretionary. Funding has never been appropriated for this program.
- Annual amounts discharged or repaid: N/A
- Annual number of beneficiaries: N/A
- Additional resources: None.

Program for the Repayment of Educational Loans

- Authority: Statute: Clay Hunt Suicide Prevention for American Veterans Act (P.L. 114-2), §4; 38 U.S.C. §7681, note. Regulations: 38 C.F.R. §§17.640-17.647.
- Federal administering agency: U.S. Department of Veterans Affairs (VA), Veterans Health Administration (VHA).

- Purpose of program: To support the recruitment of qualified psychiatrists to work at the VA and to increase veterans' access to mental healthcare.
- Eligible Loan Types: Loans used to pay all or part of the cost of tuition and reasonable educational and living expenses to obtain an education to qualify the individual for a VA position. This may include FFEL and Direct Loan program Subsidized Loans, Unsubsidized Loans, PLUS Loans to graduate students, and some Consolidation Loans; Perkins Loans; and private education loans. Parent PLUS Loans and Consolidation Loans used to repay parent PLUS Loans are excluded. In addition, loans that are in default, delinquent, or not in current payment status are ineligible.
- Qualifying service or other activity: Individuals must work full-time in permanent employment with the VA in the field of psychiatric medicine in a location determined by the VA for two or more calendar years.
- To qualify for repayment benefits, individuals must be enrolled in the final year of a post- graduation physician residency program that is accredited by the Accreditation Council for Graduate Medical Education or the American Osteopathic Association and leads to either a specialty qualification in psychiatric medicine or subspecialty qualification of psychiatry. By the time of VA employment, the individual must
  o have completed all psychiatry residency training,
  o have received a completion certificate from the program director of the core psychiatry program in which the individual trained,
  o certify intention to apply for board certification in the specialty of psychiatry within two years of residency completion, and
  o be licensed or eligible for licensure to practice medicine by meeting specified requirements.
- Maximum benefit amount: Up to $30,000 per year of service. Borrowers may not receive annual loan repayment amounts that

would exceed the amount of the principal and interest on their qualifying loans.

- Restrictions on eligibility: Repayment benefits are awarded on a competitive basis, with applicants submitting an application, letters of recommendation, and a personal statement. Program participants must be U.S. citizens or permanent residents and may not simultaneously participate in another loan repayment program.
- Post-award conditions: Borrowers must repay the full amount of the benefit received, prorated for completed service days, if they fail to complete the obligated service.
- Federal tax treatment: Undetermined, as the program has not yet been implemented.
- Budgetary classification and funding: Discretionary. This program is authorized as a pilot program that will expire three years after the date on which the Secretary of Veterans Affairs commences the pilot. The Secretary of Veterans Affairs intends to make initial awards under this program in FY2019. Funding for this program is derived from amounts available to the Secretary of the VHA for medical services.
- Annual amounts discharged or repaid: Program has not yet been implemented.
- Annual number of beneficiaries: Program has not yet been implemented.
- Additional resources: None.

Veterans Affairs Specialty Education Loan Repayment Program

- Authority: Statute: VA Mission Act of 2018 (P.L. 115-182) Title III, §303; 38 U.S.C. §§7691-7697. Regulations: None.
- Federal administering agency: U.S. Department of Veterans Affairs (VA), Veterans Health Administration (VHA).

- Purpose of program: To recruit and retain qualified physicians in medical specialties to serve in positions within the VHA for which recruitment or retention is difficult.

- Eligible loan types: Loans used to pay all or part of the cost of tuition and reasonable educational and living expenses to obtain a health professional degree to qualify the individual for the VHA position (this may include FFEL and Direct Loan program Subsidized Loans, Unsubsidized Loans, Graduate PLUS Loans, and Consolidation Loans; Perkins Loans; and private education loans).

- Qualifying service or other activity: To qualify for repayment benefits, borrowers must be VHA specialty physicians who provide full-time clinical care at a VHA facility selected from a list of VHA facilities deemed eligible by the VA Secretary. Borrowers must serve as a full-time clinical practice employee for no fewer than 24 months and for 12 months for each $40,000 in loan repayment benefits they receive.

- Maximum benefit amount: Up to $160,000 over a total of four years of service, but repayment amounts may not exceed $40,000 in each year of participation. Borrowers may not receive annual loan repayment amounts that would exceed the amount of the principal and interest on their education or training loans.

- Restrictions on eligibility: Repayment benefits are awarded on a competitive basis, with priority given to the physicians participating in residency programs in rural areas, operated by an Indian Tribe, Tribal Organization, or the Indian Health Service, or in a program affiliated with a VHA facility. The program also gives priority to veterans.

- Post-award conditions: N/A

- Federal tax treatment: Undetermined, as the program has not yet been implemented.

- Budgetary classification and funding: Discretionary. Funding for this program is derived from amounts available to the Secretary of the VHA for medical services.

- Annual amounts discharged or repaid: Program has not yet been implemented.
- Annual number of beneficiaries: Program has not yet been implemented.
- Additional resources: None.

Armed Forces National Call to Service Payment of Student Loans

- Authority: Statute: National Defense Authorization Act for Fiscal Year 2003, Div. A, Title V, Subtitle D, §531(a)(1); 10 U.S.C. §510. Regulations: None.
- Federal administering agency: Department of Defense, applicable military branch.
- Purpose of program: To serve as an incentive to individuals to enlist for active-duty service in a military occupational specialty designated as facilitating a pursuit of national service.
- Eligible loan type: Any loan used to pay all or part of the cost of attendance at a public or private, nonprofit degree-granting institution of higher education (this may include FFEL and Direct Loan program Subsidized Loans, Unsubsidized Loans, PLUS Loans, and Consolidation Loans; Perkins Loans; and private education loans).
- Qualifying service or other activity: To qualify for repayment benefits, borrowers must not have previously served in the Armed Forces and must enter into an original enlistment in which they agree to perform a period of national service. A period of national service includes 15 months of active duty in a military occupational specialty designated by the Secretary of Defense and either
  o an additional period of active duty as determined by the Secretary of Defense; or
  o 24 months of active status in the Selected Reserve.

- Additionally, borrowers must then serve the remaining period of obligated service either
  - o on active duty in the Armed Forces;
  - o in the Selected Reserve;
  - o in AmeriCorps or another domestic national service program jointly designated by the Secretary of Defense and the head of the program for purposes of the statute; or
  - o in any combination of service described above. Generally, these requirements total three years of service.
- Maximum benefit amount: Up to $18,000.
- Restrictions on eligibility: Benefits are only available for the amount of a borrower's outstanding student loan debt on the date that a service agreement is entered.
- Post-award conditions: Borrowers must repay the amount equal to the unearned portion of the loan repayments if they fail to complete their service.
- Federal tax treatment: The amount of student loan repayments received is included in gross income.
- Budgetary classification and funding: Discretionary. Amounts appropriated are included as part of the relevant military service component's personnel appropriation.
- Annual amount discharged or repaid: Information currently unavailable to CRS.
- Annual number of beneficiaries: Information currently unavailable to CRS.
- Additional resources: None.

Education Loan Repayment Program: Commissioned Officers in Specified Health Professions

- Authority: Statute: National Defense Authorization Act for Fiscal Year 1998, Div. A, Title VI, Subtitle E, §651(a); 10 U.S.C. §2173. Regulations: None.

- Federal administering agency: Department of Defense, applicable military branch.
- Purpose of program: To maintain a sufficient number of active duty commissioned officers who are qualified in specified health professions.
- Eligible loan type: A loan used to finance a health profession education; obtained from a governmental entity, private financial institutions, school, or other authorized entity; and used to pay for educational expenses (this may include FFEL and Direct Loan program Subsidized Loans, Unsubsidized Loans, PLUS Loans, and Consolidation Loans, Perkins Loans, and private education loans).
  - Qualifying service or other activity: To qualify for repayment benefits, a borrower must be fully qualified for, or hold, an appointment as a commissioned officer in one of the specified health professions and either be
  - fully qualified health care professionals in an area designated by the Secretary of the relevant military department as necessary to meet a skill shortage;
  - enrolled as full-time students in the final year of a course of study at an accredited institution leading to a degree in a health profession other than medicine or osteopathic medicine;
  - enrolled in the final year of an approved graduate program leading to specialty qualification in medicine, dentistry, osteopathic medicine, or other health profession; or
  - enrolled in the Armed Forces Health Professions Scholarship and Financial Assistance Program for a number of years less than required to complete the normal length or study.
- Borrowers must serve on active duty for at least one year or, if currently on active duty, remain on active duty for an additional period of time.
- Maximum benefit amount: Up to $60,000 per year. The maximum amount is increased annually by an amount equal to the percent increase in the average annual cost of educational expenses of a scholarship under the Armed Forces Health Professions

Scholarship and Financial Assistance Program. Cumulative amounts vary by military branch.

- Restrictions on eligibility: Students of the Uniformed Services University of Health Sciences cannot receive repayment benefits.
- Post-award conditions: Borrowers who are commissioned officers and who are relieved of their officer's active duty obligations under the program may be given alternative obligations. Borrowers who do not complete the active duty service or an alternative obligation must repay an amount equal to the unearned portion of student loan payments.
- Federal tax treatment: The amount of student loan repayments received is included in gross income.
- Budgetary classification and funding: Discretionary. Amounts appropriated are included as part of the relevant military service component's personnel appropriation.
- Annual amount discharged or repaid: Information currently unavailable to CRS.
- Annual number of beneficiaries: Information currently unavailable to CRS.
- Additional resources: National Council of Higher Education Loan Programs, Program Regulations Committee, "Matrix of Department of Defense (DOD) and Other Federal Student Loan Repayment Programs," February 2, 2012, http://c.ymcdn. com/sites/www.ncher.us/resource/collection/F4EAF7F5-F223-4EC9-9C0E-5511898606A6/02-08-13_DOD_Repayment_ Matrix.pdf.

Armed Forces Student Loan Interest Payment Program: Members on Active Duty

- Authority: Statute: National Defense Authorization Act for Fiscal Year 2003, Div. A, Title VI, Subtitle F, §651(a)(1); 10 U.S.C. §2174. Regulations: None.

- Federal administering agency: Department of Defense, applicable military branch.
- Purpose of program: To pay for interest accrued on student loans of military personnel while they are on active duty.
- Eligible loan type: Interest and special allowances that accrue on FFEL and Direct Loan program Subsidized Loans, Unsubsidized Loans, and PLUS Loans and Perkins loans.
- Qualifying service or other activity: To qualify for repayment benefits, borrowers must be members of the Armed Forces who are on active duty in fulfillment of their first enlistment or active-duty officers who have not completed more than three years of service on active duty.
- Maximum benefit allowed: Any interest and special allowances that accrue on one or more student loans to be paid for a maximum of 36 consecutive months.
- Restrictions on eligibility: Loans on which interest is to be paid may not be in default.
- Post-award conditions: N/A
- Federal tax treatment: The amount of student loan repayments received is included in gross income.
- Budgetary classification and funding: Discretionary. Amounts appropriated are included as part of the relevant military service component's personnel appropriation.
- Annual amount discharged or repaid: Information currently unavailable to CRS.
- Annual number of beneficiaries: Information currently unavailable to CRS.
- Additional resources: None.

Coast Guard Education Loan Repayment Program

- Authority: Statute: Coast Guard and Maritime Transportation Act of 2004, Title II, §218(a); 14 U.S.C. §472. Regulations: None.

- Federal administering agency: Department of Homeland Security.
- Purpose of program: To recruit and retain qualified enlisted members in determined specialty occupations.
- Eligible loan type: FFEL and Direct Loan program Subsidized Loans, Unsubsidized Loans, PLUS Loans, and Consolidation Loans and Perkins loans.
- Qualifying service or other activity: To qualify for repayment benefits, borrowers must serve in active duty as enlisted members of the Coast Guard in a determined specialty occupation. Payment is made based upon each complete year of service performed.
- Maximum benefit allowed: The greater of 33 1/3% of the outstanding student loan or $1,500 per year.
- Restrictions on eligibility: N/A
- Post-award conditions: N/A
- Federal tax treatment: The amount of student loan repayments received is included in gross income.
- Budgetary classification and funding: Discretionary. Information on previous amounts appropriated is currently unavailable to CRS.
- Annual amount discharged or repaid: Information currently unavailable to CRS.
- Annual beneficiaries: Information currently unavailable to CRS.
- Additional resources: None.

Federal Food, Drug, and Cosmetic Act Loan Repayment Program

- Authority: Statute: Federal Food, Drug, and Cosmetic Act §1005; 21 U.S.C. §395. Regulations: None.
- Federal administering agency: U.S. Department of Health and Human Services, Food and Drug Administration (FDA).

- Purpose of program: To recruit appropriately qualified health professionals to conduct research as employees of the FDA.
- Eligible loan types: Government and private loans obtained for tuition, other educational expenses, and reasonable living expenses for undergraduate education, graduate education, or both.
- Qualifying service or other activity: To qualify for repayment benefits, borrowers must be appropriately qualified health professionals who conduct research while FDA employees. Borrowers must complete at least three years of service.
- Maximum benefit amount: Up to $20,000 per year.
- Restrictions on eligibility: Borrowers must have a substantial amount of education loans relative to income (i.e., debt is more than 20% of borrower's annual federal salary).
- Post-award conditions: Borrowers must pay an amount equal to the sum of: (1) the amount of loan repayments paid to the participant for a period of service not completed; (2) $7,500 multiplied by the number of months of service not completed; and (3) the interest on the sum of (1) and (2) calculated at the maximum prevailing rate— as determined by the Treasury—from the date of the contract breach if they do not complete their service commitment.
- Federal tax treatment: The amount of student loan repayments received is excluded from gross income if the loan meets certain conditions.
- Budgetary classification and funding: Discretionary.
- Annual amounts discharged or repaid: FY2013: $2.2 million. FY2014-FY2017: Information currently unavailable to CRS.
- Annual number of beneficiaries: FY2013: 248; FY2014-FY2017: information currently unavailable to CRS.
- Additional resources: None.

National Indian Forest Resources Management Postgraduation
Recruitment Assumption of Student Loans

- Authority: Statute: National Indian Forest Resource Management Act, Title III, §315; 25 U.S.C. §3114. Regulations: 25 C.F.R. §163.41.
- Federal administering agency: Department of the Interior, Bureau of Indian Affairs (BIA).
- Purpose of program: To recruit Indian and Alaska Native graduate foresters and trained forestry technicians into the Bureau of Indian Affairs forestry programs.
- Eligible loan type: Any outstanding student loan from an established lending institution (this may include FFEL and Direct Loan program Subsidized Loans, Unsubsidized Loans, PLUS Loans, and Consolidation Loans; Perkins Loans; and private education loans).
- Qualifying activity or other service: To qualify for repayment benefits, borrowers must be Indian or Alaska Native professional foresters or forester technicians who have completed a post-secondary forestry or forestry-related curriculum at an accredited institution and enter into a service agreement with a BIA or tribal forestry program. Payment is made based upon each complete year of service performed.
- Maximum benefit allowed: Up to $5,000 per year.
- Restrictions on eligibility: N/A
- Post-award conditions: Borrowers must repay the amount, plus interest, of their loans assumed by the agency if they fail to complete their service. The amount to be repaid is adjusted based on the amount of obligated service performed.
- Federal tax treatment: The amount of student loan repayments received is included in gross income.
- Budgetary classification and funding: Discretionary. Information on previous amounts appropriated is currently unavailable to CRS.

- Annual amount discharged or repaid: Information currently unavailable to CRS.
- Annual number of beneficiaries: Information currently unavailable to CRS.
- Additional Resources: None.

American Indian Agricultural Resource Management Postgraduation Recruitment Assumption of Student Loans

- Authority: Statute: American Indian Agricultural Resource Management Act, Title II, §202; 25 U.S.C. §3732. Regulations: 25 C.F.R. §166.900 et seq.
- Federal administering agency: Department of the Interior, Bureau of Indian Affairs (BIA).
- Purpose of program: To recruit Indian and Alaska Natives for employment as natural resource and trained agriculture technicians in approved agriculture programs.
- Eligible loan type: Any outstanding student loan from an established lending institution (this may include FFEL and Direct Loan program Subsidized Loans, Unsubsidized Loans, PLUS Loans, and Consolidation Loans; Perkins Loans; and private education loans).
- Qualifying service or other activity: To qualify for repayment benefits, borrowers must be Indian or Alaska Native natural resources and agriculture technicians who have completed a post-secondary natural resources or agriculture-related curriculum at an accredited institution and enter into a service agreement with a BIA or a tribal agriculture program or related programs. Payment is made based upon each complete year of service performed.
- Maximum benefit allowed: Up to $5,000 per year.
- Restrictions on eligibility: N/A
- Post-award conditions: Borrowers must repay the amount, plus interest, of their loans assumed by the agency if they fail to

complete their service. The amount required to be repaid is adjusted based on the amount of obligated service performed.

- Federal tax treatment: The amount of student loan repayments received is included in gross income.
- Budgetary classification and funding: Discretionary. Information on previous amounts appropriated is currently unavailable to CRS.
- Annual amount discharged or repaid: Information currently unavailable to CRS.
- Annual number of beneficiaries: Information currently unavailable to CRS.
- Additional resources: None.

APPENDIX B. PROGRAMS BY ELIGIBILITY

Table B-2, Table B-3, Table B-4, and Table B-5 list federal student loan repayment and forgiveness programs by type of profession or service that qualifies borrowers for program benefits. Table B-6 lists federal student loan repayment and forgiveness programs that are based, in part, on a borrower's financial circumstances. Within each table, programs are organized according to their order of presentation in the report (i.e., in descending order intended to be reflective of potential scale of availability to borrowers and financial resources needed to provide benefits). The following tables list a brief description of the eligibility criteria, length of service commitment, qualifying loan type, maximum benefit available, and administering agency or entity. For more complete information on each program, see the program-specific details listed in Appendix A. Programs with columns denoted "undetermined" have not yet been implemented and, therefore, may have some criteria that have not yet been established. Finally, several programs (e.g., the Public Service Loan Forgiveness Program) benefit a variety of professions and, therefore, may appear in multiple tables.

Table B-1 identifies the meanings of acronyms used in the tables that follow.

Table B-1. Acronyms used in Table B-2 through Table B-6

ATSDR	Agency for Toxic Substances and Disease Registry
BIA	Bureau of Indian Affairs
BJA	Bureau of Justice Assistance
CDC	Centers for Disease Control and Prevention
CBO	Congressional Budget Office
CNCS	Corporation for National and Community Service
DL	William D. Ford Federal Direct Loan program
DHS	Department of Homeland Security
DOD	Department of Defense
DOI	Department of the Interior
DOJ	Department of Justice
DOS	Department of State
ED	Department of Education
FDA	Food and Drug Administration
FFEL	Federal Family Education Loan program
HHS	Department of Health and Human Services
HPSA	Health Professional Shortage Areas
IHS	Indian Health Service
JRJ	John R. Justice
LRP	Loan Repayment Program
NCCC	National Civilian Community Corps
NHSC	National Health Service Corps
NIFA	National Institute of Food and Agriculture
NIH	National Institutes of Health
PHSA	Public Health Service Act
STEM	Science, Technology, Engineering, and Mathematics
USCG	U.S. Coast Guard
USDA	U.S. Department of Agriculture
VA	U.S. Department of Veterans Affairs
VHA	Veterans Health Administration
VISTA	Volunteers in Service to America

Table B-2. Federal Student Loan Repayment and Forgiveness Programs Health Care and Public Health Professions

Program	Administering Agency/Entity	Eligibility	Service Commitment	Qualifying Loans	Maximum Benefit
DL Public Service Loan Forgiveness	ED	Employed full-time in a public service job, including jobs in public health	10 years	DL program Subsidized Loans, Unsubsidized Loans, PLUS Loans, and Consolidation Loans	Remaining loan balance after 10 years of qualifying payments
Federal Perkins Loan Cancellation	ED	Employed full-time as a nurse or medical technician	At least 1 year for partial benefit; 5 years for maximum benefit	Federal Perkins Loans	100% of student loan balance
IHS Loan Repayment Program	HHS/IHS	Health professionals employed at an IHS facility in a specifically identified field	At least 2 years	Loans used to finance educational expenses	$35,000 per year
NHSC LRP	HHS/HRSA	Health professionals in health professional shortage areas, including clinical social workers, family therapists, and counselors	At least 2 years	Loans used to finance educational expenses	$60,000 per year; $240,000 in total
NHSC Students to Service LRP	HHS/HRSA	Primary care physicians in health professional shortage areas of greatest need	At least 3 years	Loans used to finance educational expenses	$60,000 per year; $120,000 in total

Table B-2. (Continued)

Program	Administering Agency/Entity	Eligibility	Service Commitment	Qualifying Loans	Maximum Benefit
National Health Service Corps State LRP	HHS/HRSA	Health professionals in state-designated shortage areas	Varies by state	Loans used to finance educational expenses	Varies by state
Loan Repayments for Health Professional School Faculty	HHS/HRSA	Health professionals who agree to serve as faculty at a health professions school	At least 2 years	Loans used to finance educational expenses	$40,000 per year
General, Pediatric, and Public Health Dentistry Faculty Loan Payment	HHS/HRSA	Full-time faculty in general, pediatric, or public health dentistry	5 years	Loans used to finance educational expenses	100% of student loan balance
Substance Use Disorder Treatment Loan Repayment Program	HHS/HRS	Substance use disorder treatment providers in mental health professional shortage areas or in an area with high rates of drug overdose deaths	At least 2 years	Loans used to finance educational expenses	Up to $250,000 in total
Nursing Education LRP (NURSE Corps)	HHS/HRSA	Nurses at nonprofit health care facilities with a shortage of nurses or nurse faculty members at accredited nursing schools	At least 2 years	Loans used to finance educational expenses	85% of student loan balance
Nursing Faculty LRP	HHS/HRSA	Full-time nurse faculty at accredited nursing schools	At least 1 year	Loans used to finance educational expenses	85% of student loan balance, plus interest

Program	Administering Agency/Entity	Eligibility	Service Commitment	Qualifying Loans	Maximum Benefit
NIH Extramural LRPs	HHS/NIH	Health professionals who conduct research in specified areas	At least 2 years	FFEL, DL, Graduate PLUS, and Consolidation loans, PHSA Title VII-A and VIII-E loans, loans made by certain government and private lenders	$50,000 per year
Public Health Workforce LRP	HHS/HRSA	Full-time public health professionals	At least 3 years	Loans used to finance educational expenses	$35,000 per year
Loan Forgiveness for Service in Areas of National Need	ED	Employed as a nurse, public or mental health professional, or dentist	None	FFEL and DL program Subsidized Loans, Unsubsidized Loans, Graduate PLUS Loans, and Consolidation Loans (other than those used to repay Parent PLUS Loans)	$2,000 per year; $10,000 in total
Pediatric Subspecialist LRP	HHS/HRSA	Full-time pediatric health professionals who are employed in a HPSA or underserved area	At least 2 years	Loans used to finance educational expenses	$35,000 per year
Nursing Workforce Development Loans: Loan Cancellation	HHS/HRSA	Professional full-time nurses at eligible institutions; loans must have been received before September 29, 1995	Undetermined	Loans made to students by schools from funds established under the program's statute	85% of student loan balance

Table B-2. (Continued)

Program	Administering Agency/Entity	Eligibility	Service Commitment	Qualifying Loans	Maximum Benefit
Nursing Workforce Development Student Loans: Loan Repayment	HHS/HRSA	Borrower is unable to complete nursing studies, is in exceptionally needy circumstances, and does not resume studies within two years of withdrawal from studies	Undetermined	Loans made to students by schools from funds established under the program's statute	Undetermined
Eligible Individual Student LRP	HHS/HRSA	Licensed nurses with a master's or doctoral degree who serve as full-time nursing faculty	At least 4 years	Undetermined	$20,000 per year; $80,000 in total
LRP: Health Professions Officers Serving in the Selected Reserve with Wartime Critical Medical Skill Shortages	DOD	Officers in the Selected Reserve who are qualified, or enrolled in a program leading to qualification, in a critically needed health care profession to meet wartime combat medical shortages	At least 1 year	FFEL and DL program Subsidized Loans, Unsubsidized Loans, Graduate PLUS Loans, and Consolidation Loans, Perkins Loans, PHSA Title VII-A and VIII-B loans, Primary Care Loan Program loans, and private education loans	$60,000 per year

Program	Administering Agency/Entity	Eligibility	Service Commitment	Qualifying Loans	Maximum Benefit
Education Debt Reduction Program	VA/VHA	VHA health professionals who provide direct patient care, or services incident to direct patient case, difficult-to-fill health professions	None specified	Loans used to finance educational expenses	$200,000 in total over a five-year period
NIH Intramural LRPs	HHS/NIH	NIH employees who conduct research in specified areas	At least 2 years	FFEL, DL, Graduate PLUS, and Consolidation loans, PHSA Title VII-A and VIII-B loans, and loans made by certain government and private lenders	$50,000 per year
CDC/ATSDR Educational LRP	HHS /CDC/ATSDR	CDC or ATSDR employees in hard-to-fill positions and whose debt exceeds 20% of their salary	At least 3 years	Loans used to finance educational expenses	$35,000 per year
IHS Mental Health Prevention and Treatment LRP	HHS/IHS	IHS employees who provide mental health services	Undetermined	Loans used to finance educational expenses	Undetermined
LRP: Clinical Researchers from Disadvantaged Backgrounds	VA/VHA	VHA employees from disadvantaged backgrounds who conduct clinical research	At least 1 year	Loans used to finance educational expenses	$35,000 per year
Program for the Repayment of Educational Loans	VA/VHA	VHA health professionals who serve as qualified psychiatrists	At least 2 years	Loans used to finance educational expenses	$30,000 per year

Table B-2. (Continued)

Program	Administering Agency/Entity	Eligibility	Service Commitment	Qualifying Loans	Maximum Benefit
Veterans Affairs Specialty Education Loan Repayment Program	VA/VHA	VHA specialty physicians who provide full-time clinical care at a VHA facility	At least 2 years	Loans used to finance educational expenses	$40,000 per year; $160,000 in total
LRP: Commissioned Officers in Specified Health Professions	DOD	Members who are serving or able to serve on active duty as an officer in a specified health care profession	At least 1 year	Loans used to finance a health profession education	$60,000 per year
Federal Food, Drug, and Cosmetic Act LRP	HHS/FDA	Health professionals who conduct research as an FDA employee and whose debt exceeds 20% of their annual salary	At least 3 years	Loans used to finance educational expenses	$20,000 per year

Source: CRS analysis of relevant statutes, regulations, and program materials.

**Table B-3. Federal Student Loan Repayment and Forgiveness Programs
Education Professions**

Program	Administering Agency/Entity	Eligibility	Service Commitment	Qualifying Loans	Maximum Benefit
DL Public Service Loan Forgiveness	ED	Employed full-time in a public service job, including jobs education or school-based library services	10 years	DL program Subsidized Loans, Unsubsidized Loans, PLUS Loans, and Consolidation Loans	Remaining loan balance after 10 years of qualifying payments
Stafford Loan Forgiveness for Teachers	ED	Full-time teachers in public or private nonprofit schools or public education service agencies	At least 5 consecutive complete academic years	FFEL and DL program Subsidized Loans and Unsubsidized Loans; and portions of Consolidation Loans attributable to Subsidized Loans and Unsubsidized Loans	$5,000 in general; $17,500 for special education and STEM teachers
Federal Perkins Loan Cancellation	ED	Employed full-time in specified education services	At least 1 year for partial benefit; 5 years for maximum benefit	Federal Perkins Loans	100% of student loan balance
Loan Repayments for Health Professional School Faculty	HHS/HRSA	Health professionals who agree to serve as faculty at a health professions school	At least 2 years	Loans used to finance educational expenses	$40,000 per year
General, Pediatric, and Public Health Dentistry Faculty Loan Payment	HHS/HRSA	Full-time faculty in general, pediatric, or public health dentistry	5 years	Undetermined	100% of student loan balance

Table B-3. (Continued)

Program	Administering Agency/Entity	Eligibility	Service Commitment	Qualifying Loans	Maximum Benefit
Nursing Education LRP (NURSE Corps)	HHS/HRSA	Nurse faculty members at accredited nursing schools	At least 2 years	Loans used to finance educational expenses	85% of student loan balance
Nursing Faculty LRP	HHS/HRSA	Full-time nurse faculty at accredited nursing schools	At least 1 year	Loans used to finance educational expenses	85% of student loan balance, plus interest
Loan Forgiveness for Service in Areas of National Need	ED	Full-time teachers, librarians, school counselors, and school administrators	At least 1 year	FFEL and DL program Subsidized Loans, Unsubsidized Loans, Graduate PLUS, and Consolidation Loans (other than those used to repay Parent PLUS Loans)	$2,000 per year; $10,000 in total
Nursing Workforce Development Loans: Loan Cancellation	HHS/HRSA	Professional full-time nursing teachers at eligible institutions; loans must have been received before September 29, 1995	Undetermined	Loans made to students by schools from funds established under the program's statute	85% of student loan balance
Eligible Individual Student LRP	HHS/HRSA	Licensed nurses with a master's or doctoral degree who serve as full-time nursing faculty	At least 4 years	Undetermined	$20,000 per year; $80,000 in total

Source: CRS analysis of relevant statutes, regulations, and program materials.

Table B-4. Federal Student Loan Repayment and Forgiveness Programs Public Service Professions (Other than Health Care, Education, and Military)

Program	Administering Agency/Entity	Eligibility	Service Commitment	Qualifying Loans	Maximum Benefit
DL Public Service Loan Forgiveness Program	ED	Employed full-time in a public service job, including jobs in emergency management, public safety, public interest law, elderly, or disability services	10 years	DL program Subsidized Loans, Unsubsidized Loans, PLUS Loans, and Consolidation Loans	Remaining loan balance after 10 years of qualifying payments
Federal Perkins Loan Cancellation	ED	Employed full-time in specified public service professions, including Peace Corps and AmeriCorps VISTA	At least 1 year for partial benefit; 5 years for maximum benefit	Federal Perkins Loans	100% of student loan balance
Veterinary Medicine LRP	USDA/NIFA	Large animal veterinarians who provide short-term emergency services to the federal government	60 days of service per year for at least 3 years	Loans used to finance educational expenses	$25,000 per year
JRJ Loan Repayment for Prosecutors and Public Defenders Program	DOJ/BJA	Full-time prosecutors, public defenders, and federal defenders	At least 3 years	FFEL, DL, Graduate PLUS, Consolidation, and Perkins loans	$10,000 per year; $60,000 in total
Civil Legal Assistance Attorney Student LRP	ED	Full-time civil legal assistance attorneys	At least 3 years	FFEL and DL program Subsidized Loans, Unsubsidized Loans, Graduate PLUS, and Consolidation	$6,000 per year; $40,000 in total

Table B-4. (Continued)

Program	Administering Agency/Entity	Eligibility	Service Commitment	Qualifying Loans	Maximum Benefit
				Loans (other than those used to repay Parent PLUS Loans) and Perkins Loans	
Loan Forgiveness for Service in Areas of National Need	ED	Full-time public safety, emergency management, public interest legal services, or STEM professionals	At least 1 year	FFEL and DL program Subsidized Loans, Unsubsidized Loans, Graduate PLUS, and Consolidation Loans (other than those used to repay Parent PLUS Loans)	$2,000 per year; $10,000 in total
LRP for Senate Employees	Secretary of the Senate	Senate or Office of Congressional Accessibility Services employees	At least 1 year	FFEL, DL, PLUS, Consolidation, and Perkins loans, PHSA Title VII-A and VIII-E loans	$500 per month; $40,000 in total
LRP for House Employees	Committee on House Administration	U.S. House of Representatives employees	At least 1 year	FFEL, DL, PLUS, Consolidation, and Perkins loans, PHSA Title VII-A and VIII-E loans	$833 per month; $60,000 in total
CBO Student Loan Repayment	CBO	CBO employees	At least 1 year	Loans used to finance educational expenses	$6,000 per year; $40,000 in total
Government Employee LRP	Individual Executive Agencies	Federal executive branch agency employees and certain legislative branch agency employees	At least 3 years	FFEL, DL, PLUS, Consolidation, and Perkins loans, PHSA Title VII-A and VIII-E loans	$10,000 per year; $60,000 in total
Defense Acquisition	DOD	DOD acquisition personnel	At least 3 years	FFEL, DL, PLUS,	$10,000 per year;

Program	Administering Agency/Entity	Eligibility	Service Commitment	Qualifying Loans	Maximum Benefit
Workforce LRP				Consolidation, and Perkins loans, PHSA Title VII-A and VIII-E loans	$60,000 in total
National and Community Service Grant program, Educational Award	CNCS	Individuals who complete service in AmeriCorps, NCCC, or VISTA	Completion of service in AmeriCorps, NCCC, or VISTA	FFEL, DL, PLUS, Consolidation, and Perkins loans, PHSA title VII-A and VIII-E loans, and other loans determined necessary to finance educational expenses	Equal to the maximum Pell Grant award in effect at the beginning of the year in which the CNCS approves the individual's service position
Capitol Police LRP	Capitol Police	Capitol Police employees	N/A	Loans used to finance educational expenses	$40,000 in total
National Indian Forest Resources Management Postgraduation Recruitment Assumption of Student Loans	DOI/BIA	Indians or Alaska Natives who serve as professional foresters or forester technicians for the BIA or a tribal forestry program	At least 1 year	Loans used to finance educational expenses	$5,000 per year
American Indian Agricultural Resource Management Postgraduation Recruitment Assumption of Loans	DOI/BIA	Indians or Alaska Natives who serve as professional natural resources and agriculture technicians for the BIA or tribal agriculture program	At least 1 year	Loans used to finance educational expenses	$5,000 per year

Source: CRS analysis of relevant statutes, regulations, and program materials.

Table B-5. Federal Student Loan Repayment and Forgiveness Programs Military Service

Program	Administering Agency/Entity	Eligibility	Service Commitment	Qualifying Loans	Maximum Benefit
DL Public Service Loan Forgiveness Program	ED	Employed full-time in a public service job, including military service	10 years	DL program Subsidized Loans, Unsubsidized Loans, PLUS Loans, and Consolidation Loans	Remaining loan balance after 10 years of qualifying payments
LRP: Enlisted Members on Active Duty in Specified Military Specialties	DOD	Members who perform active duty in certain officer programs or military specialties	At least 1 year	FFEL, DL, PLUS, Consolidation, and Perkins loans, state and private education loans	The greater of 33 1/3% of the outstanding loan or $1,500 per year
LRP: Members of the Selected Reserve	DOD	Members of the Selected Reserve in certain officer programs or enlisted military specialties	At least 1 year	FFEL, DL, PLUS, Consolidation, and Perkins loans, state and private education loans	The greater of 15% of the outstanding loan or $500 per year, plus accrued interest
LRP: Health Professions Officers Serving in Selected Reserve with Wartime Critical Medical Skill Shortages	DOD	Officers in the Selected Reserve who are qualified, or enrolled in a program leading to qualification, in a critically needed health care profession to meet wartime combat medical shortages	At least one year	FFEL, DL, Graduate PLUS and Perkins loans, PHSA Title VII-A and VIII-B loans, Primary Care Loan Program loans, and private education loans	$60,000/year
LRP: Chaplains Serving in the Selected Reserve	DOD	Members serving or able to serve as a chaplain in the Selected Reserve	At least 3 years	Loans used to finance educational expenses	$20,000 per three years

Program	Administering Agency/Entity	Eligibility	Service Commitment	Qualifying Loans	Maximum Benefit
Armed Forces National Call to Service	DOD	Members who enlist and serve in a designated military occupational specialty	At least 15 months of active duty, plus additional active or reserve service	Loans used to finance educational expenses	$18,000 in total
LRP: Commissioned Officers in Specified Health Professions	DOD	Members who are serving or able to serve on active duty as an officer in a specified health care profession	At least 1 year	Loans used to finance a health profession education	$60,000 per year
Armed Forces Student Loan Interest Payment Program: Members on Active Duty	DOD	Active duty members of the Armed Forces in their first term of service	None	Interest and special allowances that accrue on FFEL, DL, PLUS, and Perkins loans	36 consecutive months of interest and special allowances
Coast Guard Education LRP	DHS/USCG	Enlisted members of the Coast Guard on active duty in specified occupations	At least 1 year	FFEL, DL, PLUS, Consolidation, and Perkins loans	The greater of 33 1/3% of the loan or $1,500 per year

Source: CRS analysis of relevant statutes, regulations, and program materials.

Table B-6. Federal Student Loan Repayment and Forgiveness Programs Borrower's Financial Circumstances

Program	Administering Agency/Entity	Eligibility	Service Commitment	Qualifying Loans	Maximum Benefit
DL Public Service Loan Forgiveness Program	ED	Employed full-time in a public organization	10 years	DL program Subsidized Loans, Unsubsidized Loans, PLUS Loans, and Consolidation Loans	Remaining loan balance after 10 years of qualifying payments
Income-Contingent Repayment (ICR)	ED	Borrowers who make the equivalent of 25 years of payments under ICR or other qualifying plans; monthly payments are generally capped at 20% of borrower's discretionary income	N/A	DL program Subsidized Loans, Unsubsidized Loans, Graduate PLUS, and Consolidation Loans	Remaining loan balance after 25 years of qualifying payments
Income-Based Repayment (IBR) Plan for Pre-July 1, 2014, Borrowers	ED	Borrowers who make the equivalent of 25 years of payments under IBR or other qualifying plans; monthly payments are capped at 15% of the borrower's discretionary income	N/A	FFEL and DL program Subsidized Loans, Unsubsidized Loans, Graduate PLUS, and Consolidation Loans (other than those used to repay Parent PLUS Loans)	Remaining loan balance after 25 years of qualifying payments
Pay-As-You-Earn (PAYE)	ED	Borrowers who make the equivalent of 20 years of payments under PAYE or other qualifying plans; monthly payments are capped at 10% of	N/A	DL program Subsidized Loans, Unsubsidized Loans, Graduate PLUS Loans, and Consolidation Loans (other than those used to repay Parent PLUS Loans)	Remaining loan balance after 20 years of qualifying payments

Program	Administering Agency/Entity	Eligibility	Service Commitment	Qualifying Loans	Maximum Benefit
		borrower's discretionary income			
Income-Based Repayment (IBR) Plan for New Borrowers on or after July 1, 2014	ED	Borrowers who make the equivalent of 20 years of payments under IBR or other qualifying plans; monthly payments are capped at 10% of the borrower's discretionary income	None	DL program Subsidized Loans, Unsubsidized Loans, Graduate PLUS Loans, and Consolidation Loans (other than those used to repay Parent PLUS Loans)	Remaining loan balance after 20 years of qualifying payments
Revised Pay-As-You-Earn (REPAYE)	ED	Undergraduate and graduate/professional school borrowers who make the equivalent of 20 and 25 years of payments, respectively, under REPAYE or other qualifying plans; monthly payments are capped at 10% of borrower's discretionary income	N/A	DL program Subsidized Loans, Unsubsidized Loans, Graduate PLUS Loans, and Consolidation Loans (other than those used to repay Parent PLUS Loans)	Remaining loan balance after 20 or 25 years of qualifying payments for undergraduate and graduate/professional school borrowers, respectively.
NIH Extramural LRPs	HHS/NIH	Health professionals who conduct research in specified areas	At least 2 years	FFEL, DL, Graduate PLUS, and Consolidation loans, PHSA Title VII-A and VIII-E loans, loans made by certain government and private lenders	$50,000 per year

Table B-6. (Continued)

Program	Administering Agency/Entity	Eligibility	Service Commitment	Qualifying Loans	Maximum Benefit
Nursing Workforce Development Student Loans: Loan Repayment	HHS/HRSA	Borrower is unable to complete nursing studies, is in exceptionally needy circumstances, and does not resume studies within two years of withdrawal from studies	Undetermined	Loans made to students by schools from funds established under the program's statute	Undetermined
NIH Intramural LRPs	HHS/NIH	NIH employees who conduct research in specified areas	At least 2 years	FFEL, DL, Graduate PLUS, and Consolidation loans, PHSA Title VII-A and VII-B loans, and loans made by certain government and private lenders	$50,000 per year
CDC/ATSDR Educational LRP	CDC/ATSDR	CDC or ATSDR employees in hard-to-fill positions and whose debt exceeds 20% of their salary	At least 3 years	Loans used to finance educational expenses	$35,000 per year
LRP: Clinical Researchers from Disadvantaged Backgrounds	VA/VHA	VHA employees from disadvantaged backgrounds who conduct clinical research	At least 1 year	FFEL, DL, PLUS, and Perkins loans	$35,000 per year
Federal Food, Drug, and Cosmetic Act LRP	HHS/FDA	Health professionals who conduct research as an FDA employee and whose debt exceeds 20% of their annual salary	At least 3 years	Loans used to finance educational expenses	$20,000 per year

Source: CRS analysis of relevant statutes, regulations, and program materials.

In: Loan Forgiveness …
Editor: Virgil Davidson

Chapter 2

THE PUBLIC SERVICE LOAN FORGIVENESS PROGRAM: SELECTED ISSUES*

Alexandra Hegji

ABSTRACT

The Public Service Loan Forgiveness (PSLF) program provides Direct Loan borrowers who, on or after October 1, 2007, are employed full-time in certain public service jobs for 10 years while making 120 separate qualifying monthly payments on their Direct Loans with the opportunity to have any remaining balance of principal and interest on their loans forgiven. The program was enacted under the College Cost Reduction and Access Act of 2007 (P.L. 110-84) to encourage individuals to enter into and remain employed in public service and to alleviate the potential financial burdens associated with federal student loans of borrowers in public service occupations who were presumed generally to earn less than their counterparts in other occupations.

With the opportunity to apply for program benefits first being made available on October 1, 2017, based on service completed and payments made prior to that date, many issues that span several aspects of the

---

* This is an edited, reformatted and augmented version of Congressional Research Service, Publication No. R45389, dated October 29, 2018.

program have been raised and have garnered congressional interest. This chapter addresses numerous issues, which are highlighted below.

Program implementation issues that have surfaced relate to how the PSLF program's statutory requirements have been operationalized, difficulties experienced by borrowers in participating in the program, and difficulties in administering the program. Some of these issues include:

- Operationally defining what constitutes a "public service job." This includes whether the definition in use is sufficiently targeted to meet congressional intent for the program and whether it has created inequities among types of borrowers. There have also been administrative difficulties associated with identifying and certifying qualifying employment.
- Determining what constitutes a "qualifying payment." Multiple criteria related to on-time payments, time periods over which payments must be made, and specific payment amounts must be met for a payment to be considered qualifying, which may cause confusion among borrowers and create administrative difficulties.
- Difficulties borrowers may face when determining which repayment plan to enroll in to maximize PSLF benefits. Payments made according to an income-driven repayment (IDR) plan may decrease the monthly dollar amount of payments made, which may ultimately lead to greater amounts of PSLF forgiveness benefits. Payments made under other plans may also qualify for PSLF but may not be as valuable to borrowers in terms of eventual PSLF forgiveness benefits.
- The effects of loan consolidation on a borrower's progress toward receiving PSLF benefits. Of particular importance, PSLF qualifying payments made prior to consolidation do not count toward forgiveness of the resulting Direct Consolidation Loan.
- The complexities and challenges that administering the program may present for the Department of Education, loan servicers, and borrowers. These include issues of communication among the parties regarding program requirements and processes, lack of coordination among loan servicers, loans servicers making errors or not completing tasks associated with the program in a timely manner, and the lack of automation of some administrative functions.

Issues pertaining to PSLF program interactions with other programs and benefits relate to whether borrowers understand the interactions well enough to make rational choices and maximize available benefits and, from the federal government's perspective, questions have arisen regarding whether the desired targeting of benefits is being achieved and about the potential costs associated with such interactions. Some of these issues include:

- There is no limit to the amount of loan forgiveness benefits an individual may realize under the PSLF program. While it is possible that many borrowers may receive limited benefits, some Direct Loan borrowers may realize large forgiveness benefits under the program. This outcome may be more likely to occur for borrowers of Direct PLUS Loans for graduate and professional students, which have no aggregate borrowing limits, and which were newly authorized to be made just prior to the enactment of PSLF. Also, the variety of IDR plans has expanded greatly since the PSLF program's inception, with several of the new IDR plans providing for lower monthly payments than under the Income-Based Repayment plan the primary IDR plan available when the PSLF program was enacted. This expansion may allow borrowers to lower monthly payments and potentially realize larger forgiveness benefits under the program. The current borrowing limits and variety of IDR plans, coupled with PSLF program benefits, have raised questions about whether certain types of students are not incentivized to limit borrowing and whether they may be less sensitive to the price of postsecondary education.
- Borrowers may receive benefits under a number of federal student loan repayment programs. Borrowers may also be able to avail themselves of certain income tax provisions to maximize PSLF program benefits. For borrowers, understanding whether the same service that qualifies for PSLF may also qualify for other loan repayment benefits is important, as is their understanding of how other benefits and tax provisions may interact with PSLF. From the perspective of the federal government, a key consideration may relate to what constitutes a "double benefit" for service performed by borrowers and the extent to which overlapping benefits might be provided.

Broad program-related issues relate to (1) how the program fits into the overall suite of federal student aid benefits and (2) the difficulty of estimating the potential participation in and costs of the program.

1) The enactment of the PSLF program is reflective of a broadening of the federal approach to student aid, providing more widely available assistance to individuals after a postsecondary education's costs have been incurred. This approach may place greater emphasis on providing aid on the basis of economic circumstances after enrollment, rather than at

the time of enrollment. It also makes some aid available on a targeted basis providing relief to individuals who pursue certain types of service or occupations, rather than providing aid more broadly to individuals who enroll in postsecondary education.

2) The granting of loan forgiveness benefits results in costs to the federal government, and there has been some speculation that the cost of PSLF could be much higher than anticipated. Limited information is available on the actual and future costs to the government of the PSLF program. It has just recently become possible to claim program benefits; thus, little is known about what the costs associated with the program will be based on the experiences of actual cohorts of borrowers. In addition, estimating potential costs may prove difficult as borrowers are not required to submit information on their intent to participate in the program until they seek forgiveness benefits after 10 years of service and qualifying payments.

INTRODUCTION

Student loan forgiveness and loan repayment programs provide borrowers a means of having all or part of their student loan debt forgiven or repaid upon satisfying certain criteria, such as having worked or served in particular fields or professions for a specified period of time.[1] Some of these programs are intended to support goals such as providing a financial incentive to encourage individuals to enter into and/or remain in a particular profession or public service. One such federal program that has received considerable attention in recent years is the Public Service Loan Forgiveness (PSLF) program.

Under the PSLF program, borrowers of the U.S. Department of Education's (ED's) Direct Loans[2] who are employed fulltime in certain public service jobs for 10 years while making 120 separate qualifying

---

[1] For information on the numerous federal student loan forgiveness and loan repayment programs, see CRS Report R43571, *Federal Student Loan Forgiveness and Loan Repayment Programs*, coordinated by Alexandra Hegji. Some loan forgiveness programs are made available to borrowers following prolonged periods during which their student loan debt is high relative to their income.

[2] For additional information on Direct Loans, see CRS Report R40122, *Federal Student Loans Made Under the Federal Family Education Loan Program and the William D. Ford Federal Direct Loan Program: Terms and Conditions for Borrowers*, by David P. Smole.

monthly payments on their Direct Loans may be eligible to have any remaining balance of principal and interest forgiven. Borrowers first became eligible to apply for PSLF forgiveness benefits on October 1, 2017, based on service completed and payments made prior to that date.

With the opportunity to apply for program benefits being made available recently, many issues that span multiple aspects of the program have been raised and have garnered congressional interest. In general, identified issues fit into the following groupings:

1) Program implementation issues, which pertain to the operationalization of statutory provisions, difficulties experienced by borrowers in participating in the program, and difficulties experienced by entities administering the program. Specific issues include operationally defining a "public service job," certifying qualified public service employment, determining qualifying payments, and administering a program with relatively complex eligibility criteria.

2) Interaction of the PSLF program with other programs and benefits, which from a borrower's perspective relates to understanding the interactions to make rational choices and maximize available benefits. This involves borrowers understanding the various loan repayment plans available, interaction between PSLF and other service benefits (e.g., loan repayment programs), deciding the amount of student loans to borrow, and the tax treatment of program benefits. From the federal government's perspective, interaction of program benefits relates to whether desired targeting of benefits is being achieved and the potential costs associated with such interactions. This issue also relates to subsequent changes to benefits (e.g., expansion of available loan repayment plans), which may substantially affect the targeting of PSLF and resulting program costs.

3) Broad program-related issues, which relate to how the program complements or fits into the overall suite of federal student aid benefits and how costly the program might ultimately be.

This chapter begins with a brief legislative and regulatory history of the PSLF program. This is followed by a brief description of how the program works. Finally, the report describes several selected program issues that have arisen in recent years. These are issues that have received recent congressional and stakeholder attention and issues identified in reviews of the program, as well as some that have been raised by researchers, analysts, and other entities outside of the government.[3] The issues discussed in this chapter are not intended to be an exhaustive list.

LEGISLATIVE HISTORY

The PSLF program was first authorized in 2007 under the College Cost Reduction and Access Act of 2007 (CCRAA; P.L. 110-84). However, at least as early as 2003, other bills, including H.R. 1306,[4] proposed authorization of a program providing loan forgiveness benefits to individuals making payments under specified repayment plans while also being employed in public service. H.R. 1306 presented findings suggesting that student loan debt was placing constraints on the career options of many college graduates, resulting in borrowers choosing higher paying jobs over public service, and that many public service professions such as teaching and nursing were facing staffing shortages.[5]

Over the years, several iterations of this construct of providing loan forgiveness benefits to individuals who were employed in public service and who made monthly payments on their loans over a specified period of time were introduced in Congress. Several of these sought to encourage individuals to enter into public service occupations and were often introduced under the presumption that borrowers may choose higher

---

[3] The policy issues discussed in this report are generally based on those identified by external researchers, think tanks, practitioner groups, media accounts of the program, and reports by the Government Accountability Office and the Consumer Financial Protection Bureau. In some instances, common and underlying themes are synthesized by CRS. No attempt is made to evaluate the policy issues discussed herein.

[4] 108th Congress, College Opportunity for a Better America Act of 2003.

[5] Ibid.

paying jobs in the private sector over public service and that this issue was at least somewhat exacerbated by student loan debt burdens. However, the means for meeting this goal differed among the proposals. For instance, some proposals would have based borrowers eligibility for forgiveness largely on the type of their employer (e.g., federal, state, or local government),[6] while others seemed to have proposed making benefits available to borrowers based largely on a borrower's job function while employed (e.g., jobs in public safety, education).[7] In addition, some proposals would have provided for the forgiveness of a borrower's entire outstanding loan balance after a specified number of years of public service employment and monthly payments,[8] while others would have provided borrowers the opportunity to have a percentage of their loans forgiven based on the number of years employed in public service (e.g., 10% of a borrower's loan balance could be forgiven for each year of employment in public service, up to 100% forgiveness).[9] Finally, some proposals would have made benefits available to borrowers whose annual income or earnings fell below a threshold amount.[10]

Congress authorized the PSLF program in 2007 to encourage individuals to enter into and remain employed in public service and to alleviate the potential financial burdens associated with federal student loans of borrowers in public service who were presumed to generally earn less than their counterparts in other types of occupations.[11] In doing so, it stated it was concerned with the number of individuals who chose not to enter into lower paying jobs, such as public service, due to increasing student loan debt.[12] Under the program, Direct Loan borrowers employed fulltime in certain public service jobs for 10 years while making 120 qualifying payments are given the opportunity to have any balance of

---

[6] See, for example, H.R. 4102 (108th Congress), Access and Equity in Higher Education Act.

[7] See, for example, S. 1614 (109th Congress), Higher Education Amendments of 2005.

[8] See, for example, H.R. 1859 (109th Congress), Education for Public Service Act of 2005.

[9] See, for example, S. 1762 (110th Congress), Higher Education Access Act of 2007.

[10] Ibid.

[11] See, for example, U.S. Congress, House Committee on Education and Labor, *College Cost Reduction Act of 2007*, report to accompany H.R. 2669, 110th Cong., 1st sess., June 25, 2007, H.Rept. 110-210, pp. 48-49.

[12] Ibid.

principal and interest that remains after those 10 years forgiven. The CCRAA specified that monthly payments made under, among others, the Income Contingent Repayment (ICR) plan[13] or the newly created Income Based Repayment (IBR) plan (discussed below) would qualify for purposes of PSLF and that only Direct Loan borrowers would be eligible for PSLF forgiveness benefits.[14]

In addition to enacting the PSLF program, the CCRAA made another change to the HEA that would have a bearing on the design and operation of the PSLF program; specifically, it authorized the Income Based Repayment plan for pre July 1, 2014, borrowers.[15] Prior to the enactment of the CCRAA, the ICR plan was the only income driven repayment (IDR) plan available to borrowers. Under ICR, a Direct Loan borrower's monthly payments are set at an amount equal to the lesser of 20% of their annual discretionary income divided by 12, or what they would pay under a repayment plan with a fixed monthly payment over a 12year period multiplied by an income percentage factor that corresponds to a borrower's adjusted gross income (AGI). Borrowers make payments on their loans for 25 years, and any loan balance remaining after that period is forgiven. The CCRAA made no changes to the ICR plan but did authorize the IBR plan for pre July 1, 2014, borrowers, under which eligible borrowers with

---

[13] As originally introduced, the CCRAA would have amended the Income Contingent Repayment plan by providing for shortened repayment terms for public sector employees and loan forgiveness of remaining outstanding balances at the end of the repayment term.

[14] Leading up to the enactment of the CCRAA, some bills that proposed a program offering loan forgiveness benefits in exchange for public service would have made benefits available to Federal Family Education Loan (FFEL) program borrowers. See, for example, H.R. 4102 (108th Congress), Access and Equity in Higher Education Act. However, it appears that PSLF benefits were only made available to Direct Loan borrowers, at least in part to act as an incentive for borrowers to switch from the FFEL program to the Direct Loan program; such a switch was predicted to result in cost savings to the federal government. See U.S. Congress, House Committee on Education and Labor, *College Cost Reduction Act of 2007*, 110th Cong., 1st sess., June 25, 2007, H.Rept. 110-210, p. 72.

[15] This Income-Based Repayment plan was made available to borrowers who had outstanding Direct Loan program or FFEL program loans prior to July 1, 2014. The HEA was later amended in 2010 by the SAFRA Act (Title II of P.L. 111-152) to offer an IBR plan to new borrowers on or after July 1, 2014, with partial financial hardships the opportunity to make monthly payments on their loans capped at 10% of their annual discretionary income divided by 12, and to receive loan forgiveness of any remaining balance at the end of 20 years of repayment. Hereinafter, these two forms of Income-Based Repayment plans are referred to as "the IBR plans" unless otherwise noted.

partial financial hardships[16] may have their monthly payments capped at 15% of their annual discretionary income divided by 12. Borrowers make payments for a maximum of 25 years, and any loan balance remaining at the end of that period is forgiven. The CCRAA specified that payments made under both the ICR and IBR plans would qualify for purposes of PSLF. In coupling PSLF with the newly created IBR plan, Congress expressed its intent to offer a suite of benefits to borrowers who entered public service that would not only offer loan forgiveness benefits after 10 years of such service, but also provide borrowers with the opportunity to make reduced monthly loan payments during that 10 years.[17]

Proponents of the PSLF provisions argued that the program would incentivize individuals to enter into and remain in those professions with shortages and that paid relatively less than other professions. In addition, proponents argued that PSLF benefits would help address the effects on borrowers of increasing tuition at institutions of higher education (IHEs) by alleviating the higher debt burden they assumed.[18] On the other hand, opponents argued that the program's benefits were not well targeted. For instance, some argued that the program would not make sufficient distinctions among types of borrowers. It was contended that higher-income students would be more likely to receive larger benefits than low-income students because higher-income individuals tend to attend higher priced IHEs and would likely borrow larger amounts of federal student loans that could then be forgiven under the program.[19] It was also argued that, because the program placed no cap on potential program benefits, it might create an incentive for individuals to borrow the maximum amount

---

[16] For purposes of the IBR plans, a borrower has a partial financial hardship when the annual amount a borrower would be required to repay on his or her eligible FFEL and Direct Loans under a Standard repayment plan with a 10-year amortization exceeds 15% or 10% of the borrower's discretionary income, respectively.

[17] See Senator Edward Kennedy, College Cost Reduction Act of 2007, Senate consideration of H.R. 2669, *Congressional Record*, daily edition, vol. 153, No. 116 (July 19, 2007), pp. S9534-S9535.

[18] Ibid., pp. S19673-S19674.

[19] Senator Jeff Sessions, College Cost Reduction Act of 2007, Senate consideration of H.R. 2669, *Congressional Record*, daily edition, vol. 153, part 14 (July 19, 2007), pp. S19696-S19697.

of federal student loans possible with the expectation of receiving program benefits.[20]

The statutory provisions of the PSLF program have remained largely unchanged since its enactment.[21] However, changes were made to the federal student loans programs both immediately prior to and several years following the enactment of PSLF that may have effects on the program. The Deficit Reduction Act of 2005 (P.L. 109-171) authorized Direct PLUS Loans to be made to graduate and professional students, with no specified aggregate borrowing limits, unlike Direct Subsidized and Unsubsidized Loans.[22] In relation to the PSLF program, there is no limit to the amount of loan forgiveness benefits that a borrower may realize under the program. Thus, it is possible that borrowers with large amounts of debt, and in particular Direct PLUS Loans for graduate and professional borrowers for whom there are no aggregate borrowing limits, may realize significant forgiveness benefits under PSLF. Because PLUS Loan eligibility for graduate and professional students was relatively new at the time PSLF was enacted, it is possible that adequate data were unavailable to fully assess the extent to which PLUS Loan availability to graduate and professional students would affect the program. In addition, the SAFRA Act (P.L. 111-152, Title II) terminated the authority to make new loans under the Federal Family Education Loan (FFEL) program[23] after June 30, 2010. Thus, as of July 1, 2010, the Direct Loan program is the primary federal student loan program. This shift to an almost all Direct Loan lending model likely had the effect of ensuring that a larger portion of federal student loan borrowers had PSLF eligible loans than might have originally been contemplated by Congress, and could increase the number of borrowers potentially eligible for PSLF benefits.

[20] Ibid.

[21] The Higher Education Opportunity Act (P.L. 110-315) made relatively minor amendments to the definition of "public service job" for purposes of the program and specifically excluded time employed as a Member of the U.S. Congress from the public service job definition.

[22] For additional information on loans made available under the Direct Loan program, see CRS Report R40122, *Federal Student Loans Made Under the Federal Family Education Loan Program and the William D. Ford Federal Direct Loan Program: Terms and Conditions for Borrowers*, by David P. Smole.

[23] Prior to the establishment of the Direct Loan program in 1992, the FFEL program was the primary federal student loan program.

Since the CCRAA's enactment, several other IDR plans have been made available. These include the Income Based Repayment plan for post July 1, 2014, borrowers, the Pay As You Earn (PAYE) repayment plan, and the Revised Pay As You Earn (REPAYE) repayment plan. Each of these programs is more beneficial to borrowers than the ICR and the IBR for pre July 1, 2014, borrowers plans in that the monthly payments are generally limited to 10% of annual discretionary income divided by 12. Also, with the introduction of each new repayment plan, larger numbers of borrowers have become eligible to utilize IDR plans. Payments made under each of these plans qualify under the PSLF program. With the expansion of the availability of more generous IDR plans, it is possible for more individuals to participate in and realize even larger forgiveness benefits under the program than what Congress might have originally contemplated. Thus, more individuals may qualify for IDR plans, and more may reduce their monthly payments below what the payments would be under ICR or IBR for pre-July 1, 2014, plans. This could result in PSLF eligible borrowers repaying a lesser total amount of their loans, and receiving larger forgiveness benefits after completing PSLF program requirements.

THE PUBLIC SERVICE LOAN FORGIVENESS PROGRAM

Section 455(m) of the Higher Education Act of 1965 (HEA; P.L. 89-329), as amended, authorizes the PSLF program. As noted previously, its purpose is to encourage individuals to enter into and remain employed in public service.[24] The program offers Direct Loan borrowers who are employed fulltime[25] in certain public service jobs for 10 years during

---

[24] U.S. Congress, House Committee on Education and Labor, *College Cost Reduction Act of 2007*, report to accompany H.R. 2669, 110th Cong., 1st sess., June 25, 2007, H.Rept. 110-210, pp. 48-49.

[25] Full-time is defined as working for one or more qualifying employers for the greater of (1) an annual average of 30 hours per week or, for a contractual or employment period of at least 8 months, an average of 30 hours per week, or (2) the number of hours the employer considers full-time. 34 C.F.R. §685.219(b).

repayment of their loans the opportunity to have any balance of principal and interest that remains after those 10 years forgiven.[26] To qualify for loan forgiveness, on or after October 1, 2007, borrowers must be employed fulltime in a public service job, which includes jobs in government, at organizations described in Section 501(c)(3) of the Internal Revenue Code (IRC) and exempt from taxation under IRC Section 501(a), and at private nonprofit organizations that provide at least one of several enumerated public services (e.g., emergency management, public safety, public interest law services).[27]

Concurrent with being employed in public service, borrowers must make 120 separate qualifying monthly payments (10 years' worth) on their Direct Loans according to qualifying loan repayment plans.[28] Qualifying loan repayment plans include any of the income driven repayment plans (IDR);[29] a standard repayment plan with a 10-year repayment period; and a standard, graduated, or extended repayment plan to the extent that monthly payments are equal to or greater than the monthly amount due as calculated according to a standard plan with a 10year repayment period. In effect, this means that payments made under the IDR plans and a standard plan with a 10year repayment period frequently are the payments that qualify for PSLF purposes. Additionally, although monthly payments made under a standard plan with a 10year repayment period, qualify for PSLF, should a borrower make payments under a such a plan for the entirety of his or her employment in public service, he or she will not realize any PSLF forgiveness benefits, because there will be no remaining loan balance to be forgiven after having made 120 (10 years' worth) of qualifying PSLF

---

[26] PLUS Loans made to parents on behalf of a dependent student and Direct Consolidation Loans that repaid a PLUS Loan made to parents may only be forgiven for service completed by the parent borrower. Office of Federal Student Aid, "Public Service Loan Forgiveness Questions and Answers," https://studentaid.ed.gov/sa/repay-loans/forgivenesscancellation/ public-service/questions, accessed December 29, 2017.

[27] In addition, employment as a full-time faculty member at a Tribal College or University as defined under Section 316(b) of the HEA and other faculty teaching in high-need subject areas, as determined by the Secretary of Education, is qualifying employment under the program.

[28] The 10 years of employment in public service and concurrent loan payments need not be consecutive.

[29] These include the income-contingent repayment (ICR) plan; the IBR plans; the Pay As You Earn (PAYE) plan; and the Revised Pay As You Earn (REPAYE) plan.

payments. Thus, individuals are most likely to qualify for PSLF program benefits while making payments under an IDR plan.

In addition, all 120 monthly payments must be qualifying monthly payments. That is, they must be required monthly payments (e.g., they cannot be payments made during a deferment or forbearance period) that are made on-time (within 15 days of the scheduled due date) and for the full scheduled monthly payment amount.[30] Payments made while a loan is in default are not qualifying payments.

Borrowers must be employed in public service at the time they apply for and receive forgiveness, and they may not be in default on loans for which forgiveness is sought.[31] Loan amounts forgiven under the program are not subject to federal income tax.[32]

Administering PSLF

ED contracts with multiple federal student loan servicers to perform the majority of administrative tasks associated with federal student loans once they have been disbursed to borrowers.[33] All federal student loan servicers are responsible for selected activities relating to PSLF, such as communicating with borrowers about the general availability of the program and enrolling borrowers in selected repayment plans that may enable them to qualify for PSLF. ED has contracted with a single loan servicer–FedLoan Servicing–to perform the majority of administrative tasks specific to PSLF.

To receive forgiveness benefits under the program, borrowers must apply for forgiveness from ED via FedLoan Servicing using an ED-developed form.[34] In general, FedLoan Servicing reviews the application

---

[30] 34 C.F.R. §685.219(c)(iii).
[31] HEA §455(m)(1).
[32] IRC, Section 108(f).
[33] For additional information on loan servicing, see CRS Report R44845, *Administration of the William D. Ford Federal Direct Loan Program*, by Alexandra Hegji.
[34] 34 C.F.R. §685.219(e).

and determines whether the borrower has met all PSLF requirements; if so, FedLoan Servicing forwards the application to ED for final review. If the application is approved by ED, ED directs FedLoan Servicing to forgive the remaining balance of the borrower's eligible loans.[35] If either FedLoan Servicing or ED denies an application, a borrower may dispute the determination[36] and/or subsequently reapply for forgiveness benefits. Borrowers were first eligible to apply for forgiveness benefits under the program on October 1, 2017.

To have eligibility status reviewed and to track progress toward forgiveness benefits, borrowers may periodically submit an Employment Certification Form (ECF)[37] to their loan servicer, which is then forwarded to FedLoan Servicing. Upon receipt of an initial ECF form, FedLoan Servicing determines whether the borrower has qualifying Direct Loans and evaluates the ECF to determine whether the borrower's employment qualifies. If the borrower has Direct Loans and PSLF employment that qualify, his or her ED held loans (including those that are not Direct Loans) are transferred to FedLoan Servicing for all servicing activities, including those not associated with the PSLF program. After transfer, FedLoan Servicing determines how many qualifying payments the borrower has made while employed in public service. Borrowers have several options to dispute payment counts and other aspects of eligibility determination.[38] Borrowers are encouraged, but not required, to submit the ECF periodically.[39]

---

[35] U.S. Government Accountability Office, *Public Service Loan Forgiveness: Education Needs to Provide Better Information for Loan Servicer and Borrowers*, GAO-18-547, September 2018, pp. 6-7.

[36] Ibid., p. 23.

[37] U.S. Department of Education, Public Service Loan Forgiveness (PSLF): Employment Certification Form, OMB No. 1845-0110, Exp. Date May 31, 2020.

[38] U.S. Government Accountability Office, *Public Service Loan Forgiveness: Education Needs to Provide Better Information for Loan Servicer and Borrowers*, GAO-18-547, September 2018, p. 23.

[39] Office of Federal Student Aid, "Public Service Loan Forgiveness" https://studentaid.ed.gov/sa/repayloans/forgiveness-cancellation/public-service#apply, accessed May 29, 2018.

SELECTED ISSUES RELATED TO THE PSLF PROGRAM

Although borrowers have been eligible to apply for PSLF forgiveness benefits only since October 1, 2017, many issues that span several aspects of the program have arisen that have garnered congressional interest. In general, as has been noted, issues fall into a few categories (1) program implementation, (2) interaction of the program with other federal programs and benefits, and (3) facets of program design. Each will be discussed in the sections that follow.

Implementation Issues

Implementation issues relate to how the PSLF program's statutory requirements have been operationalized, difficulties experienced by borrowers in participating in the program, and program administration. They include how employment in a "public service job" has been operationally defined, how qualifying payments are determined, the effects of loan consolidation on a borrower's progress towards receiving PSLF benefits, and the administrative challenges and complexities faced by ED, borrowers, and student loan servicers.

Operationally Defining Employment in Public Service

A foundational concept in the PSLF program is defining what comprises employment in public service. Statutory provisions provide broad guidance but do not precisely define what constitutes qualifying employment, and regulatory and sub-regulatory administrative decisions have resulted in operationally defining it based primarily on employer characteristics rather than borrower job functions. This has led to some perceived inequities among borrowers and difficulties in identifying eligible employers.

The HEA requires, among other criteria, that an individual be employed in a "public service job" for 10 years to be eligible for PSLF benefits. It specifies that a public service job includes full time jobs in a variety of fields including, but not limited to, government,[40] military service, law enforcement, public education, public health, and public interest law services. It adds that jobs in an organization "described in section 501(c)(3) of the Internal Revenue Code of 1986 and exempt from taxation under section 501(a) of such Code"[41] (hereinafter a "501(c)(3) organization") are also considered public service jobs.

In implementing the statutory provisions, ED added specificity to the employment requirements in regulations by focusing largely on the type of employer at which an individual is employed, rather than on the type of services rendered by the employee. Specifically, the program's regulations state that an eligible individual must be an employee of a "public service organization," which includes federal, state, local, or tribal governments[42]; most 501(c)(3) organizations; and private organizations that provide at least one of many specified types of public service (e.g., public interest law services or public health) and that are "not businesses organized for profit."[43] Thus, operationally, employment in public service is identified largely by employer type rather than the nature of the work performed by an individual.

Concerning PSLF, ED regulations define "employed" as being hired and paid by a public service organization.[44] Individuals who are hired and paid by an employer that is not a qualifying public service organization but

---

[40] Time employed as a Member of the U.S. Congress is excluded.

[41] HEA §455(m)(3)(B)(i).

[42] Employment with a foreign government or international, intergovernmental organization (e.g., the United Nations) does not qualify. Employment for a U.S. delegation to an international intergovernmental organization does qualify. U.S. Department of Education, "Public Service Loan Forgiveness Questions and Answers," https://studentaid.ed.gov/sa/repay-loans/forgiveness-cancellation/public-service/questions#qualifying-employment, accessed May 29, 2018.

[43] [43] 34 C.F.R. §685.219(b). A public service organization also includes public child or family services agencies and Tribal colleges or universities. Service in the AmeriCorps and Peace Corps is considered qualifying "employment" for PSLF. Employment with a foreign nonprofit organization that operates in the United States may qualify for PSLF. U.S. Department of Education, "Public Service Loan Forgiveness Questions and Answers," https://studentaid.ed.gov/sa/repay-loans/forgiveness-cancellation/public-service/questions#qualifying-employment, accessed May 29, 2018.

[44] 34 C.F.R. §685.219(b).

s in the private sector.[52] Moreover, even for those
oyed in higher-paying, more desirable positions, they may
large amounts relative to their income to pursue the
ary to enter their field. Thus, it is argued, in such instances
LF forgiveness benefits is proper and serves as a "public
."[53]

nore narrowly define the types of employment that could
F might be considered; however, there may be tradeoffs
g specific types of service and providing a more open-
vice employment category. There is precedent within other
rgiveness and loan repayment programs for providing
lividuals employed in specific occupations that have
tment and retention issues,[54] which result in the provision
eted benefit. Such an approach, however, may potentially
rogram eligibility other populations of borrowers perceived
occupations that also further the public interest.

e construct of determining PSLF eligibility based on
acteristics rather than services rendered may be seen as
arate treatment of borrowers perceived as being similarly
have questioned ED's interpretation of qualifying public
For example, consider a fulltime Department of Defense
yee performing computer programming tasks. Such an
nployment would qualify for PSLF because he or she is

that is under contract with and renders services for a public service
organization are ineligible for PSLF benefits.[45]

501(c)(3) Organizations

For PSLF purposes, 501(c)(3) organizations are nonprofit
organizations that qualify for tax exempt status under Section 501(c)(3) of
the IRC and that are not engaged in religious activities, "unless the
qualifying activities are unrelated to religious instruction, worship services,
or any form of proselytizing."[46] Under IRC Section 501(c)(3), a nonprofit
organization that qualifies for tax-exempt status is an entity "organized and
operated exclusively for religious, charitable, scientific, testing for public
safety, literary, or educational purposes, or to foster national or
international amateur sports competition (but only if no part of its activities
involve the provision of athletic facilities or equipment), or for the
prevention of cruelty to children or animals." In addition, no part of the net
earnings of any such entities may benefit a private shareholder or an
individual, and such entities are substantially limited in their ability to
lobby and are prohibited from engaging in political campaign activity.[47]

Many types of entities may be 501(c)(3) organizations. They can
include the following:

- hospitals;
- private nonprofit IHEs and elementary and secondary schools;
- public charities such as the American Red Cross;
- private foundations such as the Bill & Melinda Gates Foundation;
- other organizations organized for one of the purposes specified in
  IRC Section 501(c)(3), such as the American Society for the

---

, Letter from Tim Delaney, President & CEO, National Counsel of Nonprofit
to Nikki Harris, U.S. Department of Education, August 15, 2008, ED-2008-
)63, https://www.regulations.gov/document?D=ED-2008-OPE-0009-0063.
n, "Why teachers deserve a break on their student debt," *Politico*, October 3,

he John R. Justice Loan Repayment for Prosecutors and Public Defenders
ides loan repayment benefits to individuals employed as full-time prosecutors
efenders (42 U.S.C. §3797cc-21), and the National Health Service Corps
lents to Service Loan Repayment program provides loan repayment benefits to
mployed as primary care physicians at an NHSC-approved site in a federally
ealth Professional Shortage Area (42 U.S.C. §§254d-254f, 254l-1, 254m, 254n,

le, 73 *Federal Register* 63242. See also, Letter from Thomas M. Susman,
vernmental Affairs Office, American Bar Association, to Nikki Harris, U.S.
f Education, August 15, 2015, ED-2008- OPE-0009-0174.

---

[45] U.S. Department of Education, "Federal Perkins Loan Program, Federal Family Education
Loan Program, and William D. Ford Federal Direct Loan Program," 73 *Federal Register*
37705, July 1, 2008.
[46] 34 C.F.R. §685.219(b).
[47] For additional information on tax-exempt organizations, including 501(c)(3) organizations, see
CRS Report 96-264, *Frequently Asked Questions About Tax-Exempt Organizations*, by
Erika K. Lunder.

Prevention of Cruelty to Animals, the American Chemical Society, and the National Collegiate Athletic Association; and

- churches and religious organizations.[48]

In total, there are approximately 1,237,000[49] organizations serving a variety of purposes that are tax-exempt under IRC Section 501(c)(3).

Nonprofit, non-501(c)(3) Organizations

Private organizations that are not tax-exempt organizations under IRC Section 501(c)(3), including private organizations that are tax exempt under other sections of IRC Section 501(c), may nonetheless be considered qualifying employers for the PSLF program. Pursuant to regulations, to qualify, such organizations must not be (1) organized for profit; (2) a labor union; (3) a partisan political organization; or (4) an organization engaged in religious activities, unless the qualifying work engaged in by an individual is unrelated to religious instruction, worship services, or any form of proselytizing. In addition, such organizations must provide at least one of several enumerated public services (e.g., public interest law or public health). Although, the regulations do not specify the extent to which such public services must be offered at these organizations, the ECF and PSLF Application specify that a nonprofit organization that is not a 501(c)(3) organization must provide one of the several enumerated public services as its "primary purpose."

Discussion of Issues

A number of issues regarding the way in which qualifying employment is determined have surfaced. Criticisms have been raised that the PSLF

---

[48] Although churches and religious organizations may be 501(c)(3) organizations, PSLF regulations specify that organizations engaged in religious activities are not PSLF qualifying public service organizations, unless the work engaged in by an individual is unrelated to religious instruction, worship services, or any form of proselytizing. The ECF and Public Service Loan Forgiveness Application Form specify that for purposes of determining whether an individual is employed full-time at such an organization, ED will exclude time spent participating in religious instruction, worship services, or any form of proselytizing.

[49] Internal Revenue Service, *IRS Data Book: FY2016*, Table 25, "Tax-Exempt Organizations, Nonexempt Charitable Trusts, and Nonexempt Split-Interest Trusts, Fiscal Year 2016."

---

program is not well targeted be program covers a broad array of levels. Other concerns include wh service job" has created inequities employer type is a sufficient prox public service. In addition, some are fluid in nature and may make to realize intended benefits. To ad eligibility on job functions rather t However, if employer type were service status, it would seemingly that determine eligibility, which administer and may provide less qualifications for the program.

First, in enacting the PSLF pr forgiveness benefits to encourage employed in public service, as it individuals who chose not to enter i service, due to increasing student public service employment, distinc employed in government and nonpro private sector. As noted above, critic program is not well targeted and tha types are inappropriate, because quali encompasses a broad array of occu levels.[51] Some argue, however, that may be relevant, as public service p

similar position individuals empl have borrowed education necess the receipt of P service premium

Policies to qualify for PSL between targeti ended public se federal loan fc benefits to in perceived recru of a rather targ exclude from p as employed in

Second, th employer char leading to disp situated. Some service jobs.[55] (DOD) emplo individual's e

---

[50] See, for example, U.S. Congress, House Com *Reduction Act of 2007*, report to accompany 2007, H.Rept. 110-210, pp. 48-49.

[51] See, for example, Beth Akers, "It's time to axe *The Hill*, June 22, 2017, http://thehill.com/blc axe-student-loan-forgiveness-program-for-pub Service Loan Forgiveness bonanza," *Econ* (September 22, 2017), pp. 3, 6.

---

[52] See, for example Associations OPE-0009-0

[53] Mark Zuckerma 2017.

[54] For instance, program pro or public d (NHSC) Stu individuals designated l 254o).

[55] See, for exam Director, G Department

hired and paid by a qualifying public service organization. However, employment as a fulltime contractor who performs the same computer programming tasks for DOD may not qualify for PSLF if the third-party entity that hires and pays the contracted employee is not a qualifying public service organization (e.g., it is a for profit company). Yet, if the third party entity that hires and pays the same contracted employee is a qualifying public service organization (e.g., a 501(c)(3) organization), then the employment could qualify for PSLF.

In addition, some state laws prevent some types of workers from being directly employed by certain types of organizations that might otherwise be PSLF qualifying employers. For instance, in many states physicians may be employed directly by a nonprofit hospital and, thus, may qualify for PSLF based on their employment. However, some states bar physicians from being directly employed by qualifying nonprofit hospitals.[56] Physicians in such states may form physician corporations that then provide the same types of services as their counterparts in other states without such restrictions within hospital settings. They essentially operate as contract employees of the hospital. Where such physician corporations are organized as for-profit organizations that provide services within a PSLF qualifying nonprofit hospital, a physician employed by such a corporation would not qualify for PSLF based on his or her employment.

In both of the above examples, the individual might be performing similar job functions (e.g., computer programmer, physician) in support of the same type of endeavor. Nonetheless, in accordance with PSLF program rules, the determination of whether an individual's work constitutes public service is dependent on the status of the individual's employer. Employment with governments and most nonprofit organizations has been determined to be public service employment, whereas employment with for profit organizations and certain nonprofit organizations has been determined not to be public service employment.

---

[56] California Medical Association, "Texas Medical Association joins CMA to urge U.S. education secretary to fix public service loan forgiveness program," press release, May 26, 2016, https://www.cmanet.org/news/detail/?article=texas-medical-association-joins-cma-to-urge-us.

For purposes of awarding PSLF benefits, one may question whether a distinction should be made between two individuals working side by side and performing the same functions. It might be argued that the tasks performed by such individuals advance similar purposes. However, it may also be argued that even if the tasks performed are similar, there are important differences in the nature of these individuals' employment such that only employment by organizations satisfying certain criteria should be considered public service jobs. There may also be important differences in employee salary structures that might be considered. Such differences might include, for example, the extent to which an employer's mission is to advance certain goals (e.g., a particular cause or to earn profits) other than "public service." Although an employee's particular job or tasks may advance public service, the employer's overall mission may not, in its entirety, do so. Concerns could arise that such an employer's mission could overtake any public interest aspect of its operations. Another difference that might be relevant is that if a contract employee's work is split across several projects supporting different contracts, some portion of the work may support public service while others may not. Under a scenario in which a contract employee is devoting time both to projects that do and do not support public service, it may be hard to determine whether they qualify for PSLF benefits and how such an individual would document his or her work time.

Concerning 501(c)(3) organizations, there has been debate about whether a blanket qualification for all such organizations for PSLF purposes is appropriate. As described above, under the IRC a 501(c)(3) organization is one that is exclusively organized and operated for a variety of purposes including charitable and educational activities and has no part of its net earnings benefitting a private shareholder or an individual. Concerns have been raised that some 501(c)(3) organizations may not meet this criteria and that they should not be given tax-exempt status.[57] For instance, there have been questions about whether some tax exempt 501(c)(3) hospitals are truly organized and operated for a charitable

---

[57] A full discussion of the extent to which some 501(c)(3) organizations are meeting these criteria is beyond the scope of this report.

purpose, as they may be spending a small fraction of funds on charity and community benefit (one manner of determining the extent to which a hospital is operating for a charitable purpose).[58] In other instances, questions have been raised about whether some private nonprofit IHEs are organized and operated exclusively for educational purposes, because they may also engage in non educational, profit seeking activities such as patent, trademark, and copyright licensing and venture capital businesses.[59]

Operationally, under the PSLF program, an organization's 501(c)(3) status is used as a proxy for identifying employers that provide public service. However, because questions have been raised about whether some 501(c)(3) organizations are organized and operating exclusively for one of the enumerated purposes in the IRC, related concerns may arise regarding whether such organizations consistently provide a public service and, thus, should be considered qualifying employers under the PSLF program. Providing a blanket qualification for all 501(c)(3) organizations, rather than requiring a determination of each organization's characteristics, may make administering the PSLF program more efficient and clear but 501(c)(3) status may be an imperfect proxy for public service.

There may also be a need for clarification as to which nonprofit organizations that are not 501(c)(3) organizations might qualify for PSLF purposes. An organization that is not a 501(c)(3) organization may be considered a public service organization under PSLF if it, among other criteria, provides one of several enumerated public services as its primary purpose. While some limiting factors are placed on this type of organization, the definition is broad enough to potentially encompass a variety of employers. Also, there is no definition of "primary purpose." Whether a non501(c)(3) employer is a qualifying PSLF employer appears largely to be a case by-case determination. The current lack of available information regarding whether certain organizations provide public service as their primary purpose may also provide uncertainty for borrowers

---

[58] See, for example, Richard Cohen, "Debatable: How Nonprofit Are Nonprofit Hospitals?," *Nonprofit Quarterly*, December 18, 2013.

[59] Leslie A. Pappas, "Challenge to Princeton's Tax Exempt Status Will Proceed, New Jersey Tax Judge Rules," *Tax Management: Weekly State Tax Report*, vol. 2016, no. 8 (February 19, 2016).

employed at such organizations. This potentially undermines a principal purpose of the PSLF program, which is to encourage employment in public service. Some organizations may find the prospect of being designated as a PSLF eligible employer a useful recruitment tool, but without guarantee of being considered a qualifying PSLF employer, such organizations may experience difficulty in yielding intended benefits of recruiting and retaining qualified employees who wish to work in public service.[60]

To address some of the perceived inequities created by the distinction between borrowers based on employer type, policies to base PSLF eligibility on job function rather than employer types could be considered.[61] If organizational affiliation were not the primary determinant of public service status, it would seemingly be necessary to identify types of jobs that determine eligibility. Identifying all types of specific jobs that could arguably qualify under the HEA definition of a public service job might be inefficient and unwieldy, as it might require a case-by-case consideration of each individual's employment and job functions, and may provide less certainty to borrowers regarding their qualifications for the program.[62]

Qualifying Payments

To qualify for PSLF, borrowers must make, on or after October 1, 2007, 120 separate qualifying monthly payments on their Direct Loans while employed fulltime in public service. Qualifying payments are on-

---

[60] *American Bar Association v. U.S. Department of Education*, 1:16-cv-02476 (U.S. District Court for the District of Columbia), Complaint for Declaratory and Injunctive Relief, filed December 20, 2016.

[61] See, for example, Erica Blom, *Who does the Public Service Loan Forgiveness program really benefit?*, The Urban Institute, October 27, 2017, https://www.urban.org/urban-wire/who-does-public-service-loan-forgiveness-program- really-benefit.

[62] In response to criticisms of its regulatory construct, ED has stated that it derived the term public service organization from the HEA's term public service job, and in doing so, it "intended to identify broad categories of eligible jobs rather than define specific jobs under those categories," (73 *Federal Register* 63232, 63243) believing that using such a construct would be "clearer and more efficient" than defining specific jobs that may qualify (73 *Federal Register* 37694, 37704) and stating that "the term 'public service job' does not encompass every job. The nature of the employer ... [is an] appropriate consideration[]" (73 *Federal Register* 63232, 63243).

time (within 15 days of the schedule due), full, scheduled, and separate monthly payments that are made under a qualifying repayment plan.

To maximize PSLF program benefits, it may be most beneficial for borrowers to enroll in one of the IDR plans; however, borrowers may face difficulties determining which plan is most advantageous to them. In addition, requirements related to on-time payments and specific payment amounts necessary for a payment to qualify for PSLF benefit purposes may be difficult for borrowers to meet without an understanding of loan servicing practices.

Qualifying Repayment Plans

PSLF qualifying payments include payments made under the IDR plans and a standard repayment plan with a 10year repayment period (hereinafter, the Standard 10year repayment plan). Also included are payments made under a standard repayment plan with a greater than 10-year repayment period, a graduated repayment plan, or an extended repayment plan, to the extent that monthly payment amounts are equal to or greater than the monthly amount due as calculated according to a standard plan with 10-year repayment period at the time the loan entered repayment.[63] Table 1 provides general descriptive information on the types of repayment plans that are available to Direct Loan borrowers and indicates the extent to which monthly payments made under each type of plan may be PSLF qualifying, assuming all other PSLF criteria for monthly payments (i.e., they are on-time, full, scheduled, and separate payments) are met.

As noted, to maximize forgiveness benefits under PSLF, it may generally be most beneficial for borrowers to repay their Direct Loans according to one of the IDR plans.

---

[63] The point at which a loan enters repayment depends on the type of loan borrowed. For instance, repayment of a Direct Subsidized or Unsubsidized Loan begins six months and one day after the borrower first ceases to be enrolled on at least a half-time basis in an eligible school, and repayment of a Direct PLUS or Consolidation Loan begins the day that the loan is fully disbursed. 34 C.F.R. §685.207(b)-(e).

Table 1. Characteristics of Repayment Plan Types Available to Direct Loan Borrowers and the Extent to Which Monthly Payments under Them May Qualify for PSLF

Plan	Monthly Payments	Maximum Repayment Term	Extent to which monthly payments may qualify for PSLF[a]
Standard 10-year	Fixed monthly payments	Up to 10 years	Always
Income-Contingent Repayment	Generally, equal to the lesser of (a) 20% of their discretionary income,[b] divided by 12 or (b) the amount calculated according to a 12-year repayment period, multiplied by an income percentage factor that corresponds to the borrower's adjusted gross income.	Up to 25 years	Always
IBR for pre-July 1, 2014, borrowers	Generally, equal to 15% of borrower's discretionary income,[c] divided by 12	Up to 25 years	Always
IBR for post-July 1, 2014, borrowers	Generally, equal to 10% of borrower's discretionary income,[c] divided by 12	Up to 20 years	Always
Pay As You Earn	Generally, equal to 10% of borrower's discretionary income,[c] divided by 12	Up to 20 years	Always
Revised Pay As You Earn	Equal to 10% of borrower's discretionary income,[d] divided by 12	If all loans being repaid were received for undergraduate studies, up to 20 years If any loan being repaid was received for graduate or professional studies, up to 25 years	Always
Standard repayment plan for Consolidation Loans	Fixed monthly payments	10-30 years, depending on borrower's total outstanding federal student loans at the time of entering repayment	In limited circumstances

Plan	Monthly Payments	Maximum Repayment Term	Extent to which monthly payments may qualify for PSLF[a]
Graduated repayment plan	Monthly payments gradually increase over the repayment period	Up to 10 years	In limited circumstances
Graduated repayment plan for Consolidation Loans	Monthly payments gradually increase over the repayment period	10-30 years, depending on borrower's total outstanding student loan debt	In limited circumstances
Extended repayment plan	Fixed monthly payments	Up to 25 years	In limited circumstances
Extended graduated repayment plan	Monthly payments gradually increase over the repayment period	Up to 25 years	In limited circumstances
Alternative repayment plans	Varies, depending on individual borrower circumstances	Up to 30 years	Never

Source: CRS analysis of 34 C.F.R. §§685.208, 685.209, 685.219, and 685.221.

Notes:

[a] This column displays the extent to which monthly payments made under each type of plan may be PSLF qualifying, assuming all other PSLF criteria for monthly payments (i.e., they are on-time, full, scheduled, and separate payments) are met. Monthly payments may be qualifying payments for PSLF to the extent that monthly payment amounts are equal to or greater than the monthly amount due as calculated according to a standard plan with 10-year repayment period at the time the loan entered repayment.

[b] "Discretionary income" is the amount by which a borrower's adjusted gross income (AGI) (including the borrower's spouse's income, if filing jointly) exceeds the Department of Health and Human Servicers' poverty guidelines for the borrower's family size.

[c] "Discretionary income" is the amount by which a borrower's AGI (including borrower's spouse's income, if filing jointly) exceeds 150% of the Department of Health and Human Services' poverty guidelines for the borrower's family size.

[d] "Discretionary income" is the amount by which a borrower's AGI (including borrower's spouse's income, in most circumstances, regardless of whether they file jointly) exceeds 150% of the Department of Health and Human Services' poverty guidelines for the borrower's family size.

Typically, monthly payments made under an IDR plan are lower than they would be under a Standard 10-year plan, and in some instances can even equal $0. This is particularly true for borrowers with more modest income levels and for some borrowers with relatively high levels of debt. Therefore, over a 10 year period many borrowers are likely to make a lower total amount of payments on their loans than they would under the

Standard 10-year plan. This would result in larger amounts of loan principal and interest remaining outstanding at the time a borrower has completed 10 years of public service and receives PSLF forgiveness benefits.

Payments made under many of the other repayment plans available to Direct Loan borrowers may also be considered PSLF qualifying payments. However, making payments under such plans may not be as valuable to borrowers in terms of eventual PSLF forgiveness benefits. In addition, under some repayment plans only some payments may qualify, and it may be difficult for borrowers to discern whether such payments might qualify. Recent attention has been given to some of the difficulties borrowers may face when selecting a repayment plan that is beneficial to them for purposes of PSLF.[64] This section of the report discusses the extent to which loan payments made under selected repayment plans other than the IDR plans might qualify for PSLF purposes.

The HEA specifies that monthly payments made under a Standard 10-year repayment plan qualify for PSLF. However, should a borrower make payments under a Standard 10year repayment plan for the entirety of his or her employment in public service, he or she will not realize any PSLF forgiveness benefits, because there will be no remaining loan balance to be forgiven after having made 120 (10 years' worth) of qualifying PSLF payments.

The HEA also specifies that monthly payments under a standard, graduated, or extended repayment plan are qualifying PSLF payments, to the extent that the monthly payments are equal to or greater than the monthly amount due as calculated according to a Standard 10 year repayment plan. Depending on an individual borrower's circumstances, it is possible that some payments made under such plans may qualify for PSLF purposes. Below are a few examples of the circumstances under which some payments made under these plans might qualify for PSLF[65]

---

[64] See, for example, Ron Lieber, "A Student Loan Nightmare: The Teacher in the Wrong Payment Plan," *The New York Times*, October 27, 2017, https://www.nytimes.com/2017/10/27/your-money/paying-for-college/student-loanpayments.html.
[65] This section of the report describes repayment plans available to borrowers who entered repayment on or after July 1, 2006. For borrowers who entered repayment plans prior to

- Standard repayment plan for Consolidation Loans: Under this plan, Direct Consolidation Loan borrowers make fixed monthly payments on their loans for the duration of the repayment period. The repayment period can be 10-30 years in length, depending on the borrower's total outstanding student loan debt. The longer repayment periods generally result in monthly payments that are less than the amount that would be required under a Standard 10year repayment plan. Therefore, payments made with a repayment period of greater than 10 years generally do not qualify for PSLF. A 10year repayment period is only available to borrowers with total outstanding education debt of less than $7,500.[66] Thus, in limited circumstances, payments under this repayment plan may qualify for PSLF.[67]

- Graduated repayment plan: Under this plan, repayment is structured so that a borrower's monthly payment amount changes over the course of the repayment period. In general, a borrower makes smaller payments at first and larger payments later, and no payment may be more than three times the amount of any other. The repayment period cannot exceed 10 years.[68] Because monthly payments increase over time, it is possible that some payments toward the end of the repayment period may be greater than payments made under a Standard 10- year repayment plan and that those payments would qualify under PSLF.[69]

- Graduated repayment plan for Consolidation Loans: Under this plan, Direct Consolidation Loan borrowers may make graduated payments over a repayment period that is between 10 and 30 years,

July 1, 2006, repayment plans are available that are similar to the ones described herein but some terms and conditions may vary. For additional information on these repayment plans, see 34 C.F.R. §685.208.

[66] 34 C.F.R. §685.208(c).

[67] Office of Federal Student Aid, "Public Service Loan Forgiveness Questions and Answers," Qualifying Repayment Plans, https://studentaid.ed.gov/sa/repay-loans/forgiveness-cancellation/public-service/questions#qualifyingrepayment-plans, accessed May 29, 2018.

[68] 34 C.F.R. §685.208(g).

[69] Office of Federal Student Aid, "Public Service Loan Forgiveness Questions and Answers," Qualifying Repayment Plans, https://studentaid.ed.gov/sa/repay-loans/forgiveness-cancellation/public-service/questions#qualifyingrepayment-plans, accessed May 29, 2018.

depending on the borrower's outstanding student loan debt.[70] Because monthly payments increase over time, it is possible that some payments (typically toward the end of the repayment period) may be greater than payments that would be made under a Standard 10-year repayment plan and, thus, could qualify under PSLF.[71]

- Extended repayment plan: Under this plan, new borrowers with more than $30,000 of outstanding Direct Loan debt accumulated on or after October 7, 1998, may make fixed monthly payments over a repayment period not to exceed 25 years. Monthly payments made under this plan are typically lower than monthly payments made under the Standard 10-year repayment plan;[72] however, they may be greater than those made under the Standard 10year repayment plan in limited circumstances.[73]

- Extended graduated repayment Plan: Under this plan, new borrowers with more than $30,000 of outstanding Direct Loan debt accumulated on or after October 7, 1998, may make graduated monthly payments over a repayment period not to exceed 25 years.[74] Because monthly payments increase over time, it is possible that some payments (typically toward the end of the repayment period) may be greater than payments that would be made under a Standard 10 year repayment plan and, thus, could qualify under PSLF.

---

[70] 34 C.F.R. §685.208(h).

[71] Office of Federal Student Aid, "Public Service Loan Forgiveness Questions and Answers," Qualifying Repayment Plans, https://studentaid.ed.gov/sa/repay-loans/forgiveness-cancellation/public-service/questions#qualifyingrepayment-plans, accessed May 29, 2018.

[72] 34 C.F.R. §685.208(e).

[73] For instance, under certain circumstances, such as loan default, unpaid interest may capitalize. 34 C.F.R. §685.202(b)(5). It is possible that the amount of capitalized interest could cause monthly payments under the Extended repayment plan to be larger than what monthly payments under the Standard 10-year repayment would have been on the date the loan originally entered repayment.

[74] 34 C.F.R. §685.202(b)(5).

that is under contract with and renders services for a public service organization are ineligible for PSLF benefits.[45]

501(c)(3) Organizations

For PSLF purposes, 501(c)(3) organizations are nonprofit organizations that qualify for tax exempt status under Section 501(c)(3) of the IRC and that are not engaged in religious activities, "unless the qualifying activities are unrelated to religious instruction, worship services, or any form of proselytizing."[46] Under IRC Section 501(c)(3), a nonprofit organization that qualifies for tax-exempt status is an entity "organized and operated exclusively for religious, charitable, scientific, testing for public safety, literary, or educational purposes, or to foster national or international amateur sports competition (but only if no part of its activities involve the provision of athletic facilities or equipment), or for the prevention of cruelty to children or animals." In addition, no part of the net earnings of any such entities may benefit a private shareholder or an individual, and such entities are substantially limited in their ability to lobby and are prohibited from engaging in political campaign activity.[47]

Many types of entities may be 501(c)(3) organizations. They can include the following:

- hospitals;
- private nonprofit IHEs and elementary and secondary schools;
- public charities such as the American Red Cross;
- private foundations such as the Bill & Melinda Gates Foundation;
- other organizations organized for one of the purposes specified in IRC Section 501(c)(3), such as the American Society for the

---

[45] U.S. Department of Education, "Federal Perkins Loan Program, Federal Family Education Loan Program, and William D. Ford Federal Direct Loan Program," 73 *Federal Register* 37705, July 1, 2008.
[46] 34 C.F.R. §685.219(b).
[47] For additional information on tax-exempt organizations, including 501(c)(3) organizations, see CRS Report 96-264, *Frequently Asked Questions About Tax-Exempt Organizations*, by Erika K. Lunder.

Prevention of Cruelty to Animals, the American Chemical Society, and the National Collegiate Athletic Association; and

- churches and religious organizations.[48]

In total, there are approximately 1,237,000[49] organizations serving a variety of purposes that are tax-exempt under IRC Section 501(c)(3).

Nonprofit, non-501(c)(3) Organizations

Private organizations that are not tax-exempt organizations under IRC Section 501(c)(3), including private organizations that are tax exempt under other sections of IRC Section 501(c), may nonetheless be considered qualifying employers for the PSLF program. Pursuant to regulations, to qualify, such organizations must not be (1) organized for profit; (2) a labor union; (3) a partisan political organization; or (4) an organization engaged in religious activities, unless the qualifying work engaged in by an individual is unrelated to religious instruction, worship services, or any form of proselytizing. In addition, such organizations must provide at least one of several enumerated public services (e.g., public interest law or public health). Although, the regulations do not specify the extent to which such public services must be offered at these organizations, the ECF and PSLF Application specify that a nonprofit organization that is not a 501(c)(3) organization must provide one of the several enumerated public services as its "primary purpose."

Discussion of Issues

A number of issues regarding the way in which qualifying employment is determined have surfaced. Criticisms have been raised that the PSLF

---

[48] Although churches and religious organizations may be 501(c)(3) organizations, PSLF regulations specify that organizations engaged in religious activities are not PSLF qualifying public service organizations, unless the work engaged in by an individual is unrelated to religious instruction, worship services, or any form of proselytizing. The ECF and Public Service Loan Forgiveness Application Form specify that for purposes of determining whether an individual is employed full-time at such an organization, ED will exclude time spent participating in religious instruction, worship services, or any form of proselytizing.

[49] Internal Revenue Service, *IRS Data Book: FY2016*, Table 25, "Tax-Exempt Organizations, Nonexempt Charitable Trusts, and Nonexempt Split-Interest Trusts, Fiscal Year 2016."

program is not well targeted because qualifying employment under the program covers a broad array of occupations, credential levels, and pay levels. Other concerns include whether the operational definition of "public service job" has created inequities among types of borrowers and whether employer type is a sufficient proxy for identifying employers that provide public service. In addition, some aspects of the term "public service job" are fluid in nature and may make it difficult for borrowers and employers to realize intended benefits. To address some of these issues, basing PSLF eligibility on job functions rather than employer type might be considered. However, if employer type were not the primary determinant of public service status, it would seemingly be necessary to identify types of jobs that determine eligibility, which may be difficult and inefficient to administer and may provide less certainty to borrowers regarding their qualifications for the program.

First, in enacting the PSLF program, Congress intended to provide forgiveness benefits to encourage individuals to enter into and remain employed in public service, as it was concerned with the number of individuals who chose not to enter into lower paying jobs, such as public service, due to increasing student loan debt.[50] To operationally define public service employment, distinctions are made between individuals employed in government and nonprofit entities and those employed in the private sector. As noted above, criticisms have been raised that the PSLF program is not well targeted and that distinctions made among employer types are inappropriate, because qualifying employment under the program encompasses a broad array of occupations, credential levels, and pay levels.[51] Some argue, however, that a distinction among employer types may be relevant, as public service positions may be lower paying than

---

[50] See, for example, U.S. Congress, House Committee on Education and Labor, *College Cost Reduction Act of 2007*, report to accompany H.R. 2669, 110th Cong., 1st sess., June 25, 2007, H.Rept. 110-210, pp. 48-49.

[51] See, for example, Beth Akers, "It's time to axe student loan forgiveness for public service," *The Hill*, June 22, 2017, http://thehill.com/blogs/pundits-blog/education/338908-its-time-to-axe-student-loan-forgiveness-program-for-public; and Jason Delisle, "The coming Public Service Loan Forgiveness bonanza," *Economic Studies at Brookings*, vol. 2, no. 2 (September 22, 2017), pp. 3, 6.

similar positions in the private sector.[52] Moreover, even for those individuals employed in higher-paying, more desirable positions, they may have borrowed large amounts relative to their income to pursue the education necessary to enter their field. Thus, it is argued, in such instances the receipt of PSLF forgiveness benefits is proper and serves as a "public service premium."[53]

Policies to more narrowly define the types of employment that could qualify for PSLF might be considered; however, there may be tradeoffs between targeting specific types of service and providing a more open-ended public service employment category. There is precedent within other federal loan forgiveness and loan repayment programs for providing benefits to individuals employed in specific occupations that have perceived recruitment and retention issues,[54] which result in the provision of a rather targeted benefit. Such an approach, however, may potentially exclude from program eligibility other populations of borrowers perceived as employed in occupations that also further the public interest.

Second, the construct of determining PSLF eligibility based on employer characteristics rather than services rendered may be seen as leading to disparate treatment of borrowers perceived as being similarly situated. Some have questioned ED's interpretation of qualifying public service jobs.[55] For example, consider a fulltime Department of Defense (DOD) employee performing computer programming tasks. Such an individual's employment would qualify for PSLF because he or she is

---

[52] See, for example, Letter from Tim Delaney, President & CEO, National Counsel of Nonprofit Associations, to Nikki Harris, U.S. Department of Education, August 15, 2008, ED-2008-OPE-0009-0063, https://www.regulations.gov/document?D=ED-2008-OPE-0009-0063.

[53] Mark Zuckerman, "Why teachers deserve a break on their student debt," *Politico*, October 3, 2017.

[54] For instance, the John R. Justice Loan Repayment for Prosecutors and Public Defenders program provides loan repayment benefits to individuals employed as full-time prosecutors or public defenders (42 U.S.C. §3797cc-21), and the National Health Service Corps (NHSC) Students to Service Loan Repayment program provides loan repayment benefits to individuals employed as primary care physicians at an NHSC-approved site in a federally designated Health Professional Shortage Area (42 U.S.C. §§254d-254f, 254l-1, 254m, 254n, 254o).

[55] See, for example, 73 *Federal Register* 63242. See also, Letter from Thomas M. Susman, Director, Governmental Affairs Office, American Bar Association, to Nikki Harris, U.S. Department of Education, August 15, 2015, ED-2008- OPE-0009-0174.

Temporary Expanded Public Service Loan Forgiveness

On March 23, 2018, the Consolidated Appropriations Act of 2018 (P.L. 115-141) was enacted. The act provides $350 million to fund the costs of a modification to the Direct Loan program through which up to $500 million in loan forgiveness benefits may be made available to borrowers who would otherwise qualify for PSLF program benefits except for the fact that they made certain non-qualifying payments. To be eligible for the cancellation benefits, borrowers must meet the following criteria.

- They would qualify for PSLF program benefits except that some or all of the 120 required monthly payments they made do not qualify for purposes of the program because they were made in accordance with a graduated or extended repayment plan or the "corresponding repayment plan for a consolidation loan";
- The payments made under the above-described plans were less than the amount calculated under a Standard 10-year repayment plan; and
- The amounts of the monthly payments made 12 months before and immediately prior to application for loan cancellation under the act were each equal to or greater than the monthly amount that would have been calculated under an IDR plan for which the borrower would otherwise qualify. An exception to this criterion is made for borrowers who would otherwise be eligible for loan cancellation under the act's provisions but who demonstrate an "unusual fluctuation of income" over the past five years.
- In addition, according to ED's implementation of this provision, prior to applying for this newly created loan forgiveness benefits a borrower must have previously submitted a PSLF application and had the application denied because some or all of the payments made were not qualifying.

Loan cancellations will be made on a "first-come, first-served" basis. Borrowers who receive loan cancellations under this provision are prohibited from receiving loan repayment or cancellation benefits under the Stafford Loan Forgiveness for Teachers program, the Loan Forgiveness for Service in Areas of National Need program, and the Civil Legal Assistance Attorney Student Loan Repayment program for the same service performed. In addition, the Department of Defense and Labor, Health and Human Services, and Education Appropriations Act, 2019, and Continuing Appropriations Act, 2019 (P.L. 115-245) was enacted on September 28, 2018. It provides an additional $350 million to fund the costs of a modification to the Direct Loan program through which up to $500 million in loan forgiveness benefits may be made available to borrowers under the same circumstances as described above. For additional information, see Office of Federal Student Aid, "Temporary Expanded Public Service Loan Forgiveness," https://studentaid.ed.gov/sa/repay-loans/forgiveness-cancellation/public-service/temporary-expandedpublic-service-loan-forgiveness.

Media accounts[75] and a Consumer Financial Protection Bureau (CFPB) report[76] have recently highlighted the difficulties some borrowers may face when deciding which repayment plan to enroll in to maximize PSLF program benefits. For instance, a borrower may make 120 on-time monthly loan payments under the extended graduated repayment plan, believing the payments qualify for PSLF. After making 60 monthly payments (five years' worth), the borrower then learns they do not qualify for PSLF because the payments made were less than the monthly amount due as calculated according to the Standard 10-year repayment plan at the time his or her loan entered repayment. Because qualifying payments and employment must be concurrent, if the borrower wishes to continue pursuing PSLF, he or she would be required to complete at least another 10 years of employment in a public service job while making 120 qualifying payments, thus delaying his or her eligibility for forgiveness benefits. It appears that these difficulties may arise, at least in part, due to borrowers' misunderstandings of program requirements and/or administrative complexities associated with the program (discussed below).

Issues related to nonqualifying payments have been temporarily addressed in recent legislation (see below).

Payments for Less than the Amount Due

Loan payments must be for the full required monthly amount to be considered qualifying for PSLF.[77] For an individual with multiple loans, should he or she make a payment that is less than the total amount due on all such loans, the payment typically may be applied to each loan in proportion to the required monthly payment amount for each loan, unless requested otherwise.[78] For instance, if an individual had a total of eight

---

[75] See, for example, Ron Lieber, "A Student Loan Nightmare: The Teacher in the Wrong Payment Plan," *The New York Times*, October 27, 2017, https://www.nytimes.com/2017/10/27/your-money/paying-for-college/student-loanpayments.html.

[76] Consumer Financial Protection Bureau, *Staying on track while giving back: The cost of student loan servicing breakdowns for people serving their communities*, June 2017.

[77] 34 C.F.R. §685.219(c)(1)(iii).

[78] See, for example, Nelnet, "How Are Payments Allocated," https://www.nelnet.com/how-payments-are-allocated, accessed May 3, 2018, and Great Lakes, "How Payments Are

loans (e.g., a Direct Subsidized Loan and a Direct Unsubsidized Loan for each of four years of undergraduate study), each with a monthly payment equal to $50 ($400 in total), and he or she made a payment of $300 in a particular month, $37.50 would be applied to each of the eight loans. None of the payments on these loans would be considered PSLF qualifying. If the borrower made a $500 payment the next month, $100 of that payment would first be applied to the past due amount from the previous month and the rest would be applied proportionally across all loans to the current month's payments, thereby bringing all of the loans into current repayment status. The amount of the payment applied to the past due amount from the previous month would not be considered PSLF qualifying, but the remaining amount applied to the current month's payments would be considered PSLF qualifying, as it would be for the full scheduled monthly amount.

However, an individual could request that a payment for less than the amount due be applied in a specific way, such that the monthly payment made on some loans would be considered to be for the full amount and, thus, qualify for PSLF purposes. In the above example, for instance, the borrower could specify that the $300 payment be applied to six of the eight loans. The payments on the six loans would be considered full payments that qualify for PSLF, while the remaining two loans would be considered delinquent and, thus, not be PSLF qualifying. If the borrower made a $500 payment the next month, unless otherwise specified, $100 would be applied to the past due amount and $400 would be applied across all of the loans; the amount of payment applied to the past due amount would not be considered PSLF qualifying, but the remaining amount applied to the current month's payments would be considered PSLF qualifying.

In such instances, the timing of when a particular loan may be eligible to be forgiven under PSLF may vary.

Applied," https://mygreatlakes.org/educate/knowledgecenter/how-payments-are-applied.html, accessed May 3, 2018.

Payments Made When Not Due

In general, loan payments must be scheduled payments to be considered qualifying for PSLF.[79] Scheduled payments are those that are made while a borrower is in repayment on his or her loan and a payment is required.[80] Thus, loan payments made while an individual is in an in-school[81] or other type of deferment, grace status,[82] or forbearance are not considered qualifying payments.

One instance in which this may be particularly relevant is when an individual previously entered repayment on his or her Direct Loan and subsequently returned to school while being employed in public service. Direct Subsidized and Unsubsidized Loans are considered as having entered repayment upon the expiration of the grace period; PLUS Loans are considered to have entered repayment when the loan is fully disbursed.[83] Although Direct Loan borrowers are automatically placed in an in-school deferment upon enrolling on at least a half-time basis in an eligible program, an individual may decline the in-school deferment for those loans that previously entered repayment, such that he or she may continue making qualifying payments while employed in public service concurrently with his or her enrollment.[84] However, if the individual borrowed a new Direct Subsidized or Unsubsidized Loan for his or her return to school, the individual would be unable to decline the initial in school deferment and the grace period and, thus, may not be able to make PSLF qualifying payments on those loans while enrolled in school, as the loans would not be considered to have entered repayment. If the individual

---

[79] 34 C.F.R. §685.219(c)(1)(iii).

[80] U.S. Department of Education, Public Service Loan Forgiveness (PSLF): Employment Certification Form, OMB No. 1845-0110, expiration date May 31, 2020.

[81] Borrowers of Subsidized and Unsubsidized Direct Loans typically are not required to make payments on their loans while they are enrolled on at least a half-time basis in an eligible program. 34 C.F.R. §685.211(b) & (c).

[82] The repayment period for Subsidized and Unsubsidized Direct Loans typically begins six months and one day after the borrower first ceases to be enrolled on at least a half-time basis in an eligible program. This six-month period is commonly referred to as the grace period. 34 C.F.R. §685.207(b) & (c).

[83] 34 C.F.R. §685.211.

[84] U.S. Department of Education, Office of Federal Student Aid, "Public Service Loan Forgiveness Questions and Answers," https://studentaid.ed.gov/sa/repay-loans/forgiveness-cancellation/public-service/questions, accessed May 2, 2018.

borrowed a PLUS Loan for his or her return to school, the PLUS Loan would be considered to have entered repayment upon full disbursement. Thus, the borrower could decline an initial in school deferment on that loan and would be able to make PSLF qualifying payments on those particular loans while enrolled in school.

Lump Sum Payments

Loan payments must be separate monthly payments to be considered qualifying for PSLF.[85] Thus, making a monthly payment that is greater than the required monthly amount will not make a borrower eligible for PSLF forgiveness benefits any sooner, as it will not count as more than one qualifying payment. However, regulations for the PSLF program provide for several exceptions. In instances of a borrower making a lump sum payment using the proceeds of an AmeriCorps Segal Education Award, a Peace Corps transition payment, or through certain DOD programs, the lump sum payment may be counted as up to 12 required monthly payments. In such instances, the number counted as qualifying monthly payments is determined by taking the lesser of the amount of funds from one of the above sources that was applied toward a lump sum payment, divided by the required monthly payment amount under a qualifying repayment plan, or 12 monthly payments.[86]

Aside from these exceptions, any excess amount paid may be applied to cover all or part of one or more future monthly payments, unless the borrower requests otherwise. Depending on how much extra the borrower pays, the borrower's next payment due date could be advanced a month or more in the future from the date the extra payment amount was made. This is called being "paid ahead." Generally, payments resulting in a borrower's paid ahead status only count as one qualifying PSLF payment, even if the payments could equal multiple months' worth of payments.[87] In addition, subsequent payments made during a period when a borrower is paid ahead

---

[85] 34 C.F.R. §685.219(c)(1)(iii).

[86] 34 C.F.R. §685.219(c)(2) and (3).

[87] Office of Federal Student Aid, "Public Service Loan Forgiveness," What is a qualifying monthly payment?, https://studentaid.ed.gov/sa/repay-loans/forgiveness-cancellation/public-service#qualifying-repayment-plan, accessed December 29, 2017.

will not qualify for PSLF. However, if a borrower requests that the extra payment amount not be applied to future scheduled payments (e.g., the borrower requests that the excess payments be applied to reduce outstanding loan principal), the excess amount would not advance the due date of the next scheduled payment, and any subsequent monthly payments made would count toward the required 120 payments.[88] It has been reported that some borrowers, particularly those whose loan payments are automatically debited from their bank accounts, may not realize that the advanced payments they have made do not qualify for PSLF and, thus, they may not have made the progress toward PSLF they expected.[89]

Loan Consolidation

Loan consolidation may also affect a borrower's eligibility for and receipt of PSLF benefits. Only borrowers of Direct Loans are eligible to receive PSLF benefits, but borrowers of other types of federal student loans (e.g., Federal Family Education Loans, Perkins Loans, and Public Health Service Act loans) may consolidate their loans into a Direct Consolidation Loan[90] to pursue PSLF benefits. While loan consolidation may be a useful option for individuals considering PSLF, the timing of it may be an important factor in borrower eligibility for and receipt of program benefits. When a borrower consolidates multiple loans into a Direct Consolidation Loan, its proceeds are used to pay off the borrower's previous loans. Thus, no PSLF qualifying payments made on Direct Loans and non-Direct Loans prior to consolidation will count towards the required 120 PSLF payments. In addition, because a Direct Consolidation Loan is an entirely new loan with potentially different terms and conditions than the underlying loans, benefits uniquely associated with the underlying loans may be no longer be available upon consolidation. For instance,

---

[88] 34 C.F.R. §685.211(a).

[89] See, for example, Consumer Financial Protection Bureau, *Staying on track while giving back: The cost of student loan servicing breakdowns for people serving their communities*, June 2017, pp. 42-43.

[90] For additional information on Direct Consolidation Loans, see CRS Report R40122, *Federal Student Loans Made Under the Federal Family Education Loan Program and the William D. Ford Federal Direct Loan Program: Terms and Conditions for Borrowers*, by David P. Smole.

Perkins Loan[91] borrowers may have a portion of these loans cancelled after service in qualifying occupations (e.g., teachers in low-income schools). When a borrower consolidates his or her Perkins Loan into a Direct Consolidation Loan, the Perkins Loan cancellation benefit is no longer available to the individual. There have been reports that some borrowers may not have been aware of the effects of consolidation on their PSLF eligibility when they consolidated their loans and that had they been aware, they would have consolidated their loans earlier or would not have consolidated them at all in order to preserve their qualifying payments or other loan benefits.[92]

Administrative Complexities and Challenges

The administration of the PSLF program presents complexities and some challenges for ED, its loan servicers, and borrowers. Receipt of program benefits is dependent on an individual fulfilling multiple requirements related to qualifying employment and qualifying payments. An overarching administrative issue faced by ED, loan servicers (tasked with administering various aspects of the PSLF program), and borrowers is communications among the parties regarding PSLF eligibility requirements and processes. Borrowers sometimes seem to have imperfect information about the program's requirements,[93] which may make attainment of program benefits difficult. Loan servicers also seemingly are troubled by imperfect information related to a borrower's employment status,[94] which may make aspects of program administration difficult or inefficient. In

---

[91] For additional information on the Perkins Loan program, see CRS Report RL31618, *Campus-Based Student Financial Aid Programs Under the Higher Education Act*, by Joselynn H. Fountain.

[92] See, for example, Consumer Financial Protection Bureau, *Staying on track while giving back: The cost of student loan servicing breakdowns for people serving their communities*, June 2017, p. 38.

[93] See, for example, U.S. Government Accountability Office, *Public Service Loan Forgiveness: Education Needs to Provide Better Information for Loan Servicer and Borrowers*, GAO-18-547, September 2018 and Consumer Financial Protection Bureau, *Staying on track while giving back: The cost of student loan servicing breakdowns for people serving their communities*, June 2017.

[94] See, for example, U.S. Government Accountability Office, *Public Service Loan Forgiveness: Education Needs to Provide Better Information for Loan Servicer and Borrowers*, GAO-18-547, September 2018.

addition, the program's overall complexity, lack of automation in administrative functions, lack of coordination among loan servicers, and fragmented guidance issued by ED to loan servicers may lead to mistakes, inefficiencies, and inconsistent administration of the program that could affect borrower eligibility for program benefits.

All contracted federal student loan servicers are responsible for selected activities relating to PSLF, such as communicating with borrowers about the general availability of the program and enrolling borrowers in selected repayment plans that may enable them to qualify for PSLF. ED has contracted with a single loan servicer—FedLoan Servicing—to perform the majority of administrative tasks specific to PSLF, including determining whether an individual's employment and/or payments qualify for the program and processing forgiveness applications.

Communication Issues

PSLF can offer borrowers significant benefits to help ease the financial burdens associated with student loan debt, but borrowers can only avail themselves of the program if they actively seek forgiveness benefits. Therefore, knowledge of the program's availability is one aspect that contributes to a borrower's successful utilization of the program. Additionally, even if borrowers are aware of the program's availability, imperfect information on program eligibility requirements can negatively affect a borrower's progress toward loan forgiveness. Multiple reports have highlighted communication issues among parties regarding the program.[95]

One communication issue faced by some borrowers may be their general lack of knowledge of the existence of the program. One report found that ED has not notified all borrowers who have entered repayment about the program. It also found that while ED primarily relies on its loan servicers to communicate with borrowers who have entered repayment, it

---

[95] See, for example, U.S. Government Accountability Office, *Federal Student Loans: Education Could Do More to Help Ensure Borrowers Are Aware of Repayment and Forgiveness Options*, GAO-15-663, August 2015; U.S. Government Accountability Office, *Public Service Loan Forgiveness: Education Needs to Provide Better Information for Loan Servicer and Borrowers*, GAO-18-547; and Consumer Financial Protection Bureau, *Staying on track while giving back: The cost of student loan servicing breakdowns for people serving their communities*, June 2017.

has established few requirements related to the information the servicers should provide to borrowers about PSLF and when those communications should occur. It is reported that ED has taken some steps intended to help increase borrower awareness of the program, such as developing requirements for servicers to include information about PSLF in initial communications to borrowers.[96] However, servicers are not required to provide PSLF information in ongoing communications with borrowers beyond the initial communications,[97] which could affect a borrower's ability to participate in the program at a future point should he or she forget the information provided earlier in the repayment process.

In addition to issues relating to communicating about the general availability of the program to borrowers, reports suggest communications about program requirements between borrowers, ED, and loan servicers may be imperfect.[98] Imperfect communications may lead to borrower confusion about program requirements and could result in a borrower making extra payments, prolonging a borrower's potential time to forgiveness, or rendering a borrower's loans ineligible for PSLF. Issues experienced by borrowers relating to communication about PSLF eligibility requirements include the following:

- loan servicers not informing borrowers of the availability of PSLF and/or its requirements, despite knowing a borrower was employed in public service;
- loan servicers not explaining to borrowers that their FFEL or Perkins Loan program loans do not qualify for PSLF or that they are not enrolled in a qualifying repayment plan, despite borrowers informing the servicer that they are pursuing PSLF and believing they otherwise meet PSLF program requirements; and

---

[96] U.S. Government Accountability Office, *Federal Student Loans: Education Could Do More to Help Ensure Borrowers Are Aware of Repayment and Forgiveness Options*, GAO-15-663, August 2015, pp. 34-36.

[97] Communications between CRS and FedLoan Servicing, September 28, 2018.

[98] See, for example, U.S. Government Accountability Office, *Public Service Loan Forgiveness: Education Needs to Provide Better Information for Loan Servicer and Borrowers*, GAO-18-547, September 2018, p. 13.

- loan servicers not explaining to borrowers that if they consolidate their loans, any previous PSLF qualifying payments made will be lost.[99]

ED takes several approaches to conduct outreach to inform borrowers about PSLF requirements, but at least one report concluded that there remains a need for ED to provide borrowers with clear and sufficient information about how to qualify for the program.[100] For example, GAO found that multiple loan servicers that are not the primary servicer responsible for administering the program have policies not to answer specific questions about an individual borrower's PSLF eligibility due to the complex nature of the program.[101] While such an approach may help avoid the risk of a nonPSLF loan servicer providing inaccurate information, it may hinder a borrower's ability to make informed decisions regarding his or her pursuit of PSLF benefits.

Recently, the Consolidated Appropriations Act of 2018 (P.L. 115-141) and the Department of Defense and Labor, Health and Human Services, and Education Appropriations Act, 2019, and Continuing Appropriations Act, 2019 (P.L. 115245) each authorized $2.3 million for the Secretary of Education to conduct activities that may help to address some of the issues described in this section. The acts direct the Secretary to conduct outreach to borrowers "who may intend to qualify" for PSLF to ensure that they are meeting program terms and conditions. They also direct the Secretary to communicate to all Direct Loan borrowers all PSLF program requirements and to improve the process for filing the ECF by providing improved outreach and by creating an option for all borrowers to complete the employment certification process on a centralized website.

[99] Consumer Financial Protection Bureau, *Staying on track while giving back: The cost of student loan servicing breakdowns for people serving their communities*, June 2017.
[100] U.S. Government Accountability Office, *Public Service Loan Forgiveness: Education Needs to Provide Better Information for Loan Servicer and Borrowers*, GAO-18-547, September 2018, pp. 13-14.
[101] U.S. Government Accountability Office, *Public Service Loan Forgiveness: Education Needs to Provide Better Information for Loan Servicer and Borrowers*, GAO-18-547, September 2018, pp. 13-14.

Additional Issues Faced by Student Loan Borrowers

A 2017 CFPB report also highlighted a variety of challenges related to the administration of the PSLF program that borrowers may face. Some complaints highlighted in the report include the following:

- Borrowers consolidating federal student loans that are otherwise ineligible for PSLF into Direct Consolidation Loans in order to become eligible for PSLF report delays in the loan consolidation process. In some instances, borrowers report the process taking more than six months to complete because their original loan servicer did not provide the information necessary to complete the consolidation.

- Some borrowers report that after submitting materials to enable them to become eligible for PSLF (e.g., applications to enroll in a qualifying repayment plan or to consolidate PSLF ineligible loans into a Direct Consolidation Loan), servicers either incorrectly denied their applications or did not give them a chance to correct deficiencies in their applications.

- Some borrowers who have had their loans transferred to FedLoan Servicing after having their employment certified as PSLF qualifying report issues related to the transfer process. In some instances, borrowers have reported that during transfer and without notice, their loans were removed from an IDR plan. Thus, when they continued to submit payments during transfer, such payments did not qualify for PSLF. In other instances, borrowers have reported that their full payment history may not be received by FedLoan Servicing from the transferring servicer, which may impede FedLoan Servicing's ability to accurately track qualifying payments.

- Some borrowers report that FedLoan Servicing has provided inaccurate counts of the number of qualified payments they have made towards PSLF forgiveness and that they have experienced difficulty in having those errors corrected.

- Borrowers report that loan servicers have failed to process IDR plan recertification paperwork in a timely manner and have placed them in repayment plans or statuses (e.g., forbearance) that do not qualify for PSLF, despite servicers being required to keep the borrower in the same IDR plan until the recertification paperwork can be processed.[102]

Provisional Qualifying Employment Determination

Another administrative issue that may affect borrowers (and their employers) is a recent lawsuit between ED and the American Bar Association (ABA) that brings into question the extent to which some borrowers may be able to rely on FedLoan Servicing's determination of whether their employment qualifies for PSLF. In December 2016, the ABA filed a lawsuit against ED stating that FedLoan Servicing had notified several ABA employees that their employment with the ABA qualified for purposes of PSLF, and that subsequently ED retroactively revoked that determination. In response, ED stated that FedLoan Servicing's determination of employment eligibility was "provisional guidance" and that ED retains the right to make a final determination as to an employer's status.[103] The lawsuit has not yet been resolved, but it has called into question the extent to which some borrowers may rely on FedLoan Servicing's determination that their employment qualifies for PSLF.[104]

This issue may be of particular concern for individuals who are employed at nonprofit organizations that are not 501(c)(3) organizations but who might otherwise qualify for PSLF, as determining whether such organizations are qualifying is not always a straight-forward exercise (see discussion below regarding administrative issues with determining employer eligibility). Upon receipt of notification from FedLoan Servicing

---

[102] Consumer Financial Protection Bureau, *Staying on track while giving back: The cost of student loan servicing breakdowns for people serving their communities*, June 2017.

[103] *American Bar Association v. United States Department of Education*, Case 1:16-cv-02476-RDM (U.S. District Court for the District of Columbia), July 31, 2017.

[104] For additional information, see Stacy Cowley, "Student Loan Forgiveness Program Approval Letters May Be Invalid, Education Dept. Says," *The New York Times*, March 30, 2017, https://www.nytimes.com/2017/03/30/business/student-loan-forgiveness-program-lawsuit.html.

that their employment qualifies for PSLF, such individuals could remain in a job in which they might not have otherwise remained but for the availability of PSLF. Should ED then make a subsequent determination that their employment did not qualify, they may be delayed in qualifying for forgiveness benefits. Additionally, the benefit for which they may ultimately qualify may be reduced if borrowers made more unqualified payments (i.e., payments not made while concurrently employed in a qualifying public service job) on their loans than they would have with reliable information about the employer's eligibility status.

The ABA lawsuit may have implications for employers as well. Employers may use PSLF as a recruitment tool by informing potential employees that their current employees have been informed that employment with them qualifies for PSLF. If job-seeking borrowers feel they cannot rely on FedLoan Servicing's determination, they may choose employment elsewhere and public service organizations may not benefit from recruiting and retaining qualified employees as intended by PSLF.

Need for 10 Years of Individual Recordkeeping

A final administrative issue potentially faced by borrowers is individual recordkeeping. Overall, loan servicers and ED are responsible for determining whether an employer qualifies for PSLF and how many qualifying payments an individual has made. However, in some instances, a loan servicer may provide inaccurate or incomplete information to borrowers regarding their PSLF qualifications. Borrowers who are adept at recordkeeping (e.g., maintaining employment records such as paystubs, keeping track of payments previously made) may be better able to substantiate and resolve any issues or complaints brought to the loan servicer's and/or ED's attention than those who are not.

One instance in which individual recordkeeping may be useful is when a borrower believes his or her PSLF qualifying loan payments have been miscounted. In some instances, FedLoan Servicing may not provide borrowers with sufficient information to catch payment counting errors easily. In addition, previous loan servicers may have provided inconsistent prior-payment information to FedLoan Servicing, which could result in payment counting mistakes. FedLoan Servicing relies on borrowers to catch payment counting errors resulting from issues with information provided by previous loan servicers.[105] If a borrower has not kept records of individual payments made over time, he or she may face difficulties in disputing payment counts with FedLoan Servicing or ED.

Addressing Administrative Issues Faced by Borrowers

Proposed policies to address many of these administrative issues faced by borrowers often center around strengthening loan servicing standards related to PSLF and other aspects of loan servicing that may affect PSLF eligibility, such as borrower enrollment in qualifying repayment plans. Suggestions to strengthen servicing standards include, for instance, earlier servicer engagement with borrowers regarding the general availability of PSLF, better communication of PSLF eligibility requirements, and accessible tracking of payments toward PSLF.[106] Other policy options center around actions ED may take to strengthen the administration of the program, such as strengthening outreach to borrowers to increase awareness about the program.[107] While strengthened borrower engagement and outreach may enable some borrowers to navigate the PSLF process more easily, one might consider whether such information could be targeted to specific subgroups of borrowers, such as those individuals known to be employed in public service. Using a one size fits-all approach to providing PSLF information to all borrowers, regardless of whether they may be eligible for or interested in PSLF, may lead to borrower confusion and imprudent decision making about whether to pursue PSLF.

---

[105] U.S. Government Accountability Office, *Public Service Loan Forgiveness: Education Needs to Provide Better Information for Loan Servicer and Borrowers*, GAO-18-547, September 2018, pp. 22-23.

[106] Ibid., pp. 44-47, and Consumer Financial Protection Bureau, *Staying on track while giving back: The cost of student loan servicing breakdowns for people serving their communities*, June 2017.

[107] U.S. Government Accountability Office, *Federal Student Loans: Education Could Do More to Help Ensure Borrowers Are Aware of Repayment and Forgiveness Options*, GAO-15-663, August 2015, p. 37.

Issues Faced by Student Loan Servicers

Loan servicers may face additional issues, aside from the communication issues described above, in administering the PSLF program. Key administrative issues faced by loan servicers pertain to the complexity of the PSLF program requirements and the lack of automation of many functions related to determining a borrower's PSLF eligibility, and the fragmented guidance provided by ED to FedLoan Servicing in administering the program.[108]

Determining Employment Eligibility

One administrative task potentially affected by the lack of automation is determining whether a borrower's employment is eligible for PSLF. When FedLoan Servicing receives a borrower's ECF and determines that the borrower has an eligible Direct Loan, it then makes an initial determination of whether the borrower's employer is PSLF qualifying. ED has not provided FedLoan Servicing with a definitive source of information for determining which employers qualify for PSLF. Although ED has provided FedLoan Servicing with some resources to assist it in identifying qualifying employers, the sources are not comprehensive, and sometimes FedLoan Servicing must consult other sources and make its own determination.[109] FedLoan Servicing has expressed that a master list of qualifying employers supplied by ED that it could reference when making initial PSLF employment determinations or other data matching initiatives (such as with the IRS) could help streamline the process and add a layer of certainty to its determinations,[110] especially in light of the current ABA lawsuit.

---

[108] This section is based on conversations between CRS and FedLoan Servicing, November 2, 2017.

[109] U.S. Government Accountability Office, *Public Service Loan Forgiveness: Education Needs to Provide Better Information for Loan Servicer and Borrowers*, GAO-18-547, September 2018, pp. 18-20.

[110] Ibid., p. 19.

Counting Payments

Another administrative task potentially affected by lack of automation is counting the amount of PSLF qualifying payments a borrower has made. Once a borrower has submitted an ECF and his or her employment has been determined qualifying by FedLoan Servicing, his or her loans are transferred, along with any relevant documentation such as information on previous monthly payments made, from the borrower's current servicer to FedLoan Servicing. FedLoan Servicing then counts the number of PSLF qualifying payments the borrower has made and notifies him or her of the tally. However, FedLoan Servicing reports it does not always receive consistent information regarding prior payments from other loan servicers. This may be due in part to a lack of standard definitions and terminology among loan servicers and to them operating different IT systems to complete loan servicing tasks.[111] As described above, qualifying payments are on-time, full, scheduled, and separate monthly payments that are made under a qualifying repayment plan. Monthly payments that are greater or less than the required monthly amount may result in a borrower being in paid-ahead or delinquent status, respectively, and payments made while in these statuses are not qualifying for PSLF purposes. Due to the complexity of determining precisely what constitutes a qualifying payment and the inconsistencies in reporting among loan servicers, this process can be work intensive, which could delay FedLoan Servicing's ability to notify a borrower of the number of qualifying payments made. In addition, it could lead to miscounting payments. Were a more consistent and automated process to be developed, FedLoan Servicing might be able to tally and notify borrowers of qualifying loans payments in a more accurate and timely manner.

Fragmented and Incomplete Guidance

An overarching issue faced by FedLoan Servicing in administering the PSLF program is the fragmented and incomplete guidance ED has provided it. GAO reports that ED provides guidance and instructions to

---

[111] Ibid., pp. 21-22.

FedLoan Servicing in a piecemeal manner across multiple documents, including ED's original contract with FedLoan Servicing, contract updates, and emails. FedLoan Servicing has indicated to GAO that the use of email to communicate guidance and instructions is especially problematic, as information in the emails may not be disseminated to all relevant individuals.[112] GAO also reports that there are gaps in ED's guidance to FedLoan Servicing, which may leave the servicer uncertain about how to administer aspects of the program.[113] Such a fragmented and incomplete approach to communicating guidance and instructions may create a risk of inconsistent interpretations of law and procedures, which could negatively affect borrowers' abilities to benefit from PSLF. GAO indicates ED has taken steps (e.g., conducting regular meetings with FedLoan Servicing to discuss administrative issues) to ensure it is providing clearer and more consistent guidance and instructions.[114] However, a central source of guidance and instructions, such as a PSLF processing manual, may be helpful to further address additional administrative concerns and could provide additional levels of certainty that the PSLF program will be consistently administered.

Interaction with Other Programs and Benefits

Issues have surfaced related to the interactions between PSLF and other federal programs and benefits. From a borrower's perspective, these relate to their need to understand the interactions to make rational choices and maximize program benefits. This involves borrowers' understanding of the various loan repayment plans available and the interaction between PSLF and other service benefits (e.g., loan repayment or forgiveness programs); deciding the amount of student loans to borrow; and being able to avail themselves of certain income tax provisions to maximize PSLF program benefits.

---

[112] Ibid., pp. 16-17.
[113] Ibid., 17.
[114] Ibid., p. 18.

From the federal government's perspective, program interaction issues relate to whether desired targeting of benefits is being achieved. They may also relate to consideration of how large PSLF program benefits should be, as well as consideration of the extent to which overlapping benefits might be provided and whether any may constitute an unintended "double benefit" for the same service. Other issues relate to subsequent changes to "interacting benefits" (e.g., expansion of available loan repayment plans), which may substantially affect the targeting of PSLF benefits and associated costs.

Loan Limits and Repayment Plans

For borrowers, key issues relating to PSLF program interactions with loan limits and repayment plans are deciding the amount of student loans to borrow and understanding how loan repayment plans interact with PSLF to maximize PSLF program benefits. For the federal government, key issues relate to the amount of student loans forgiven, whether the benefits provided may be outsized for certain borrower populations, and the associated costs with providing benefits. Another issue for the federal government is subsequent changes to benefits, which may substantially affect the targeting of benefits and associated costs.

There is no limit to the amount of loan forgiveness benefits that a borrower may realize under PSLF. As such, it is possible that borrowers with large amounts of Direct Loan debt may realize significant forgiveness benefits under the program.[115] While this outcome potentially could occur for a variety of individuals borrowing different types of Direct Loans, it may be more likely for individuals who borrowed Direct PLUS Loans as

---

[115] It is difficult to estimate the potential amount of PSLF benefits that could be realized by an individual, as a variety of factors must be taken into consideration, including an individual's loan balance, interest rate, repayment plan, current and future earnings, and family size. Nonetheless, some have attempted to provide illustrative examples of the amount of forgiveness benefits that might be realized under the PSLF program. See Office of Federal Student Aid, "Repayment Estimator," https://studentloans.gov/myDirectLoan/ mobile/repayment/repaymentEstimator.action; Student Loan Hero, "Public Service Loan Forgiveness Calculator, https://studentloanhero.com/calculators/public-service-loan-forgiveness-calculator/; and Jason Delisle and Alexander Holt, *Zero Marginal Cost: Measuring Subsidies for Graduate Education in the Public Service Loan Forgiveness Program*, New America, September 2014.

graduate or professional students, because there are higher aggregate borrowing limits for Direct Unsubsidized Loans for graduate and professional students and there are no aggregate limits to the amount of PLUS Loans an individual may borrow.[116]

Table 2 depicts the average cumulative amount of federal student loans borrowed by academic level of the borrower for the cohort of students who began undergraduate study during academic year (AY) 2003-2004. Based on these data, it appears that individuals who borrowed to pursue a graduate or professional education may have the potential to realize larger PSLF loan forgiveness benefits than those who borrowed only to pursue an undergraduate education. Moreover, it appears that individuals who borrowed Direct PLUS Loans as graduate and professional students have the potential to realize an even larger PSLF loan forgiveness benefit than their counterparts who did not borrow Direct PLUS Loans as graduate and professional students.

Table 2. Average Cumulative Federal Student Loans Borrowed, by Academic Level As of June 1, 2015

Academic Level	Average Cumulative Amount Borrowed[a]
Undergraduate	$16,612
Graduate/Professional[b]	$74,476
Did not borrow PLUS Loans for graduate study	$50,981
Borrowed PLUS Loans for graduate study	$132,199

Source: CRS analysis of U.S. Department of Education, National Center for Education Statistics, 2003-04 Beyond Postsecondary Students Longitudinal Study, Second Follow-up (BPS: 04/09).

Notes: Estimates in nominal dollars.

[a] Represents the average cumulative amount of all federal loans received within 12 years of beginning postsecondary education.

[b] Estimates include undergraduate debt for loan borrowers.

---

[116] Conversely, there are aggregate borrowing limits placed on Direct Subsidized and Unsubsidized Loans, the only types of Direct Loans undergraduate students may borrow. For additional information on loan limits, see CRS Report R40122, *Federal Student Loans Made Under the Federal Family Education Loan Program and the William D. Ford Federal Direct Loan Program: Terms and Conditions for Borrowers*, by David P. Smole.

To realize PSLF program benefits, a borrower must make 120 qualifying monthly payments. When Congress first authorized the PSLF program, it specifically cited the concern that public service professions paid comparatively less than other professions. By permitting borrowers to maximize PSLF program benefits by tying monthly payments to income, as is done under an IDR plan, the issue of disparate pay among employment types (i.e., public service versus nonpublic service) may be further addressed. For individuals enrolled in IDR plans, their monthly payments are often less than what they would be under a Standard 10year repayment plan. Also, under several of the IDR plans, borrowers' monthly payments may be capped not to exceed the monthly amount a borrower would have repaid under a Standard 10year repayment plan at the time the borrower began repaying under the IDR plan.[117] Thus, depending on individual circumstances and the repayment plan chosen, a borrower may maximize the amount of loan forgiveness received under PSLF by lowering monthly payments. Some speculate this may encourage student over borrowing, as the amount a borrower repays on a loan under the IDR plans is largely based on the borrower's income and family size, once a certain amount has been borrowed. Some individuals may borrow at a high enough level that, provided qualified service and on-time payment requirements are met, borrowing additional sums may not result in a borrower incurring any increases in future loan payments. Consequently, such individuals may have little incentive to limit their borrowing.[118] In addition, some hypothesize that the lack of student incentive to limit borrowing may also make some students less sensitive to the price of education.[119]

Criticisms have been raised that the level of program benefits provided is not well targeted because it may depend on borrower characteristics (e.g., amount of debt and repayment plan) and allows borrowers potentially

---

[117] Monthly payments made under the IBR plans and the Pay As You Earn (PAYE) plans are capped at the amount the borrower would pay under the Standard 10-year repayment plan.

[118] Jason Delisle and Alexander Holt, *Zero Marginal Cost: Measuring Subsidies for Graduate Education in the Public Service Loan Forgiveness Program*, New America, September 2014.

[119] Ibid., p. 21.

to accrue large amounts of debt and subsequently receive large dollar amounts of benefits, through both reduced monthly payments in IDR plans while performing public service and eventual loan forgiveness following 10 years of public service. Critics often argue that the program's design may provide outsized benefits to certain types of borrowers who have the opportunity to accrue large amounts of debt; specifically, graduate and professional student borrowers who tend to borrow more cumulatively and also tend to have higher earning potential than individuals without graduate or professional degrees. These two factors may enable such borrowers to realize the greatest amount of benefits (in terms of dollar amount forgiven) under the program and they may face little incentive to curtail their borrowing.[120] However, even for borrowers with modest amounts of debt but very low incomes, and who repay their loans according to an IDR plan, the amount repaid on their loans could be as low as $0, and the amount forgiven could be substantial compared to the amount borrowed.[121] On the other hand, some argue that the opportunity to make lower monthly payments under an IDR plan, coupled with the potential for an unlimited amount of debt forgiveness, makes the PSLF program attractive to individuals with debt repayment responsibilities who may not otherwise consider entering public service due to the amount of their debt.[122]

The evolution of the federal student loan programs since the PSLF program's enactment may also have a bearing on the types of individuals who receive program benefits and the amounts of debt relief they may realize under the program. PSLF originally was designed so that it would primarily be borrowers whose post-enrollment income (from employment in public service) was low enough for them to qualify for the pre-July 1, 2014, IBR plan (i.e., they demonstrated a partial financial hardship (PFH)), with monthly payments based on 15% of their discretionary income, who

---

[120] See ibid. and Jason Delisle, "The coming Public Service Loan Forgiveness bonanza," *Economic Studies at Brookings*, vol. 2, no. 2 (September 22, 2017), p. 3.

[121] Jason Delisle and Alexander Holt, *Zero Marginal Cost: Measuring Subsidies for Graduate Education in the Public Service Loan Forgiveness Program*, New America, September 2014, p. 21.

[122] Christopher P. Chapman, "Scrapping loan forgiveness for public servants hurts our democracy," *The Hill*, November 1, 2011, http://thehill.com/opinion/civil-rights/358258-scrapping-loan-forgiveness-for-public-servants-hurtsour-democracy.

would qualify for PSLF benefits. Since that time, additional IDR plans with varying terms have become available that make it easier for individuals to qualify for IDR repayment plans. Repayment term changes encompassed by these new plans include basing monthly payments on 10% of a borrower's discretionary income (i.e., post-July 1, 2014, IBR; PAYE; REPAYE) and not requiring borrowers to demonstrate a PFH to qualify for certain repayment plans (i.e., REPAYE). These changes enabling additional borrowers to qualify for IDR plans and to repay their loans at a lower rate mean that individuals may also be more likely to qualify for PSLF benefits.

With the expansion of the various types of IDR plans under which monthly payments made generally qualify for PSLF, one could argue that PSLF benefits have been tilted toward high-income participants, as monthly payments required under the various IDR plans have decreased from 15% to 10% of discretionary income, while the amount of nondiscretionary income excluded from monthly payment calculations has remained the same~150% of the federal poverty guidelines. Nonetheless, the enhancement of such programs may still amplify PSLF benefits for some low-income borrowers as well. In addition, under the two IBR and PAYE plans, monthly payment amounts are capped at the amount a borrower would have paid under a Standard 10-year repayment plan at the time he or she entered repayment under the plan. This characteristic may provide an outsized benefit to borrowers with very large debts who initially have low AGIs but then experience a substantial growth in income (e.g., doctors who experience significant income growth upon completion of their residencies). In some instances, without this IDR benefit, individuals who are employed in public service and experience rapidly rising income trajectories would otherwise be required to make payments sufficient to pay off a much larger portion of their loans within the qualifying 10year period of service. Finally, the amounts of debt that may be forgiven under PSLF are likely to be higher due to the lower rates at which outstanding balances may be repaid under several of the more generous IDR plans under which an individual is required to make monthly payments equal to 10% of his or her discretionary income.

Other student loan program factors may also lead to higher amounts of debt being forgiven under PSLF. First, later cohorts are borrowing larger amounts of student loans than previous cohorts.[123] Second, with the end of the FFEL program and the switch to 100% Direct Loan lending, many more borrowers have Direct Loans, the only loans eligible for PSLF.

Receipt of Multiple Benefits

Another issue related to PSLF interaction with other programs or benefits pertains to whether borrowers can or should be able to receive loan repayment or forgiveness benefits under other programs for the same service used to qualify for PSLF program benefits. For borrowers, key aspects of this issue include whether the same service that qualifies them for PSLF may also qualify them for other benefits and their understanding of how other benefits may interact with PSLF. For the federal government, key aspects are the need to decide what constitutes a "double benefit" for borrower service performed and the extent to which overlapping benefits might be provided.

In general, borrowers receiving loan repayment benefits under one of a number of federal student loan repayment programs[124] may use the monetary benefits provided under such programs to make payments on their Direct Loans, and payments made using those funds could count as a qualifying payment under PSLF. In some instances, the service performed to receive the monetary benefit under the loan repayment program may also be considered qualifying employment for purposes of PSLF. This is often the case for loan repayment programs that operate on a fairly limited scale and that typically target individuals employed in specific fields. For example, under the Nurse Corps Loan Repayment Program, the Student Loan Repayment Program for House Employees, or the Student Loan Repayment Program for Senate Employees borrowers perform specified service to receive monthly loan repayment benefits, and the service

---

[123] See CRS In Focus IF10158, *A Snapshot of Student Loan Debt*, by David P. Smole.

[124] For information on authorized federal student loan repayment programs, see CRS Report R43571, *Federal Student Loan Forgiveness and Loan Repayment Programs*, coordinated by Alexandra Hegji.

performed would likely qualify as a public service job under the PSLF program. Individuals could use funds provided under these programs to make scheduled monthly payments on their Direct Loans, and payments made with those funds could count toward the required 120 payments under PSLF. This could be viewed as providing multiple benefits to an individual for the same service performed. Borrowers and employers might consider this an additional benefit that could further aid in the recruitment and retention of employees. Alternatively, this could be viewed as providing overlapping or double benefits across multiple federal programs with the same or substantially similar goals and activities, which could be considered akin to a windfall.

Although some federal student loan repayment programs do not prohibit individuals from receiving benefits under multiple programs for the same service performed, several federal student loan forgiveness and repayment programs authorized under HEA, Title IV do prohibit borrowers from receiving a reduction in their loan repayment obligations through more than one program for the same service.[125] For instance, the HEA prohibits individuals from receiving PSLF benefits for the same service under the PSLF program and the Loan Repayment for Civil Legal Assistance Attorneys programs. Programs with such prohibitions typically operate on a rather small scale, but one, the Teacher Loan Forgiveness program, provides benefits to a relatively large number of beneficiaries approximately 43,000 individuals in FY2017.[126]

Under the Teacher Loan Forgiveness program, individuals must teach full-time for five complete and consecutive academic years in certain

---

[125] The HEA, Title IV loan forgiveness and loan repayment programs that have coordinated language specifying the ineligibility of borrowers for double benefits are the FFEL Teacher Loan Forgiveness program (HEA, §428J), the Loan Forgiveness for Service in Areas of National Need program (HEA, §428K), the Loan Repayment for Civil Legal Assistance Attorneys program (HEA, §428L), the Direct Loan Public Service Loan Forgiveness program (HEA, §455(m)), and the Direct Loan Teacher Loan Forgiveness program (HEA, §460). The Loan Forgiveness for Service in Areas of National Need program has never been funded, and the Loan Repayment for Civil Legal Assistance Attorneys program was last funded in FY2010 and, thus, is not currently operational. Due to these circumstances, neither of these programs is addressed further in this report.

[126] U.S. Department of Education, Office of Federal Student Aid Data Center, "Teacher Loan Forgiveness Report," https://studentaid.ed.gov/sa/node/874.

qualifying teaching positions to receive up to $17,500 in forgiveness benefits. Typically, such service would likely be considered qualifying employment for PSLF. Because receipt of benefits under both the PSLF and Teacher Loan Forgiveness programs for the same service performed is specifically prohibited, however, an individual may be required to choose between the two benefits, either choosing a defined benefit after five years under Teacher Loan Forgiveness or a potentially greater amount of loan forgiveness after a longer 10year period under PSLF. In addition, depending on an individual's knowledge of the availability of the Teacher Loan Forgiveness and PSLF programs, it may be difficult for some individuals to determine which program is most beneficial to them. Consequently, some individuals may be unable to maximize program benefits.

Other Loan Repayment Programs and Lump Sum Payments

As described earlier in this chapter, PSLF qualifying payments are on time, full, scheduled, and separate monthly payments that are made under a qualifying repayment plan.[127] In certain instances, a lump-sum payment made by a borrower may result in him or her being "paid ahead,"[128] which generally results in a borrower's paid ahead status only counting as one qualifying PSLF payment, even if the amount paid equaled multiple months' worth of payments.[129] In addition, subsequent payments made during a period when a borrower is paid ahead will not qualify for PSLF. In instances in which an employer provides lump-sum loan repayment benefits to an employee, the current policies regarding the application of lump sum payments may have the effect of partially limiting an individual's ability to benefit from more than one program for the same service. Such circumstances may occur with both private employer loan repayment benefits and certain federal student loan repayment programs,

---

[127] 34 C.F.R. §685.219(c)(1)(iii).

[128] A borrower may request that the extra payment amounts not be applied to future scheduled payments (e.g., the borrower requests that the excess payments be applied to reduce outstanding loan principal). 34 C.F.R. §685.211(a).

[129] Office of Federal Student Aid, "Public Service Loan Forgiveness," What is a qualifying monthly payment?, https://studentaid.ed.gov/sa/repay-loans/forgiveness-cancellation/public-service#qualifying-repayment-plan, accessed December 29, 2017.

such as lump sum payments received by certain federal employees under the Government Employee Student Loan Repayment Program. It can be argued that such policies decrease the effectiveness of these programs[130] that are intended to aid in the recruitment and retention of qualified employees, in that the value of an employer's loan repayment benefit and the PSLF program's benefit to the borrower may be lessened. However, it can also be argued that such policies are appropriate and that the provision of double benefits to individuals employed in public service would be akin to a windfall.

Federal Income Tax

In addition to amounts of PSLF benefits being excluded from an individual's gross income for purposes of federal income taxation,[131] other federal income tax provisions may provide additional benefits, both in terms of lowering income tax liability and reducing loan burdens. These, in turn, could have the effect of increasing PSLF benefits received by certain individuals. A full discussion of every applicable tax provision is beyond the scope of this chapter, but at least one education tax benefit the student loan interest tax deduction may be particularly relevant as it relates to the overall federal effort in postsecondary education.[132] Monthly payments under an IDR plan are based on an individual's adjusted gross income (AGI) as reported to the Internal Revenue Service on a borrower's federal income tax return. Various federal income tax provisions may be used to reduce an individual's AGI, which could reduce an individual's monthly IDR payments. This, in turn, could increase the total amount of debt forgiven under PSLF due to lower rates at which outstanding balances are paid under the IDR plans. The student loan interest tax deduction could

---

[130] Consumer Financial Protection Bureau, *Public Service & Student Debt: Analysis of Existing Benefits and Options for Public Service Organizations*, August 2013, p. 12, http://files.consumerfinance.gov/f/201308_cfpb_public-serviceand-student-debt.pdf.

[131] IRC §108(f).

[132] For additional information on federal education tax benefits, see CRS Report R41967, *Higher Education Tax Benefits: Brief Overview and Budgetary Effects*, by Margot L. Crandall-Hollick.

have this effect, as it enables eligible taxpayers to deduct up to $2,500 in out-of-pocket student loan interest payments from their gross income.[133]

In addition, under most of the IDR plans (ICR, the IBR plans, and PAYE), if a borrower and his or her spouse file separate federal income tax returns (i.e., their federal income tax filing status is "Married Filing Separately"), then the borrower's monthly payments will be calculated using only the borrower's AGI. If a borrower and his or her spouse file jointly, however, the borrower's monthly payments will be calculated using the spouses' combined AGI.[134] Two similarly situated households (i.e., those with similar combined spousal incomes) could pay significantly different monthly payments on their federal student loans, and, thus, could potentially receive significantly different PSLF benefits based on their federal income tax filing status. In addition, some borrowers who are enrolled in these plans and whose tax filing status is Married Filing Separately may end up making "artificially low monthly payment[s]."[135] In promulgating regulations for the REPAYE plan, ED sought to address the issues of disparate treatment of individuals based on tax filing status and the potential for some individuals making artificially low monthly payments. The regulations require married individuals enrolled in the REPAYE plan to use their combined spousal AGI when calculating their monthly loan payments.[136] The other IDR plans, however, continue to calculate a borrower's AGI based on the federal income tax filing status of the borrower.[137]

---

[133] IRC §221.

[134] 34 C.F.R. §§685.209(a)(1)(i) and (b)(2), and 685.221(a)(1).

[135] U.S. Department of Education, "Student Assistance General Provisions, Federal Family Education Loan Program, and William D. Ford Federal Direct Loan Program," 81 *Federal Register* 67210, October 31, 2015.

[136] Only the borrower's AGI will be used to calculate monthly payments if the borrower is separated from his or her spouse and the borrower is unable to reasonably access the spouse's income information. 34 C.F.R. §685.209(c)(1)(i).

[137] Approximately 5.4 million borrowers with approximately $259 billion in outstanding Direct Loans are enrolled in the two IBR plans, the ICR plan, and the PAYE plans. Approximately 2 million borrowers with outstanding Direct Loan debt totaling $169 billion are enrolled in the REPAYE plan. U.S. Department of Education, Office of Federal Student Aid, Data Center, "Portfolio by Repayment Plan (DL, FFEL, ED-Held FFEL, ED-Owned," 2018 Q1.

Broad Program-Related Considerations

There are multiple broad program-related considerations pertaining to PSLF. One issue relates to how the program fits into the overall suite of federal postsecondary education benefits and a broadening of the federal approach to student aid by providing aid after enrollment. Other issues include the difficulty in estimating the potential participation in and costs of the program due to individuals only recently being eligible to apply for and receive program benefits and that borrowers are not required to submit information on their intent to participate in the program until they seek forgiveness benefits after 10 years of service and qualifying payments.

Expansion of Post-Enrollment Benefits

To a large extent, federal policy related to supporting students pursuing postsecondary education has historically centered on providing up-front, in-school assistance to individuals and their families. This assistance helps provide access to postsecondary education and encourages persistence by providing a range of monetary benefits to help students and their families finance its costs. Federal efforts to provide such support to certain types of postsecondary students (e.g., veterans) can be traced back to at least the enactment of the Serviceman's Readjustment Act of 1944 (P.L. 82550), which authorized the first veterans' educational assistance program (the GI Bill). Over the next several decades, additional federal student aid programs were enacted that made postsecondary education benefits available to low income students (e.g., National Defense Student Loan, Basic Educational Opportunity Grants (now known as Pell Grants)), and federal need analysis procedures were developed for the purpose of making such aid available to students on the basis of their demonstrated financial need. Later, certain types of federal student loans were made available without regard to financial need.

Today, a number of federal student aid grants and loans are available to students who demonstrate financial need or low income status (e.g., Pell Grants, Direct Subsidized Loans) and to students without regard to financial need or low income status (e.g., Direct Unsubsidized and Direct

PLUS Loans, TEACH Grants). The largest of these programs are the Federal Pell Grant program, which provides need-based[138] aid to students that is not required to be repaid; and the Direct Loan program, which provides both need based and non-need based loans to students and their families that must be repaid.

Over time, reliance on federal student loans as a means to finance increasingly costly postsecondary education has increased.[139] At the same time, the number and availability of programs to alleviate the repayment burden associated with such loans has also increased. Such programs are often aimed at providing debt relief to borrowers and/or incentivizing individuals to enter into and remain in particular occupations or professions. The first major federal effort of this type was established under the National Defense Education Act of 1958 (P.L. 85864), which authorized the forgiveness of a portion of an individual's federal student loan for those who taught full-time in public elementary or secondary schools. Today, over 50 federal loan forgiveness and loan repayment programs are authorized, at least 30 of which are operational as of October 1, 2015.[140] Based on the types of employment that may qualify an individual for program benefits and the potentially large amounts of debt that may be forgiven under the program in the future, it appears that the PSLF program could be the largest student loan forgiveness program in terms of scope.

The expansion of such loan forgiveness and loan repayment programs may be viewed as a broadening of federal policy toward providing more widely available assistance to individuals after postsecondary education costs (i.e., student loan debt) have been incurred and to alleviate some or all of the financial burdens associated with borrowing to pursue postsecondary education. Federal student aid awards are currently constructed on the basis of an individual's need at the time of enrollment;

---

[138] Need-based aid is aid for which a student's eligibility is based on his or her demonstrated need for the funds.

[139] For additional information, see CRS In Focus IF10158, *A Snapshot of Student Loan Debt*, by David P. Smole.

[140] See CRS Report R43571, *Federal Student Loan Forgiveness and Loan Repayment Programs*, coordinated by Alexandra Hegji.

whereas, loan repayment and forgiveness program benefits are provided to individuals based on post-enrollment economic circumstances. The expansion of such benefits may signal a greater emphasis being placed on providing aid to individuals based on their post-enrollment economic circumstances by creating a system in which individuals may only be required to repay a portion of the loan amount they were originally expected to repay. These programs' expansion may also signal a broadening of the federal effort to provide more targeted aid to encourage service or specific occupational pursuits, versus providing aid that is more generally available to qualified students to pursue a wide variety of eligible postsecondary programs, regardless of students' future employment plans. As HEA reauthorization deliberations evolve and program configurations are contemplated, consideration might be given to the relative emphasis to be placed on providing more widely available aid at the time of a student's enrollment versus providing more targeted aid post-enrollment.

Estimating Potential Costs and Participation

Granting loan forgiveness benefits results in costs to the federal government. Given that it has only recently become possible to claim benefits, little is known about what the costs associated with the program will be based on the experience of actual cohorts of borrowers.[141] Estimating such potential costs is difficult, as the estimates must take into consideration a variety of factors including borrower participation in certain repayment plans and their career trajectories. In a 2008 notice of proposed rulemaking to implement the PSLF program, ED estimated a cost to the government of $1.5 billion over the five-year period from FY2008 to

---

[141] ED's Office of the Inspector General issued a report in January 2018 finding that ED should have provided to decisionmakers and the public more detailed and easier to understand information on IDR plans and some loan forgiveness plans, including PSLF, to fully inform them about current and future program management and the resulting costs of such programs. U.S. Department of Education, Office of Inspector General, *The Department's Communication Regarding the Costs of Income-Driven Repayment Plans and Loan Forgiveness Programs*, EDOIG/A09Q0003, January 31, 2018, https://www2.ed.gov/about/offices/list/oig/auditreports/fy2018/a09q0003.pdf.

FY2012,[142] but it did not provide additional details associated with the estimated cost, such as the number of borrowers expected to receive loan forgiveness benefits. In addition, the estimate was made prior to many Direct Loan program changes, such as the expansion of IDR plans and the switch to 100% Direct Loan lending. Since that time, no other estimates of the program's potential costs have been made publicly available by ED. Despite this, some policymakers speculate that the cost of the PSLF program to the federal government could be much higher than originally expected.[143]

Because borrowers first became eligible to apply for PSLF forgiveness benefits on October 1, 2017, limited information is available on the actual and future costs to the government of the PSLF program.[144] The number of borrowers receiving PSLF forgiveness benefits and the amount of their loan balances are likely to be large drivers of the program's costs.[145] This section of the report discusses two datasets that have been published by ED that provide limited insight into how the PSLF program is performing and actual and future costs of the program. The section concludes with a brief presentation of other data that have been made publically available that may provide some additional insight into the characteristics of borrowers who have had at least one ECF approved, which may be useful when attempting to conceptualize potential program costs.

---

[142] Of this amount, $1.2 billion was associated with loans made prior to FY2008. U.S. Department of Education, "Federal Perkins Loan Program, Federal Family Education Loan Program, and William D. Ford Federal Direct Loan Program," 73 *Federal Register* 37709, July 1, 2008.

[143] See, for example, Jason Delisle, "The spiraling costs of a student loan relief program," *Politico*, July 21, 2017, http://www.politico.com/agenda/story/2017/07/21/public-service-loan-forgiveness-cost-double-000478.

[144] Although borrowers were first eligible for PSLF forgiveness benefits on October 1, 2017, data on whether or the extent to which any individual has actually received forgiveness benefits has not been made available.

[145] See U.S. Government Accountability Office, *Federal Student Loans: Education Needs to Improve Its Income-Driven Repayment Plan Budget Estimates*, GAO-17-22, November 2016, pp. 45-47; and Susan Shain, "Public Service Loan Forgiveness Might Cost $24 Billion--But Who's Paying for It?," Student Loan Hero, August 10, 2017, https://studentloanhero.com/featured/public-service-loan-forgiveness-changes/.

Data on Public Service Loan Forgiveness Applications

ED recently made available some program data related to the number of individuals who have applied for and received loan forgiveness under the program. The data show that FedLoan Servicing has processed approximately 28,913 forgiveness applications, and 1% of these applications were approved. However, it is possible that some portion of the individuals who submitted denied applications could qualify for forgiveness under the program in the future as borrowers complete program requirements or provide missing information from their applications.

Specifically, the data show that in total, between October 1, 2017, and June 30, 2018, ED received 32,601 forgiveness applications from 28,081 individuals. Of the 28,913 applications that have been processed by FedLoan Servicing, 20,521 (71%) were denied due to the individual not meeting program requirements and 8,103 (28%) were denied due to missing information on the application. FedLoan Servicing approved 289 applications for individuals who had met all PSLF program requirements.[146] After FedLoan Servicing has approved an application, it forwards it to ED for a final review. If ED approves the application, it directs FedLoan Servicing to forgive the remaining balance of the borrower's eligible loans.[147] Of the applications approved by FedLoan Servicing, 96 unique borrowers' applications have been fully reviewed and processed by ED, and those individuals have received program benefits totaling of $5.52 million in loan forgiveness.[148] The remaining 193 applications approved by FedLoan Servicing had been forwarded to ED for final approval but remained in process as of June 30, 2018; thus, the loans associated with those applications had not yet been forgiven.

While these data provide an initial impression of the number of individuals who have thus far received loan forgiveness under the program

---

[146] The remaining applications (3,688) were pending processing by FedLoan Servicing.

[147] U.S. Government Accountability Office, *Public Service Loan Forgiveness: Education Needs to Provide Better Information for Loan Servicer and Borrowers*, GAO-18-547, September 2018, pp. 6-7.

[148] U.S. Department of Education, Office of Federal Student Aid, "Public Service Loan Forgiveness Data," PSLF Report, https://studentaid.ed.gov/sa/about/data-center/student/loan-forgiveness/pslf-data, accessed September 20, 2018.

and the benefits received, limited conclusions regarding future participation in and costs of the program can be drawn from them. First, individuals have just recently become eligible to apply for forgiveness benefits. It is possible that the first cohort of individuals eligible to receive PSLF benefits is smaller than future cohorts, as borrowers with older loans may be more likely to have FFEL program loans, which do not qualify for PSLF.[149] This first cohort of borrowers also had less qualifying repayment plan options (i.e., less IDR plans) available to them when they would have likely entered repayment, which may make it less probable that they would have paid according to a PSLF qualifying plan for the previous 10 years. Second, although 28,624 processed applications have been denied, this does not necessarily preclude denied borrowers from receiving PSLF forgiveness benefits in the future. Some applications were denied for being incomplete; a borrower may submit a new and complete application and then be determined to meet PSLF requirements. In addition, some borrowers whose applications were initially denied for not meeting PSLF program requirements may meet the requirements at a later time.[150] For instance, an application may have been denied because the borrower had made 100 of the required 120 qualifying payments. The borrower could subsequently make 20 additional qualifying payments and then be eligible for loan forgiveness.

It may also be reasonable to expect that should communications issues, servicing, and other administrative challenges identified earlier in this chapter be addressed, a larger share of borrowers would be able to submit successful applications in the future.

---

[149] For nearly two decades, both FFEL and Direct Loan program loans were available to borrowers. In 2010, the SAFRA Act, part of the Health Care and Education Reconciliation Act of 2010 (P.L. 111-152), terminated the authority to make new FFEL program loans beginning July 1, 2010. A recent GAO report indicates that, for individuals who applied for forgiveness between October 2017 and April 2018, one common reason for denial was that a borrower did not have a qualifying loan. U.S. Government Accountability Office, *Public Service Loan Forgiveness: Education Needs to Provide Better Information for Loan Servicer and Borrowers*, GAO-18-547, September 2018, p. 11.

[150] Borrowers may also dispute the determination, which could potentially lead to a reversal of the denial.

Data on Borrowers Who Have Made Some Progress toward PSLF

Previously, ED published data on the number of individuals who have submitted PSLF employment certifications forms.[151] As of March 31, 2018, approximately 874,000 individuals had submitted at least one PSLF ECF, have had at least one ECF approved, and have at least one qualifying Direct Loan.[152] These data may provide a general estimate of the potential number of individuals who have made some progress toward meeting the PSLF program employment requirements, but they do not provide a good estimate of the number of individuals who may ultimately be eligible for and receive forgiveness benefits under the program for a variety of reasons:

1) Borrowers may, but are not required to, submit ECFs at any point in time to assist them in tracking their progress towards PSLF eligibility requirements. Some borrowers may choose to wait until they believe they have met all program criteria before submitting documentation about their employment. Thus, submission of an ECF by an individual indicates that he or she has self-identified as interested in PSLF, not that he or she necessarily meets all program requirements.

2) Although an individual may have an ECF approved, this does not guarantee that the borrower will receive forgiveness benefits under the program, as he or she may subsequently cease to be employed in a position that qualifies for PSLF, fail to meet other program requirements (e.g., make payments under a nonqualifying repayment plan), or decide not to otherwise participate in the program. Also, disapproval of an ECF does not guarantee that a borrower will not qualify for PSLF benefits in the future, as the borrower's ECF may have been disapproved for administrative

---

[151] ED stopped publishing these data in its FSA Data Center when data on the number of individuals who have applied for and received forgiveness under the program became available.

[152] U.S. Department of Education, Office of Federal Student Aid, "Loan Forgiveness Reports," Public Service Loan Forgiveness Employment Certification Forms, https://studentaid.ed.gov/sa/about/data-center/student/loan-forgiveness, accessed June 22, 2018.

reasons (e.g., submission of an incomplete form), or the borrower may later become employed in a PSLF qualifying job.

3) While employed in public service, an individual must simultaneously make qualifying payments on his or her Direct Loans. An ECF's approval does not indicate whether a borrower was making qualifying payments while simultaneously employed in public service.

Data on Amount Borrowed and Borrower Income

Other data that have been made publicly available provide some additional insight into the characteristics of borrowers who have had at least one ECF approved and may be useful when attempting to conceptualize potential program costs. Data from two such datasets are provided below. It should be noted, however, that while this information may provide additional context pertaining to the PSLF program and the characteristics of individuals who have expressed interest in using it, the insight provided is limited for many of the reasons described above.

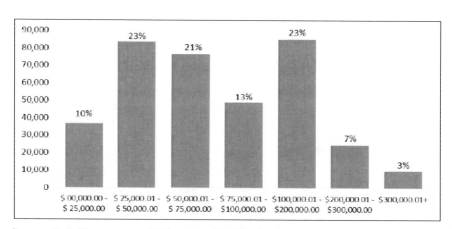

Source: U.S. Department of Education, "Public Service Loan Forgiveness Policy and Operations," 2016 FSA Training Conference for Financial Aid Professionals, November 2016, p. 28, http://fsaconferences.ed.gov/conferences/library/2016/2016FSAConfSession18.ppt.

Figure 1. Distribution of Individuals with Qualifying Direct Loans Who Have Had at Least One ECF Approved, by Amount Borrowed; As of September 2016.

Figure 1 presents the amount borrowed by individuals who have qualifying Direct Loans and have had at least one ECF approved. This information may be useful in conceptualizing potential program costs because the amount of debt to be forgiven is a function of the total amount borrowed by an individual.

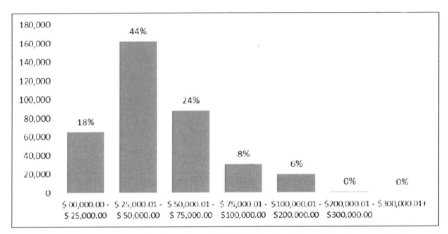

Source: U.S. Department of Education, "Public Service Loan Forgiveness Policy and
   Operations," 2016 FSA Training Conference for Financial Aid Professionals,
   November 2016, p. 29, http://fsaconferences.ed.gov/conferences/library/
   2016/2016FSAConfSession18.ppt.

Figure 2. Distribution of Individuals with Qualifying Direct Loans Who Have at Least
One Approved ECF and Are Enrolled in an IDR Plan, by Annual Adjusted Gross
Income; As of September 2016.

Figure 2 depicts the annual AGI[153] of borrowers who have qualifying Direct Loans, have had at least one ECF approved, and are enrolled in an IDR plan. As described earlier in this chapter, to maximize forgiveness benefits under the PSLF program it may be most beneficial for borrowers to repay their Direct Loans according to one of the IDR plans. The information provided in Figure 2 may be useful in conceptualizing potential program costs because qualifying PSLF monthly payments are

---

[153] Borrowers· AGI amounts depicted in Figure 2 represent the borrowers· current AGI in
   September 2016. The AGIs depicted would not reflect the borrowers· AGIs at the time such
   individuals may ultimately receive PSLF program forgiveness benefits.

most likely to be made under an IDR plan in order to maximize potential borrower benefits, and payments made under these plans are a function of a borrower's AGI.

INDEX

Repayment of Student Loans: Federal Plans and Forgiveness Options and Issues for Older Americans

Editor: George L. Payne

Series: Financial Institutions and Services

Book Description: This book discusses how participation in Income-Based Repayment and Pay As You Earn compares to eligibility, and to what extent Education has taken steps to increase awareness of these plans; and what is known about Public Service Loan Forgiveness certification and eligibility, and to what extent Education has taken steps to increase awareness of this program.

Softcover ISBN: 978-1-63484-922-7
Retail Price: $62

Student Loans: Borrower Default, Rehabilitation, Federal Terms and Conditions

Editor: Crystal Rollins

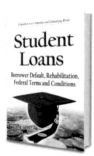

Series: Education in a Competitive and Globalizing World

Book Description: This book examines how Education assists borrowers in rehabilitating defaulted student loans; the upgrade of its defaulted loan information system affected loan rehabilitation; and Education oversees private collection agencies in implementing loan rehabilitation.

Hardcover ISBN: 978-1-63321-267-1
Retail Price: $140

FEDERAL STUDENT LOANS: ELEMENTS AND ANALYSES OF THE DIRECT LOAN PROGRAM

EDITOR: Gabriella Bradford

SERIES: Education in a Competitive and Globalizing World

BOOK DESCRIPTION: This book discusses major provisions of federal student loans made available through the DL program and previously made through the FFEL program. It focuses on provisions related to borrower eligibility, loan terms and conditions, borrower repayment relief, and loan default and its consequences for borrowers.

HARDCOVER ISBN: 978-1-63321-223-7
RETAIL PRICE: $140